Collaborations for Student Success

Beta Phi Mu Scholars series

Founded in 1948, Beta Phi Mu is the international library and information studies honor society. Its mission is to recognize and encourage scholastic achievement among library and information studies students.

The Beta Phi Mu Scholars series publishes significant contributions and substantive advances in the field of library and information science. Series editor Andrea Falcone is committed to presenting work which reflects Beta Phi Mu's commitments to scholarship, leadership, and service. The series fosters creative, innovative, and well-articulated works that members of the field will find influential.

Recently published titles in the series are:

Book Banning in 21st-Century America by Emily J. M. Knox
Young Adult Literature, Libraries, and Conservative Activism by Loretta M. Gaffney
School Librarianship: Past, Present, and Future edited by Susan W. Alman
Six Issues Facing Libraries Today: Critical Perspectives by John M. Budd
Access to Information, Technology, and Justice: A Critical Intersection by Ursula Gorham
Collaborations for Student Success: How Librarians and Student Affairs Work Together to Enrich Learning by Dallas Long

Collaborations for Student Success

How Librarians and Student Affairs Work Together to Enrich Learning

Dallas Long

ROWMAN & LITTLEFIELD
Lanham • Boulder • New York • London

Published by Rowman & Littlefield
An imprint of The Rowman & Littlefield Publishing Group, Inc.
4501 Forbes Boulevard, Suite 200, Lanham, Maryland 20706
www.rowman.com

6 Tinworth Street, London SE11 5AL

Copyright © 2019 by Dallas Long

All rights reserved. No part of this book may be reproduced in any form or by any electronic or mechanical means, including information storage and retrieval systems, without written permission from the publisher, except by a reviewer who may quote passages in a review.

British Library Cataloguing in Publication Information Available

Library of Congress Cataloging-in-Publication Data

Names: Long, Dallas, author.
Title: Collaborations for student success : how librarians and student affairs work together to enrich learning / Dallas Long.
Description: Lanham : Rowman & Littlefield, [2019] | Series: Beta Phi Mu scholars series | Includes bibliographical references and index.
Identifiers: LCCN 2019018233 (print) | LCCN 2019022262 (ebook) | ISBN 9781538119075 (cloth) | ISBN 9781538158395 (pbk)
Subjects: LCSH: Academic librarians—Professional relationships—United States. | Student affairs administrators—Professional relationships—United States. | Libraries and colleges—United States. | Libraries and colleges—United States—Case studies.
Classification: LCC Z682.4.C63 L66 2019 (print) | LCC Z682.4.C63 (ebook) | DDC 027.7—dc23
LC record available at https://lccn.loc.gov/2019018233
LC ebook record available at https://lccn.loc.gov/2019022262

Contents

Acknowledgments		vii
Introduction		ix
1	Overlapping Values	1
2	Review of the Literature	29
3	The Research Methodology	57
4	The Librarians' Stories	75
5	The Student Affairs Professionals' Stories	109
6	The Diverging and Sometimes Intersecting Worlds of Librarians and Student Affairs Professionals	133
7	Recommendations for Practice	161
References		175
Index		185
About the Author		191

Acknowledgments

First, I wish to thank my husband, Jason, and my family for their encouragement and patience as I worked on this book and during all of my academic endeavors. This book would certainly not have been possible without their understanding. I am so fortunate.

I am also grateful for the support of my current and former deans, Drs. Shari Zeck and Dane Ward, for the gift of time and for their confidence in my contributions. Perhaps most importantly, I owe a debt of gratitude to the many outstanding student affairs colleagues I have had over the course of my career for their willingness to teach me about their work. Not least, I thank Jim Palmer, Phyllis McCluskey-Titus, and Scott Walter for their interest in my research, for their ideas, and for the generosity of their time.

And, of course, I thank the librarians and student affairs professionals who so generously were part of my learning and gave me insights into their passions and professionals lives.

Introduction

Librarians are exploring new roles and new partnerships on college campuses in order to improve students' experiences and enable learning outside the classroom. Other than faculty members, who should be librarians' potential partners? Student affairs professionals are one group of educators with much to offer. They are responsible for many tasks ranging from the management of residence halls to connecting students with service learning opportunities to helping students explore future careers. They make up one of the fastest growing groups in higher education. They are the experts in student development and the student experience.

Librarians and student affairs professionals know very little of each other's roles in the academic enterprise. The purpose of *Collaborations for Student Success: How Librarians and Student Affairs Work Together to Enrich Learning* is to explore the roles of librarians and student affairs professionals in student success and learning and to identify their respective perceptions of each other's work. At its heart, this book is about collaboration. Opportunities for collaboration between librarians and student affairs professionals are potentially rich and offer the promise of improved and high-quality student experiences. What this book is not about is examining specific collaborations between librarians and student affairs professionals; readers seeking ideas to replicate at their institutions will find case studies in my review of the literature. Rather, I am exploring the potential barriers and conditions that will impede or facilitate collaboration between librarians and student affairs professionals. You cannot collaborate with people whose work you do not yet understand.

The idea for *Collaborations for Student Success*, and the research that girds it, arose from my own lived experiences as a librarian inhabiting the world of student affairs professionals. For four years, I was the residential life librarian, fully and entirely embedded in a major research university's undergraduate residence halls. I partnered with student affairs colleagues from residence life and university housing, career services, the student union, counseling and health services, Greek life, and minority student services. Together, we created avenues for programming, library outreach, and specialized services for undergraduate students.

This work was not without challenges. Often my student affairs colleagues had a limited understanding of my work as a librarian and my ability to work outside the confines of a library. Worse, I had barely come into contact with student affairs professionals prior to accepting this new assignment. Suddenly I was a stranger in a strange land—at sea with a professional language I did not speak, little knowledge of the values or traditions that inspired my colleagues, and limited insight into how they taught, advised, and enabled students into increasingly sophisticated cognitive and psychosocial skills and identity development. It was only after I took the time to learn about their training, the core values that guide their work, their approaches to teaching and mentoring, and their specialized language that I was able to successfully forge connections that allowed us to build programming and initiatives together.

This book plumbs the identities of librarians and student affairs professionals and their unique contributions to student learning and success. It identifies the potential opportunities and barriers for prospective collaborations and addresses gaps in the higher education literature regarding librarians and student affairs professionals' familiarity with each other. This work is based on my original research. Using multiple focus groups in a phenomenological study design, I describe the experiences and perceptions of librarians and student affairs professionals at several four-year residential public and private universities in the American Midwest region. The implications should provide educators with a framework for collaboration between librarians and student affairs profesisonals as well as insight into making collaborations more effective for student development and learning. It is my hope that this book will offer a theoretical road map for fruitful, long-lasting collaborations that enrich students' lives.

EXPLORING COLLABORATION IN SEARCH OF STUDENT SUCCESS

Tinto (1987) theorized that student success—or persistence to graduation—is most favorable when students' intellectual endeavors and social experiences are tightly integrated. Additionally, Kuh (1996) proposed students learn best in "seamless" learning environments, in which the curricular goals of higher education institutions and students' experiences outside the classroom are interwoven and facilitate students' cognitive, psychosocial, and identity development. The *Powerful Partnerships* report contends that when the domains of student affairs and academic affairs work together, significant progress is made towards student learning and, as a result, student persistence (American Association for Higher Education, Task Force on Student Learning, 1998). Consequently, many faculty members and student affairs professionals have heeded the call and engaged in collaborations that enrich the student experience.

However, relatively few librarians and student affairs professionals have partnered to find ways to advance student learning and success. At first, librarians and student affairs professionals may not appear to share common purposes and goals. Librarians collect, preserve, and disseminate knowledge while almost invariably working within the framework of a library. Student affairs professionals help students navigate and adjust to campus environments. They tend to students' advising, housing, recreation, and health needs, among other areas.

Yet both groups of professionals are integral to student success and are as focused on student learning as the English professor who strives to improve students' writing skills. Librarians and student affairs professionals shape student learning and development outside of the traditional classroom environment. Librarians teach information literacy and critical thinking skills that influence students' cognitive development. They influence the campus climate by designing libraries that are dynamic learning spaces and by crafting collections that support curricular needs and reflect students' interests and identities. Similarly, student affairs professionals guide students' cognitive, ethical, psychosocial, and identity development through their counseling of students in crises and through their instillment of citizenship, diversity, and leadership skills. Additionally, they contribute to how students experience the campus climate by interpreting student culture, advocating for students, facilitating discussions with student groups, and remedying conflicts.

While relatively few examples of collaboration between librarians and student affairs professionals are detailed in the scholarly and professional literature, both groups stand to improve student learning and student success by working together. For example, career services counselors are concerned that students lack knowledge of the industries and employers with whom they interact at career fairs (Ledwith, 2014). Their lack of preparation leaves employers with poor impressions of the students and results in missed opportunities for formal job interviews (Ledwith, 2014). Librarians teach students research skills and information literacy as part of higher education institutions' established curriculum, while career services counselors help students think about career paths and interviewing skills. By partnering together, librarians could teach students to apply their information-seeking skills to researching careers and prospective employers, providing the students with better-informed information prior to interviews, while the career services counselors could gain deeper familiarity with the resources librarians make available for students to research different careers and employment sectors. As a result of the collaboration, students may benefit by being better prepared at career fairs and making favorable impressions on employers.

A key to identifying opportunities for prospective collaboration between the two groups and to identifying the conditions that impede or facilitate prospective collaboration is understanding librarians' and student affairs professionals' perceptions of their own and each other's roles in student learning and success. Using focus groups, I spoke with 30 librarians and 25 student affairs professionals at five higher education institutions about these perceptions. Their responses provided insight into the diverging and intersecting areas of librarians' and student affairs professionals' work and the feasibility of collaboration between these two professional groups.

Although librarians and student affairs professionals have common ground on which to base potential collaborations and partnerships, relatively little collaboration seems to have taken place (Hinchliffe & Wong, 2012; Swartz, Carlisle, & Uyeki, 2007). When librarians and student affairs professionals have attempted collaboration, many of these collaborations are reportedly not successful and do not persist (Strothman & Antell, 2010). In Arcelus's (2008) and Kezar and Lester's (2009) studies of successful collaboration between interdisciplinary groups, perceptions influence the willingness and ability of different professional groups to work together. In order for a collaboration focused on improving the student experience to be successful, actors must have a shared understanding of student learning and an appreciation for the expertise that each group brings to the collaboration (Kezar & Lester, 2009). Therefore, an important concern for building successful collaborations between librarians and student affairs professionals is ensuring that both groups have insight into each other's expertise and then finding value in the contributions each could make to improving student learning and student success.

However, higher education literature suggests librarians' and student affairs professionals' perceptions of each other are not well understood. Tenofsky (2007) and Walter (2007) claim librarians and student affairs professionals are largely unfamiliar with each other's work and do not understand how each contributes to student learning and to student success. In the relatively few case studies of collaborations, only the librarians' voices are heard (Aguilar & Keating, 2009; Elguindi & Sandler, 2013; Lampert, Dabbour, & Solis, 2007). The student affairs professionals' contributions and perspectives are almost entirely unknown. *Collaborations for Student Success* addresses the question of how librarians and student affairs professionals view each other and what their perceptions might mean for potential collaborative ventures between the two groups. With this book's findings, librarians, student affairs professionals, and other educators should be able to develop insights into whether and how successful collaborations to improve the student experience may be approached.

Kuh (1996) proposed that students perceive their educational experiences as disjointed and unconnected. When students are able to bridge their curricular and extracurricular learning experiences, they are able to apply critical thinking skills to their social and personal lives and make better-informed decisions and display greater autonomy and competence (Kuh, 1996). Similarly, students are able to apply lessons learned from their extracurricular experiences to complex problem-solving and collaborative work in their classroom experiences. Consequently, Kuh (1996) argued that student affairs and academic affairs must forge collaborations to bridge the divide between students' classroom and out-of-class experiences.

Pascarella and Terenzini (2005) proposed that students' development and learning are affected by the frequency, content, and quality of their interactions with faculty. Tinto (1987) claimed that students persist to graduation at greater rates when they integrate socially and intellectually with the culture of the campus. Accordingly, student affairs professionals have partnerships with faculty members to promote such learning environments. Many of these partnerships are highly structured and formal in design, ranging from faculty involvement in living–learning communities in residence halls, to faculty-in-residence programs, to first-year experience programs (Streit, Dalton, & Crosby, 2009).

Librarians are largely absent from these structured, formal partnerships with student affairs professionals (Walter, 2009; Hinchliffe & Wong, 2012). Moreover, the library profession is experiencing profound changes: Student behavior, modes of research, learning styles, and technology are rapidly transforming expectations of librarians and libraries. In 2010, the Association of College and Research Libraries issued *The Value of Academic Libraries* as a response to growing calls in higher education for libraries to demonstrate their importance to student learning. In the report, Oakleaf (2010) stated:

> [P]arents and students expect [libraries] to propel students into successful careers with high earning potential, and the general public expects [libraries] to change lives ... these constituents expect libraries to achieve these goals but to also demonstrate evidence of doing so. (p. 4)

Oakleaf (2010) proposed that the most effective ways librarians could demonstrate their success are by increasing their impact on student persistence, on academic performance, and on student learning inside and outside of the classroom. If librarians are now asking "How are students changed by the library and by librarians?" they must look toward other groups in higher education for guidance. Oakleaf offered no road map for librarians, but encouraged librarians to move outside the confines of the library and to collaborate with those who are most deeply engaged in student persistence and student learning outside of the classroom—namely, student affairs professionals.

Although collaborations between librarians and faculty members are plentiful in higher education literature, collaborations between librarians and student affairs professionals are relatively scarce and less explored (Hinchliffe & Wong, 2012; Swartz, Carlisle, & Uyeki, 2007). All of the literature is written by and for practitioners, and virtually all of it from librarians' perspectives. Why have librarians and student affairs professionals not yet embraced each other as partners in student learning and success?

Walter (2007) proposed student affairs professionals and librarians are generally not aware of each other's educational roles. However, librarians and faculty members are better acquainted with each other's respective roles because of librarians' close support of the curriculum and of faculty research endeavors. At higher education institutions where librarians hold faculty rank and status, librarians and faculty members also participate together in tenure and promotion deliberations and in campus governance (Walter, 2007). On the other hand, student affairs professionals and librarians are arguably less visible to each other. Moreover, student affairs professionals and librarians appear to have narrow understandings of each other's domains. Student affairs professionals view librarians as largely concerned with the custody of books and journals and rarely willing or able to engage with students outside the library, whereas librarians consider student affairs professionals to be "babysitters" concerned with student entertainment and discipline and also possibly lacking in the academic rigor necessary to shape students' cognitive development (Tenofsky, 2007).

Finally, studies on interdisciplinary collaboration suggest that perceptions matter greatly. For collaborations between different groups to be successful, both groups must share common philosophical ground and a deep appreciation for the knowledge, skills, and expertise that each brings to the collaboration (Arcelus, 2008; Kezar, 2006; Kezar & Lester, 2009). Therefore, explorations of librarians' and student affairs professionals' perceptions of each other are crucial so each group can develop keener insight into the common values and philosophies they share and can craft successful, long-lived collaborations that improve the student experience.

Librarians and student affairs professionals do not appear to be deeply familiar with each other's educational roles. Therefore, the following questions arose for me:

- How do librarians and student affairs professionals describe student learning and student success?

- How do librarians and student affairs professionals perceive their own and each other's roles in student learning and student success?
- Where do they see the work of librarians intersect, if at all, with the work of student affairs professionals?
- How might they approach collaborations in these intersecting areas?
- How might the work and identities of librarians and student affairs professionals change because of these collaborations?

I utilized focus groups to provide rich descriptions of how librarians and student affairs professionals understand and explain their own and each other's roles in student learning and success, and how they might collaborate with each other in ways that benefit students. Focus groups are especially effective when the topic of the study concerns group interaction. This research was concerned with collaboration, which certainly requires one or more actors working together to create meaningful experiences for the benefit of students.

I drew the sample of focus group participants from five higher education institutions in the American Midwest region. The institutions selected for the book represent a range of institutional types, including size of student enrollment and private or public institution, as denoted by Carnegie classification. Participants in my research were librarians and student affairs professionals employed full-time at those five higher education institutions who had been employed in their respective fields for three or more years. In all, I conducted 10 focus groups, involving 30 librarians and 25 student affairs professionals.

Because the book ultimately explores perceptions of professional identity, I employed Whitchurch's (2010) concept of third-space professionals as the underpinning framework. Whitchurch (2008a) argued that three categories of people are typically employed at higher education institutions: faculty or instructional staff who engage in teaching, research, and service; support staff who perform largely clerical duties or manual labor; and professional staff who attend to the institutions' needs for professional services. Whitchurch (2010) proposed that professional staff are increasingly responsible for student learning and postulated that a "third space" has emerged between the professional and the academic domains:

> [T]he blurring of boundaries between functional areas, professional and academic activity, and internal and external constituencies have contributed to the creation of a third space between the professional and the academic. In this space, the concept of non-instructional staff has become reoriented towards one of partnership with academic colleagues and the multiple constituencies with whom institutions interact. (p. 378)

Whitchurch (2008a) developed her concept based on a qualitative study of 54 professionals employed at 12 U.K. and U.S. higher education institutions.

The institutions varied in missions, size, history, and teaching and research orientations. Her participants included accountants, human resources officers, student services staff, and public relations officers. Whitchurch determined that some participants were *bounded* professionals; their professional activities were limited to the scope of their position descriptions and, in essence, they practiced their craft within the context of higher education. These bounded professionals were predominantly human resources officers, accountants, and public relations officers and rarely interacted with students in the course of their duties.

Other participants were *cross-boundary*: They assumed some responsibility for teaching and student learning outside the classroom. This assumption of responsibility appeared to be the participants' individual choice and was largely circumstantial, such as volunteering to facilitate first-year experiential courses for supplementary stipends (Whitchurch, 2008a). *Blended* professionals saw teaching and student learning as distinctly within their purview, and the practice of their profession was largely shaped by this belief. Student services staff and librarians were among the blended professionals, regardless of institution or institutional type (Whitchurch, 2013). They occupied the "third space," in which professional identity coalesced with those of their faculty colleagues (Whitchurch, 2008a).

Whitchurch's (2008a) findings suggested that professional staff are differentiated in their professional identity according to their function, and "blended professionals" perform roles that marry professional services with teaching or student development components. Blended professionals have a sense of simultaneously "belonging and not belonging entirely to either professional domains or academic domains" and "working in ambiguous conditions with a multi-layered reality of the academic enterprise" (Whitchurch, 2009, p. 408).

Within her conceptual framework of third-space professionals, Whitchurch (2013) expanded her prior study on blended professionals to a much larger phenomenological study in order to understand how blended professionals make sense of their identities and work lives. Whitchurch (2013) employed four research questions (paraphrased): How do they understand their work? What is the "space" they fill in their institutions? How do they perceive themselves? How do faculty and administrators perceive third-space professionals?

Applying social capital and actor–network theories as frameworks to interpret participants' stories, Whitchurch (2013) proposed four dimensions of third-space professional identity. In the *spaces* dimension, blended professional staff recognize the multiple realities of their institution and the ambiguity of their working conditions, and redefine physical, virtual, and cognitive spaces that are "safe" and accommodate the duality of the professional and academic identities. In the *knowledges* dimension, blended professional staff integrate their professional and academic knowledge into theory-to-practice. In the *relationships* dimension, they experience weakening ties to the professional bodies that exist outside of higher education and fashion strong alliances to new networks that support their work. The *legitimacies* dimension concerns their ability to achieve credibility with faculty members and to challenge the status quo.

Whitchurch's (2010) concept of third-space professionals is an appropriate lens with which to explore the research problem. At its heart, the concept of third-space professionals emphasizes the themes of professional identity and identity tension. Becher and Trowler's (2001) study of the cultures of academic disciplines serves as a framework for many investigations of academic identities. Indeed, their study has proven helpful for understanding the barriers that impede interdisciplinary collaboration among faculty members (Arcelus, 2008; Kezar & Lester, 2009). However, Whitchurch's (2010) concept of third-space professionals may prove more helpful because it specifically explores the professional identities of staff who do not belong to the professoriate and are not encumbered by the barriers to collaboration that Becher and Trowler (2001) identified, such as inflexible reward systems that prize peer-reviewed publications, among others. Rather, Whitchurch's (2010) concept of third-space professionals explores how blended professionals navigate spaces, relationships, and territories that bring them out of their traditional roles and allow them to forge new alliances that integrate the institutions' needs for services with an educational component oriented toward student growth and learning. This emphasis on identity tension is crucial, as the definition of collaboration pursued here relies upon the creation of something new that changes the way collaborators work and view themselves and their roles rather than merely a collaboration that relies on a co-location of services.

As librarians respond to the profession's call to demonstrate their impact on student learning and success by partnering with student affairs professionals, they must develop greater awareness of the expertise of student affairs professionals and envision new ways of working together. However, higher education literature suggests that librarians have little awareness of student affairs professionals, and vice versa. When librarians and student affairs professionals are aware of each other, the literature indicates they may hold unfavorable or inaccurate perceptions of each other's roles in students' lives and may not fully appreciate their own capabilities in enriching students' experiences outside of their traditional settings and responsibilities. Additionally, student affairs professionals' voices are almost entirely lacking in librarians' depictions of the few collaborations treated in library literature, and often librarians concede these collaborations have uncertain futures. It is difficult to discern what roles student affairs professionals have played in such collaborations, aside from being guarantors of space and access to students.

Collaborative experiences will benefit the librarians and student affairs professionals as individuals and will ultimately benefit the students. Although student affairs professionals are certainly educators, Moore and Marsh (2007) describe student affairs as teaching from "afar" by creating environments and experiences for students (p. 7). Moore and Marsh (2007) advocated for student affairs professionals to adopt a stronger teacher identity rather than an educator identity and to design individual interactions with students to develop students' cognitive and psychosocial skills. Librarians have expertise in curriculum design and teaching activities, which they could transfer to student affairs professionals so that student affairs might create more intentional teaching moments. At most higher education institutions, librarians belong to academic affairs; perhaps by working more closely with librarians, student affairs professionals will forge stronger connections with other faculty as well. Finally, student affairs professionals might benefit from the information that librarians manage. Librarians could help them remain current in professional and scholarly literature.

Student affairs professionals also have much to offer to librarians. Although librarians have a strong teaching identity, they must find new ways of connecting with students outside of the library. Librarians could benefit from student affairs professionals' knowledge of student development theories. They could apply this knowledge to help students locate and evaluate information that in turn helps students navigate college or make better-informed decisions about their extracurricular experiences. Finally, student affairs professionals can teach librarians advising skills that help librarians more appropriately diagnose and understand students' information needs.

Seven chapters comprise this book. In the introduction, I have introduced the research, provided an overview of the work of librarians and student affairs professionals, and described the purpose of the research. Next, the first chapter explores the intersection between the academic library and the student affairs professions. This chapter describes the core values of both professions, highlighting the commonalities in the ways each profession enriches students' lives and meets the missions of their higher education institutions. This chapter is also a primer to readers who may be unfamiliar with either or both professions.

The second chapter serves as the literature review. The review consists of four sections and begins with a discussion of collaboration within the context of higher education generally. The second and third sections discuss collaborations between academic librarians and student affairs professionals, respectively, with other actors in higher education institutions. In the final section of the literature review, collaborations specifically between academic librarians and student affairs professionals are addressed. A critical analysis of the literature as a whole concludes the literature review. Gaps in the literature are identified and discussed, warranting a study of the phenomena explored in my research. Lastly, implications are drawn for research questions that guided the book.

The third chapter describes in greater detail the research method used throughout the book. Based on the gaps in the literature reviewed in this introduction, the following research questions will be addressed: How do librarians and student affairs professionals describe student learning and student success? How do librarians and student affairs perceive their own and each other's roles in student learning and student success? Where do they see the work of librarians intersect, if at all, with the work of student affairs professionals? How might they approach collaborations in these intersecting areas? How might the work and identities of librarians and student affairs professionals change because of these collaborations?

In the fourth and fifth chapters, the librarians and the student affairs professionals share their perspectives on each other and their perceived roles in student learning. They reveal how collaboration was successful between the groups and why, and, perhaps more importantly, why it was not. These chapters present key findings that inform my interpretation of their stories. In chapter six, I return to the book's research questions and discuss the intersecting ways librarians and student affairs professionals perceive their work and the potential connections they could make in the service of student success, such as librarians developing expertise in advising skills and taking roles in more active programming. All three of these chapters discuss the distinctive barriers each group faces in collaborating with each other, including competing reward systems and differing perceptions of student learning.

The final chapter explores ways librarians and student affairs professionals can overcome the barriers identified in the previous chapters. While strategies for successful collaboration in higher education, such as finding common language and a common vision of student success, are essential to success, this chapter focuses on the specific ideas each group had for productive, fruitful collaborations that are student-centered. The recommendations push the boundaries for librarians and student affairs professionals to grow in skill sets, such as librarians becoming active participants in student culture and student affairs professionals developing expertise in teaching.

Chapter One

Overlapping Values

Becher and Trowler (2001) noted that different groups are more likely to work together if those groups have comparable values. Kezar and Lester (2009) concluded that interdisciplinary collaboration is most successful when different groups ground their partnership in a mutual goal or value that both groups recognize as fundamental to their groups' professional purpose. Yet academic librarianship and student affairs are distinctly different professions with their own functions, professional training, and culture. Where do these two professions intersect? The core values of service, community development, and social justice are where academic librarianship and student affairs appear to overlap. Certainly, these are not the only core values of each profession, but these fundamental values have shaped the histories, and perhaps the futures, of both groups.

THE CHANGING ROLE OF FACULTY AND THE RISE OF THIRD-SPACE PROFESSIONALS: THE EVOLVING ROLE AND NATURE OF FACULTY

"The faculty *are* the university." This simple phrase invokes ideas and images that are nearly universal in American colleges and universities: the autonomous and tenured professor, inspiring undergraduates in the classroom and bringing new ideas to the world through research and writing. Schuster and Finkelstein (2006) laud the faculty as "the academy's most valuable asset" (p. 3). Donoghue (2018) describes the rise of the American research university more than a century ago as "animated" by the discipline-based scholar (p. 15). Bok (2015) deems faculty the essence of higher education and remarks, "Trustees, presidents, deans, registrars, secretaries, janitors and the like are not, strictly speaking, part of the university at all" (p. 19).

However, American higher education has transformed in recent years, and with it, the nature of faculty work. Faculty are increasingly pressured to produce research and scholarship (Donoghue, 2018). States provide declining support for higher education institutions, so in turn higher education institutions look toward faculty research endeavors for income-producing activities (Donoghue, 2018; Bok, 2015). However, the demands on faculty for greater research productivity are not motivated merely by higher education's desire to produce income through entrepreneurial activities. Rather, higher education institutions are competing with each other for ranking, for talented students, and for grant funding (Finkelstein, Conley, & Schuster, 2016). Higher education institutions raise their profile in all three areas by stimulating faculty research productivity (Finkelstein, Conley, & Schuster, 2016). In 2010, faculty at research institutions reported spending as much as 50% less time on teaching activities than their counterparts at comprehensive universities, and faculty at comprehensive institutions reported spending less time on teaching activities than faculty at liberal arts colleges (Bozeman & Boardman, 2013). Although research productivity varies by institutional type, by discipline, and by faculty rank, Bozeman and Boardman (2013) concluded that faculty at nearly every type of higher education institution spent more time engaged in research activities than on teaching or service-related activities.

At the same time that faculty are pressured to be more productive in research and scholarship, record numbers of students are enrolling in higher education. Enrollment in baccalaureate programs increased by 36% (from 2.2 million to 2.9 million) between 2000 and 2016 (National Center for Education Statistics, 2018). The growing student body is also more diverse. The number of students over the age of 25 has grown faster than the number of traditional-aged students (18–24 years old) (National Center for Education Statistics, 2018). The number of Latino students increased from 3% to 17%, black students from 9% to 14%, and Asian students from 2% to 7% between 1976 and 2015 (National Center for Education Statistics, 2016). Female students outpaced male students and comprised 63% of students enrolled in baccalaureate programs in 2009 (National Center for Education Statistics, 2016). Accordingly, pedagogy has grown more diverse to accommodate the differing perspectives, academic skills, technology facility, and needs of students. Faculty are challenged to "reculturate" and adopt teaching methods that are appropriate for the educational outcomes defined for diverse groups of students (Hailu, Mackey, Pan, & Arend, 2017). These teaching methods encompass a wide array of pedagogical strategies, including multicultural competencies for instructors, student-centered learning, culturally responsive curricula, active learning, reflective learning, and online learning (Hailu et al., 2017).

Despite the growing number of students, there are fewer full-time tenured and tenure-track faculty. In 1975, full-time tenured and tenure-track faculty accounted for 57% of all faculty positions at four-year higher education institutions (Donoghue, 2018). By 2015, tenured and tenure-track faculty had dwindled to 29% of faculty positions (Donoghue, 2018). More than half of full-time faculty positions were not on the tenure track despite employment at institutions with tenure systems. Full-time nontenure faculty and part-time, or contingent, faculty constituted 67% of teaching positions (American Association of University Professors, 2017).

Although the number of full-time nontenure faculty and part-time contingent faculty have grown significantly, their impermanence and lack of engagement with the institution inhibits their ability to socialize students. Nontenure and contingent faculty might teach subject matter content excellently, but research on student learning draws on powerful connections between teacher, student, subject matter, learning environment, and institutional mission (Quaye, 2016). Tenured faculty tend to remain at the institutions that granted their tenure for the duration of their careers and are more likely to develop lasting relationships with students, stay current in the emerging research of their disciplines, involve students in research activities, and connect institutional mission to curricula than their nontenure and contingent counterparts (Donoghue, 2018). Such qualities transcend teaching and demonstrate socialization. Donoghue (2018) defines the socialization of students as the institution's desire and ability to foster students' teamwork, leadership skills, perspective-taking, cultural competencies, and citizenship. Donoghue (2018) suggests that higher education has a critical interest in imbuing students with these skills: Students need these skills to participate successfully in the knowledge economy, and higher education needs students to succeed in their post-college years in order to maintain the public's trust in its purpose.

If tenured and tenure-track faculty are more effective at facilitating student learning than nontenure and contingent faculty, but such faculty are declining in number and spending more of their time on research productivity than on teaching, who is becoming responsible for student learning?

THE EMERGENCE OF "THIRD-SPACE" PROFESSIONALS

Trowler (2012) acknowledges the teaching and research functions have become "separated" (p. 30) in higher education, but such socialization of students (or student learning, as Trowler defines it) still takes place. Trowler (2012) speculates on the "invisible college," where students are learning the skills necessary for the knowledge economy but not necessarily inside the classroom (p. 38). Three groups of people are typically employed at higher education institutions: the faculty (and administrators, who historically rose from the faculty); the support staff, who attend to the institution's clerical needs; and professional staff, who meet the institution's need for services (Whitchurch, 2010). Whitchurch (2010) proposes that student learning is increasingly the responsibility of higher education's administrative or professional staff.

Whitchurch (2008a) mentions that professional staff occupy specialist roles that typically exist in great numbers outside of higher education, such as human resources, accounting, and architecture, but fulfill the institution's needs for those services. Just as faculty identify strongly with their disciplines, professional staff identify strongly with their professional organizations (Whitchurch, 2008a). Whitchurch (2008b) suggests faculty members' relationships with their disciplines are flexible because most academic disciplines do not exist in great numbers outside of higher education; these disciplines are therefore shaped by higher education's "way of working" (p. 381). For professional staff, the opposite is true. They belong to professions that serve distinct purposes outside of higher education. The practitioners who work inside higher education are comparatively few compared to their "civilian" counterparts (Whitchurch, 2008b, p. 381). These practitioners *must* work according to the rules and norms of their profession in order to maintain their credentials and continue to practice in their fields. However, they must also navigate higher education's way of working. Whitchurch (2010) postulates that a "third space" has emerged between the professional and the academic domains. In this space, nonacademic staff navigate their work through a framework of partnership with others in their institutions.

Zahir (2010) casts third-space professionals as simply professionals who practice their profession within the context of higher education. Trowler (2012) refers to this as "academic practice" (p. 30). Cownie (2012) and Greary (2008) describe an "identity tension" for professionals practicing their craft within higher education because academic practitioners must be familiar with models of governance and organization, pedagogy, and the nature and problems of students, and must embrace the institutional mission. However, Whitchurch (2008b) describes academic practice as a concept distinct from simply meeting the institution's needs for professional service. Rather, academic practice blends professional service and educational purpose, forging "entirely new identities" that are more akin to academic disciplines than to professions (p. 393). Regrettably, Whitchurch (2008b) does not elaborate on this similarity to academic disciplines. However, Whitchurch (2008b) states that the third space is not simply composed of professionals who practice their craft within higher education but "extended their roles beyond their given job descriptions and were likely to operate on the borders of academic space, undertaking teaching, research, and peripheral education activities like outreach or tutoring" (p. 384). Whitchurch (2008a) proposed that academic practitioners occupy a third space not because of personal inclinations or altruism toward education or students, but because shifting responsibilities within higher education demand such a space exists.

Neither Whitchuch (2010) nor Trowler (2012) have offered a definition of a profession, despite their emphasis on professionals operating within the context of higher education. It seems necessary to define "profession" before the concept of third-space professionals is fully explored. Abbott (1988) defines a profession as an occupational group with some special skills that apply "somewhat abstract knowledge to particular cases" (p. 7). The tasks of the professions are to "provide expert service to amend human problems" (p. 3). Greary (2008) distinguishes between the learned professions, such as medicine and law, and quasi-professions, such as nursing and social work. Learned professions have highly specialized knowledge that requires significant training, enjoy privileged communication in law, and operate autonomously from organizations (Greary, 2008). Quasi-professions have a less specialized body of knowledge requiring less rigorous training, enjoy little or no privileged communication, and have less autonomy from the organizations that typically employ them in great numbers, such as hospitals, schools, libraries, or government agencies (Greary, 2008).

Flexner (1916) describes the nature of a profession as intellectual aspirations oriented toward a public service, sociological in orientation, and empirically grounded in science and learning rather than philosophically grounded. Professions evolve in stages: establishment, in which members create criteria to keep out the unqualified; identification, in which members call themselves by a name different than the vernacular in an effort to reduce the occupational status; ethical development, in which members assert the social utility of their vocation; legal recognition, in which practice is limited by law to those who pass certification or examination; and control, in which the dominant professional association has direct control of, or oversight for, training facilities and programs (Flexner, 1916). Flexner (1916) suggested that fields have assumed professional status when they can answer the question "what can X offer that people need but cannot receive from any other professional in the whole system of higher education?" (p. 35). To answer this question, Flexner (1916) suggested that a profession must be examined in light of its members and their required skills and training, its history and paradigms, its values and objectives, and in the public's perceptions of the profession. These dimensions will guide the descriptions of the professions addressed later in this paper.

A significant gap exists in the higher education literature exploring the identities of third-space professionals. Trowler (2012) suggests few studies specifically examine the identities of professional staff employed in "academic practice" against their prevailing profession (p. 38). Becher's (1989) and Becher and Trowler's (2001) studies on the cultures of academic disciplines serve as frameworks for many investigations of academic identities.

However, their work omits the professions working within higher education entirely. Becher and Trowler (2001) confess, "There is an almost total neglect of the professions in terms of documentation of their cultures. This may be connected with the fact that their academic embodiment is far from easy to demarcate from the domain of professional practice" (p. 53). Elsewhere, Becher and Trowler (2001) claim, "with the exception of an interesting discussion of lawyers and law professors by Campbell and Wiles in 1975, the attempt at a literature search on academic professions drew a complete blank" (p. 60).

Kleiman (2012) explores the identities of performing artists who transition from actively performing their arts to teaching about the arts in higher education. Ylijoki (2000) interviewed Finnish library science professors who entered higher education after practicing librarianship outside of higher education. However, Ylijoki's (2000) study is limited because Finnish librarianship and library education are distinct from American and British traditions. Cownie (2012) studied the epistemological and sociocritical perspectives of practicing lawyers and law professors. None of the studies are truly on point because those instructing students in their craft are often no longer actively practicing the craft itself. Whitchurch (2008b) claims a lack of understanding about the roles and identities of academic practitioners as third-space professionals has been "fostered by the absence of a precise vocabulary to describe staff who increasingly" are charged with student learning (p. 379). Cownie (2012) proposes an ethnography of academic practitioners is needed for "disciplines torn between the academic and the vocational," which "sit uncomfortably on the sidelines of the academy" (p. 60).

The need for research in this area begs the question: Who, exactly, occupies this "third space?" Based on her study of bounded, cross-boundary, and blended professionals, Whitchurch (2008a) developed a set of criteria to identify third-space professionals. Third-space professionals:

- possess credentials required for their professional practice, but also academic credentials—such as master's or doctoral degrees—that are not strictly required for professional practice
- assume some responsibility for student learning
- carry out institutional initiatives that emphasize educational outcomes but require specialist professional expertise
- have the possibility of moving into an academic management role that affects institutional mission and faculty's "way of working," such as a vice president for academic affairs, chief information officer, or vice president of finance

Whitchurch (2008a) identified student affairs professionals as third-space professionals in her study. Based on Whitchurch's (2008a) criteria, academic librarians could also be considered third-space professionals: increasingly they hold advanced degrees in fields other than library science, teach information literacy skills, and rise to roles outside of the library such as chief information officer or vice president of academic affairs (Alire & Evans, 2010). Using Flexner's (1916) framework for investigating professions, I explore the fields of academic librarianship and student affairs in the following parts of this chapter against the context of Whitchurch's concept of third-space professionals.

ACADEMIC LIBRARIANSHIP

Who are the people that comprise academic libraries at colleges and universities, and what are their functions? What are the pivotal moments of librarianship? What are the core values that guide their work? What are the emerging trends and issues that are transforming academic librarianship today? This section answers each question with an overview of the history, values, functions, and new directions for academic librarianship.

Librarianship is the practice of collecting, preserving, and disseminating knowledge, and librarians almost invariably work within the organization of a library (Shera, 1967). Librarians and libraries are inextricably linked. Maxwell (2006) claims libraries and librarians "are treated almost as one and the same, with some questionable leaps of logic" (p. 17). Since it is virtually impossible to discuss librarians without also discussing libraries, and because libraries predate the profession of librarianship considerably, the history and function of libraries must be briefly described.

There is no question that libraries are ancient cultural institutions. According to Leckie and Buschman (2007), libraries were a feature of almost every society and during almost every time period. The Library of Alexandria was already three hundred years old when Julius Caesar burned the city in his war against Ptolemy XIII in 48 B.C. (Battles, 2004). Under the careful eye of scribes and monks, libraries flourished in the monasteries of medieval Europe. These early libraries were little more than "storehouses of men's work of the past and the present" and probably staffed, if at all, by stewards charged with protecting the collections from harm, whether by visitors or by weather (Cossette, 2009, p. 31).

The function of libraries expanded beyond their role as storehouses in the 17th century, when the British military deemed libraries at garrisons to be vital strategic assets for the competitive advantage maps, legal codes, and historical and scientific works they gave their armies. The information utility of libraries is believed to have emerged from this innovation (Tetreault, 2007). The desire to foster community spirit and to socialize recent immigrants led to the founding of public libraries in early 19th century New

England; thus the concept of the library as a social center was established (Davies, 1974). The collection, information services, and community development functions of libraries are still contemporary. The American Library Association (ALA) offers this definition of the modern library:

> A library is a collection of resources in a variety of formats that is organized by information professionals who provide convenient physical, digital, bibliographic, or intellectual access; offer targeted services and programs with the mission of educating, informing, or entertaining a variety of audiences; with the goal of stimulating individual learning and advancing society as a whole. (Eberhart, 2006, p. 2)

The ALA's definition of libraries puts a striking emphasis on the role of the librarian and the librarian's relationship with people. Despite the antiquity of libraries, librarians are relatively modern. Until the mid-19th century, academic libraries were generally staffed by men, and occasionally women, who tended the book collections for a few hours each day as part of their larger teaching or administrative responsibilities; these people were generally called "book men" and merely controlled access to collections (Battles, 2004). Meanwhile, private and public libraries were often staffed by volunteers on a rotating basis (Davies, 1974). The year 1876 is often called the "extraordinary year" in librarianship (Gorman, 2015). In that year, Melvil Dewey published his Dewey Decimal Classification system for the organization of library materials, founded the first school of library education at Columbia University, and cofounded the American Library Association to "exchange views, reach conclusions, induce cooperation in all departments of bibliotecal science, and dispose the public mind to the founding and improving of libraries" (Thomison, 1978, p. 4).

LIBRARIANS' DEMOGRAPHICS AND TRAINING

Who are librarians today? The U.S. Bureau of Labor Statistics estimates 178,200 librarians are employed in the U.S. labor market (U.S. Department of Labor, 2016). The ALA records 166,164 credentialed librarians employed in public libraries, primary and secondary education, higher education, museums, and federal, state, and local agencies (American Library Association, 2018). Credentialed librarians possess a degree in library and information science from an ALA-accredited graduate program. Librarianship is not a particularly diverse profession: 82% of librarians are women, and 89% of librarians are Caucasian (Davis & Hall, 2012). Despite comprising only 18% of the profession, male librarians hold 48% of the leadership positions (Davis & Hall, 2012). The majority of librarians are employed outside of higher education, with approximately 74% employed in public libraries, primary and secondary education, private industry, government agencies, and nonprofit organizations (Davis & Hall, 2012).

Librarians employed at four-year and two-year higher education institutions are generally described as academic librarians. The National Center of Educational Statistics (2016) estimates 26,253 librarians are employed at higher education institutions—approximately one of every four librarians. Many academic librarians engage in the same core activities as their peers in public and school libraries. Certainly, academic librarians are responsible for facilitating students' and scholars' access to information through careful selection, bibliographic description, and preservation of information sources. Academic librarians share their nonacademic counterparts' desire to promote community, protect intellectual freedom and uplift society, and inform and entertain through programming (Gorman, 2015). Cossette (2009) noted the "library-ness" of libraries—which he defined as preservation, information access, and community—created overlapping missions between types of libraries. Indeed, significant movement of librarians between academic and public libraries occurs.

Academic librarians are indeed different than their peers outside of higher education. The sharpest distinction is teaching. Cossette (2009) claims teaching is a role unique to academic librarians because public librarians instruct users on how to find materials in the library but not on how to evaluate, synthesize, or use information. Cossette (2009) states, too, that academic libraries are designed for teaching because their collections are "viewpoint-neutral," whereas public libraries remain "hegemonic" by largely collecting materials that reflect the viewpoints and demographics of their communities and are challenged when they stray too far from their base (p. 45). However, academic libraries are rarely challenged on the grounds of indecency or obscenity (Gorman, 2015).

Alire and Evans (2010) propose the chief role of the academic librarian is "the formation of the intellectual aptitude of the student" (p. 285). Every facet of the academic library, and thus the librarian, is focused on the education of the student. Rubin (2015) states: "The academic library does not have an independent purpose; its functions, collections, and services are directly related to the larger academic institution in which it is embedded" (p. 200). Shera (1967) acknowledged library collections and services should reflect the institutional emphasis, but he asserted strongly the primary role of the academic librarian is to emphasize teaching, learning, and a well-rounded student. Shera's stress on teaching and student learning is certainly resonant in contemporary academic librarianship: The teaching of information literacy to students has become since the late 1970s the most widely accepted and integrated core activity among academic librarians (Kuhlthau, 2004).

Arguably more so than any other type of librarian, academic librarians are cultural stewards: collecting and preserving rare or unique collections that are generally related to the institution's history, disciplinary strengths, or distinctive regional identity (Alire & Evans, 2010). Although many academic librarians are generalists, academic librarians employed at research institutions develop subject specialties (Alire & Evans, 2010). They foster relationships with faculty and students affiliated with specific academic disciplines, know the disciplines' literature, teach faculty and students how to use specialized resources, and make faculty aware of new scholarship. Approximately 42% of academic librarians are expected by their institutions to engage in research productivity, service to the institution and to the profession, and to participate in institutional governance (Bolin, 2008).

Unlike librarians in public libraries and private industry, academic librarians are likely to perform very specific roles that carry out administrative or programmatic functions of the library. Forty-nine percent of academic librarians work in services designed to help people meet their information needs, such as reference, media services, circulation, interlibrary loan, and bibliographic instruction (Griffiths & King, 2009). Eighteen percent of librarians work in technical functions, such as cataloging, preservation, or the collection development; 12% in library administration; 3% in archives or records management; and the remainder in technology positions (Griffiths & King, 2009). Academic librarians tend to be specialized by function because academic libraries are generally larger and more complex organizations than other types of libraries (Alire & Evans, 2010).

Most academic librarians hold master's degrees, and many higher education institutions require a master's degree or higher from a graduate program accredited by the American Library Association for entry-level positions. ALA-accredited graduate programs offer degrees in fields that are variously called library and information science, librarianship, and information studies. Many of these programs are offered through colleges or schools of education, information, or library and information science (Greary, 2008).

Although programs associated with schools or colleges of education may stress pedagogy, and programs associated with colleges of information technology may stress information science, all programs teach core skills, such as information evaluation (American Library Association, 2008). Most graduate programs will provide opportunities for graduate students to participate in an assistantship or practicum, either at their home campus or with a partner campus, as a way of providing students with professional experiences. Many students enrolled in library and information science graduate programs will find their first position after graduation based on the context and strength of their assistantship and practicum experiences (American Library Association, 2008). There is some criticism that little training exists in graduate programs to prepare academic librarians for their roles (Alire & Evans, 2010). This implies that differences between academic librarians and librarians working outside of higher education must be inculcated "on the job" for academic librarians.

Shera (1967) was a strong proponent for academic librarians holding a second master's degree: "A librarian . . . is never just a librarian. He is a librarian of something" (p. 144). Shera (1967) argued that an academic librarian should hold at least a master's degree in a separate discipline in order to join the intellectual discourse of higher education. Ferguson (2016) reported that only 15% of academic librarians were required by their institutions to hold an advanced degree in a second discipline, but the number of position advertisements requiring a second advanced degree had increased by 21% over five years.

HISTORICAL UNDERPINNINGS OF ACADEMIC LIBRARIANSHIP

Competitive Collection-Building

The history of academic librarianship has evolved somewhat independently from librarianship outside of higher education. Academic library collections were impoverished at higher education institutions throughout much of the 19th century. Resources were scarce at many colleges, and few books were purchased. Many libraries were merely reading rooms, and collections consisted predominantly of bibles and other theological treatises. Justin Winsor is credited as the first professional academic librarian, appointed to Harvard University in 1877 (Weiner, 2005).

Darwin's theory of evolution, the intrusion of scientific inquiry into the curriculum, and a new emphasis on research had a profound and "almost immediate" effect on college libraries (Atkins, 2003, p. 14). The promotion of faculty became tied to scholarship, and scholarly journals and monographs became the medium through which the findings of research were communicated (Weiner, 2005). Atkins (2003) declares, "By 1910 it had become apparent that the prestige associated with research was indicative of the quality of the university" (p. 14). Library collections grew rapidly and substantially, as colleges and universities invested in building expansive collections on a variety of subjects. Weiner (2005) describes this era of the late 19th and early 20th centuries as "competitive collection-building" (p. 5).

By the 1920s, collections had grown too large to remain in reading rooms. Smaller collections were located apart from the central library and were comprised of technical materials (Thompson, 1942). Law, medical, and theological collections were among the first departmental libraries at many colleges and universities, but other disciplines such as chemistry, history, and journalism soon boasted departmental libraries of their own (Thompson, 1945). Thompson (1945) notes departmental libraries were predominantly faculty spaces. Although graduate students were encouraged to study at departmental libraries, to interact with faculty, and to "become part of the community of scholars," undergraduate students were "rarely seen and less often welcomed" (p. 58).

Bibliographic Instruction

The spurious collections-building of the 1920s and 1930s resulted in erratic collections "appropriate to a research profile but wholly outside the scope of the undergraduate's reading and relevance to general coursework" (Atkins, 2003, p. 240). Weiner (2005) credits student restlessness in the 1960s for the birth of bibliographic instruction, and ultimately information literacy, as a core component of academic librarianship. Weiner (2005) describes bibliographic instruction as a "way of answering students' call for relevance," as students demanded recruitment of more students of color, and as veterans and older students entered higher education in high numbers (p. 33). Weiner (2005) claims that "bibliographic instruction weaved together new disciplines in area studies and ethnic and gender studies into a coherent whole from many academic and intellectual threads" (p. 35). Librarians adopted bibliographic instruction as a mode of instruction, helping students navigate interdisciplinary work. Interestingly, 93% of library deans and directors reported in 2016 that teaching information literacy to students is the most important role for academic librarians (Wolff-Eisenberg, 2017). Yet faculty perceived librarians' role as buyers of materials as their most important role, demonstrating a conflict between the perspective of library deans and directors and one of their most important constituencies (Wolff-Eisenberg, 2017).

The Rise of the Internet

Rubin (2010) describes the emergence of the Internet in the 1990s as the best and worst moment in contemporary librarianship. The Internet competes with academic librarians as an information service: Since the late 1990s, undergraduate students rank the Internet higher than librarians for accessibility, ease of use, and convenience (Rubin, 2010). Academic libraries have seen their gate counts and circulation transactions fall dramatically, and full-text journal articles and books are increasingly available in online collections. Some pundits speculate that we may be reaching the end of the traditional functions of information services and stewardship (Alire & Evans, 2010; Rubin 2010). Other pundits claim academic libraries and librarians are in a period of reorientation, and the library as a "place" is becoming the most important function as librarians struggle to make libraries a meaningful destinations for reasons other than the fulfillment of information needs (Leckie & Buschman, 2007; Maxwell, 2006).

CORE VALUES OF ACADEMIC LIBRARIANSHIP

Rubin (2010) writes, "Our values provide a framework for our conduct, policies, and services . . . Values structure our experience and provide insight when we must make important decisions affecting the future" (p. 405). Shera (1967), Gorman (2015), Maxwell (2006), Cossette (2009), and Rubin (2010) examined the values that guide librarianship, and this section discusses briefly the core values upon which they agree. However, some values espoused by some pundits are not consistently embraced by others. For example, Shera (1967) and Gorman (2015) emphasized the encouragement of literacy and lifelong reading as fundamental values of librarianship regardless of the type of library, and Maxwell (2006) noted that librarians "provide not just the knowledge to users but the inspiration to act on what they discover" (p. 37). Cossette (2009) and Rubin (2010) disagree, acknowledging the passive, ephemeral role of librarians in users' learning. The following are values that clearly overlap in the writings of each library thinker: stewardship, service, social justice, community development, and intellectual freedom. All of these values are humanistic because they emphasize respect for the human condition and for the works of mankind (Raganathan, 1931).

Stewardship of Human Knowledge

Librarians collect certain materials because those materials possess extraordinary qualities, such as epitomizing cultural or scientific achievements, representing controversial or ignored viewpoints, or contributing to human understanding in a new way. The value of stewardship frames the work of academic librarians especially. Librarians at research institutions collect widely and deeply on specific subjects to create robust collections, while those at liberal arts colleges collect the seminal works of the humanities and social sciences. The seminal works "are often prized by libraries, even when their circulation levels are low" because they form the core for general education and critical thinking (Rubin, 2010, p. 413).

The most enduring value of librarianship is also perhaps its oldest function—the preservation of the human record. The value is commonly referred to as preservation, which implies both curation and active measures of conservation. However, the proliferation of digital resources has uncoupled the philosophical value from the act of preservation. Stewardship is perhaps a more appropriate term because the word suggests a careful management without the implication of permanence. Gorman (2015) refers to stewardship as a value unique to librarians, as no other profession is responsible for safeguarding the totality of scientific, creative, and literary works, historical artifacts, and ephemera. Cossette (2009) claims stewardship is the foundational value of librarianship, for without texts "librarians can do nothing and can attain none of their goals" (p. 43).

Additionally, Cossette (2009) argues the status of librarians has lowered in society because the proliferation of digital resources has diminished the importance of the book. Rubin (2010) observes stewardship remains an unchanged value because information is still transmitted textually, even if the transmission is "merely words on a screen" (p. 417). Given the profession's nascent interest in data curation strategies (even the Library of Congress plans to record all the tweets published on Twitter), stewardship endures as a core value of the library profession.

Service

If the purpose of librarianship is to communicate information to people, then service to others is an essential value. Davies (1974) claims the service orientation of librarianship arose partly because public libraries in 19th-century America were intended to socialize the "unruly masses of immigrants" by sponsoring programs on U.S. history and culture, classes on learning English, and lessons on navigating available social services (p. 54). Ranganathan is credited with infusing service into the enduring dominant philosophy of librarianship (Rubin, 2010). Ranganathan (1931) said libraries had little value, and librarians were merely custodians, if people did not use books. Ranganathan (1931) asserted librarians should have excellent, firsthand knowledge of the people they served and build collections that serve the community's interests and needs.

Additionally, Ranganathan (1931) recommended that librarians facilitate relationships between people and books by making books as accessible as possible, through open shelving, displays, advisory services, and catalogs. Finally, Ranganathan (1931) advocated that librarians should save the time of the people by recommending the right books for the right people and mastering techniques to identity people's information needs by asking leading questions. Shera (1967) argued that librarians must serve the public good because the transmission of knowledge benefits more than the intellectual or informational needs of the individual, but also influences the growth and advancement of society.

Social Justice

Librarians serve the public good, but they also recognize the power of information to transform society and uplift people. Librarians actively reach out to those who could benefit from library services, often out of a recognition that access to information is unevenly distributed among groups of people. In public libraries, librarians practice social justice through bridging the "digital divide": making computers and the Internet available to those who cannot afford access, and teaching people how to use technology. Additionally, librarians in public libraries create programs and information services targeted especially to disadvantaged groups, such as the unemployed, homeless, or people living with HIV/AIDS (Pateman & Vincent, 2010). Librarians play more active roles in social justice in a burgeoning area called community informatics. Pateman and Vincent (2010) describe librarians in Chicago partnering with salons patronized by African American women in impoverished areas. The librarians establish computer kiosks for the women, after determining the women's information needs.

Community

Librarians craft a sense of community between people as one of the values that guides their work. Gorman (2015) notes the library is often a focus point of neighborhoods and is centrally located within schools, where people come together to participate in programs, lectures, and cultural events or to simply run into friends and neighbors by serendipity. Leckie and Buschman (2007) describe academic libraries as the "intellectual heart" of colleges and universities, and often the geographic heart of the campus as well. Maxwell (2006) describes the library's role in community as paradoxical, as it is a place where people come to read privately in the presence others who also want to be alone. Librarians design these experiences intentionally, enriching the social fabric of the communities they serve by hosting lectures and musical performances and sponsoring game and trivia nights, books, and children's activities.

Academic librarians contribute to community development in a slightly different sense. They may not create the great numbers of educational, cultural, or recreational programs found in public libraries, but they make deliberate decisions in their use of library space and relationships with students. Spaces are designed to balance active and collaborative learning styles with quiet, reflective areas; offices are increasingly allocated to student organizations, academic advisors, and career counselors (Leckie & Buschman, 2007). Librarians engage in outreach to student communities, which brings librarians into student spaces such as residence halls and student unions. Recently, librarians have begun connecting with student communities by organizing raves and dance parties in libraries during final examination periods ("Flashmobs in Libraries," 2010).

Intellectual Freedom

Librarians defend the right of individuals to seek and receive information from all points of view without restriction. Librarians practice intellectual freedom in different ways, such as ensuring collections represent diverse perspectives and lobbying against censorship. The tradition of academic freedom in higher education shields most academic libraries from censorship, but academic librarians struggle to protect students' right to privacy. Federal and state investigators have challenged a number of academic librarians to turn over records of students' reading habits or browsing histories associated with computer workstations since the passage of the Patriot Act (Rubin, 2010).

PARADIGMS OF LIBRARIANSHIP

Librarianship is in transition. Shera (1967) described the profession as grounded in a positivist framework where knowledge is archived, classified, and preserved, placing significant emphasis on the container rather than the content. Dewey and Ranganathan contributed profoundly to the profession's positivist traditions by emphasizing rationalism and the scientific method in their respective classification schema and Ranganathan's *Five Laws of Library Science* (Gorman, 2015). Kuhlthau (2004) describes this period in librarianship as the bibliographic paradigm, where librarians' practice focused on the description, organization, mediation, and use of books and other information sources. Library services were designed around the protection and appropriate use of the book, not on the patron's needs. Kuhlthau (2004) suggests the bibliographic paradigm is still pervasive in the profession, given the lack of appropriate vocabulary librarians have for the people who need and use their services. Kuhlthau (2004) says,

> [t]he first library school was founded well over a century ago, and the library profession still cannot agree on what to call its clientele. "User" is the most common word, but its sheer genericness implies that all clientele are exactly the same—interchangeable, faceless. Personal differences and learning styles are irrelevant. (p. 9)

The bibliographic paradigm is still prevalent to some extent in academic libraries because many librarians have roles that pertain to collection management, including acquiring, cataloging, preserving, and circulating information sources. Given Griffiths and King's (2009) demographics of academic librarians' specializations, nearly one-third of academic librarians are focused on those functional areas. The bibliographic paradigm must surely be entrenched in higher education.

At odds with the bibliographic paradigm is the user-centered paradigm. Kuhlthau (2004) credits the bibliographic instruction trend in academic libraries in the 1970s and 1980s as shifting librarianship's emphasis from the book to the person. Although Shera (1972) acknowledged the transformative relationship that exists between information and the general public, the user's perspective on information seeking was not well investigated. Studies on the cognitive process and the affective experience in information seeking led librarians to design library services that were flexible and responsive to the needs of library users. In academic libraries, these services included library instruction tailored to students' programs of study. Technology was designed to lessen the burden on users during their information-seeking processes. Library policies retreated from controlling people's behavior, such as banning food and drink, and library spaces became more comfortable, inviting, and designed to enable programs rather than accommodate book stacks.

Many contemporary library pundits agree that the paradigm for librarianship is shifting again, and the concept of embedded librarianship is taking shape (Alire & Evans, 2010; Rubin, 2010). Embedded librarianship involves focusing on the needs of a specific group of people, developing a deep understanding of their work, and providing information services that are highly customized, intrusive in people's lives, and present in their natural settings. Alire and Evans (2010) suggest embedded librarianship took root in the early 2000s when private industry dismantled corporate libraries and sent librarians to work among scientists and engineers. Librarians became physically located in the laboratories and played an active role in the research activities. They participated in project planning, built long-term relationships with their clientele, and interviewed their colleagues at critical junctures in research projects to identify emerging information needs, rather than responding to requests only when solicited (Alire & Evans, 2010).

Academic librarians are beginning to explore the concept of embedded librarianship. The proliferation of mobile devices, the preference of the millennial generation for digital formats, and the push to digitize physical collections have diminished the importance of the library as a destination for users. Collections and journals are widely accessible electronically, but librarians are not. Currently, some academic librarians are leaving the library behind and seeking office spaces in academic departments, attending meetings, teaching classes, and essentially being a part of the academic department. This allows librarians to develop a better understanding of what faculty and students need, while the faculty and students learn more about what sorts of assistance librarians can offer. Krkoska, Andrews, and Morris-Knower (2011) claim the relationship between librarians and faculty is strengthened because "faculty might know how to find electronic tools through the library's website, but might not know how to use them in the most effective ways" (p. 121).

STUDENT AFFAIRS

Much like librarians, student affairs professionals focus on student learning outside of the classroom. They are often responsible for functional areas of colleges and universities that are designed to support students during their time on campus. As academic advisors and career center staff, they help students articulate academic and career goals and create plans of study and find internships. As housing and residential life staff, they manage on-campus living options and create safe environments for students. As admissions and financial aid staff, they help recruit prospective students and think through choices for financing their higher education. Student affairs professionals are responsible for orienting students to the college or university, coordinating campus and recreational activities, advising student government associations, and creating communities for students who belong to underrepresented groups and may require advocates for equitable services, programs, and inclusive campus climates. Underpinning all of these services and programs is an intent to further students' learning and sense of self. Student affairs professionals use theories of student development to guide students' growth in critical thinking and decision-making abilities, communication and interpersonal skills, and leadership and citizenship. They help students explore career possibilities, pursue wellness, and establish self-identities.

This section serves as a primer on the student affairs profession. Who are the people and functions that comprise student affairs? How did student affairs evolve as a profession? What are the core values that guide the work of student affairs professionals? What are the emerging trends and issues that are transforming student affairs today? This section answers each question with an overview of the history and values of the field of student affairs.

Student Affairs Demographics and Training

Student affairs comprises a broad suite of services and functions designed to help students navigate higher education successfully and to create cocurricular experiences that facilitate students' cognitive, psychosocial, and identity development. The two most prominent student affairs associations, the National Association of Student Personnel Administrators (NASPA)–Student Affairs Administrators in Higher Education and the American College Personnel Association (ACPA)–College Student Educators International, regard the following functional areas as core domains of student affairs: academic advising, admissions and enrollment management, campus ministries, career services, Greek affairs, health services, housing and residential life, judicial affairs and student conduct, leadership programs, multicultural student services, orientation and new student programs, recreation and fitness, student activities, and student unions. Student affairs professionals tend to specialize in at least one of these core domains.

The Bureau of Labor Statistics estimates that 180,000 student affairs professionals are employed at higher education institutions (U.S. Department of Labor, 2018). The student affairs profession is heavily female at 71%, although men hold nearly half of executive leadership positions (Pritchard & McChesney, 2018). Racial and ethnic minorities are underrepresented in the profession, as nearly 70% of the profession is white (Pritchard & McChesney, 2018). Most colleges and universities require a master's degree for entry-level student affairs positions. Graduate programs that prepare people for careers in student affairs are typically found in colleges or schools of education and are called by a variety of names, including higher education administration, college student personnel administration, and college student development. Most graduate programs will provide opportunities for graduate students to participate in an assistantship or practicum.

How do people discover student affairs as a profession? Just as in librarianship, many people are introduced to the profession through their experiences in student employment. Student unions, residence halls, career centers, admissions offices, and other core areas are significant sources of employment for undergraduate students. Many student affairs professionals say they found their way into the profession through the exposure and mentoring they received from their managers and colleagues, who made the profession look personally meaningful and rewarding (Taub & McEwen, 2006).

HISTORICAL UNDERPINNINGS OF STUDENT AFFAIRS

Like librarianship, the roots of the student affairs profession reach back to the colonial era of American higher education. Students at the colonial colleges were much younger (sometimes as young as 14) than their European counterparts because families desired the colleges to take charge of unruly students and instill discipline and moral character (Cohen & Kisker, 2010). Consequently, the concept of "in loco parentis," or "in place of the parent," emerged as one of the colleges' primary roles (Cohen & Kisker, 2010). In addition to their teaching roles, the faculty were expected to inculcate students with morals and ethics that would prepare them to participate in civic life as sophisticated, upstanding citizens. The faculty and students were rarely apart, as they took meals together and lived in the dormitories. To control the students, the faculty developed closely observed rules and expectations that governed students' conduct, dress, and activities (Cohen & Kisker, 2010).

By the mid-1800s, American colleges and universities had changed radically. In order to prevent an increasing exodus of students to more prestigious European universities, American colleges and universities transformed to replicate the European experience and its perceived higher quality. As part of this transformation, presidents encouraged faculty to develop scholarly ambitions and integrate the creation of new knowledge into the curriculum and their teaching. In order to be better trained as researchers, American faculty earned doctorates in large numbers, particularly at German universities. As they did so, they adopted the European perspective on the role of faculty members. They developed deep expertise in specific disciplines rather than broad knowledge in a variety of subjects. They pursued research and began to maintain active research agendas. As the faculty's interest in research grew, they had increasingly little time for or interest in student discipline or for participating in the daily lives of the students (Thelin, 2010).

By the turn of the 20th century, faculty involvement in student discipline had all but ceased. In the 1920s, the first administrators who might be appropriately called student affairs professionals were hired. The presidents of many of the largest universities appointed the first "deans of men" (and later "deans of women") to investigate student misbehavior and to ensure university rules and decorum were followed (Thelin, 2010). The deans of men and women rose in prominence and importance as student life became more diverse. Coeducation, fraternity life, and the admissions of small numbers of African American students began in earnest during the early 20th century (Cohen & Kisker, 2010). The homogeneity of American higher education was changing. As more students with different needs, challenges, and interests entered higher education, a greater number of students came into conflict both with each other and with the norms and expectations of their institutions (Rentz, 1994). Faculty members agitated for the hiring of staff to specifically meet student needs that fell outside the curriculum and the classroom.

Student Affairs Professionals as Service Providers

Clothier (1931) advocated for college personnel to guide and counsel students rather than to enforce rules strictly or to mete out discipline. Clothier (1931) claimed students brought to higher education personal histories that warranted attention, understanding, and—where necessary—adjustment. Crowley (1936) asserted guidance was insufficient, and college personnel should instead design services that tended to students' maintenance and remove "frustrations and confusion," such as the need for lower income students to work to pay for meals, thereby allowing students to focus more fully on their academic studies (p. 61). Specifically, Crowley (1936) suggested college student personnel should bear responsibility for admissions, orientation, student housing, and student health. In the 1930s, colleges and universities hired medical doctors and nurses to tend to students' health, becoming one of the first services many higher education institutions provided for students that was not specifically linked to the curriculum. After World War II, the American Council on Education issued a revised *College Student Personnel Point of View* (CSPPV), which proposed a comprehensive suite of student services that represented 33 functional areas, including student loans, dormitories, dining halls, administration of scholarship, student organizations, athletics management, counseling, career counseling, and coordination of student employment opportunities at the institution. The CSPPV stressed that coordination of these services supported students' holistic well-being and that staff should be dedicated exclusively to these distinctive functional areas. These staff were commonly referred to as student personnel. This marked the contemporary beginnings of the student affairs profession.

Student Affairs Professionals as Educators

The relationship between American higher education institutions and students changed significantly during the 1960s. The philosophy of in loco parentis had permitted colleges and universities to exert strict control over the behavior and conduct of students under the belief that a fundamental purpose of American higher education was to shape students' character. Sometimes colleges and universities took disciplinary action against students without the benefit of a hearing or an appeal. Students who promoted civil rights or who engaged in activism were especially punished by colleges and universities, often without notification of charges or evidence against them (Lee, 2011). After a series of lawsuits, the courts began to afford constitutional protections to students. In the seminal case of *Dixon v. Alabama* in 1961, Alabama State College expelled a group of African American students for participating in a civil rights demonstration after they were refused service at a cafeteria. The college expelled the students without any notice or hearing. The U.S. Supreme Court found that students had a constitutional right to due process, and colleges and universities could no longer suspend or expel students without notification of charges, hearings, presentation of evidence, and opportunities for appeal. Subsequent court decisions reinterpreted the relationship between students and colleges and universities as largely contractual in nature—if students paid their tuition and met the college or university's published academic requirements, they were entitled to a diploma. The concept of in loco parentis was seriously eroded by the courts, and colleges and universities took less active positions in regulating students' behavior (Lee, 2011).

Simultaneously, student activism proliferated on campuses. Crises erupted at many universities, such as Kent State University, and resulted in student deaths, injuries, and property damage. As pressures in the campus environments increased, student personnel were tasked with greater roles in conflict resolution, communication, and social justice (Rentz, 1994). The critical purpose of student personnel turned to educating students on making appropriate choices and decisions (Rentz, 1994). No longer were student personnel focused exclusively on the provision of services and on student maintenance. Instead, they were viewed as intermediaries between students and higher education institutions. Student personnel began to be heavily involved in the fabric of campus life and recognized that they influenced students' decisions, maturity, and likelihood to persist to graduation. Slowly, the nomenclature used to describe the field shifted from student personnel to student affairs to reflect that such specialized staff served a deliberate educational purpose rather than merely the provision of services (Dungy & Gordon, 2011).

In the 1960s and 1970s, the student affairs profession established a theoretical base as the framework for its knowledge and practice. Many theories that explained student development emerged in the fields of education, psychology, and sociology. Student affairs professionals and their professional associations embraced the advances in student development theories, and graduate programs were founded that included student development theories as the cornerstone of the curriculum (Rentz, 1994). However, many student affairs professionals adopted these theories by creating campus environments, programs, and experiences they hoped would spur development simply by students' interactions with the institutions and each other. Moore and Marsh (2007) referred to student affairs professionals' strategies as "hands-off" teaching or teaching "far" from students (p. 3).

The marriage of professional practice and theory received profound attention in the student affairs field with the release of the American College Personnel Association (ACPA)'s 1972 report *Student Development in Tomorrow's Higher Education: A Return to the Academy* (Rentz, 1994). The report argued that student affairs professionals could not have a significant impact on students' intellectual, psychosocial, or emotional growth without first understanding the motivations, abilities, and environments that drive, create, and define students (Rentz, 1994). Consequently, the report called for student affairs professionals to collaborate with faculty, participate actively in the learning process, and create curricular experiences that spur student development inside as well as outside the classroom.

The Rise of Technology and Social Change

The rapid growth of technology is reshaping how student affairs professionals design their services and connect with students. Many students expect to conduct appointments with academic advisors, career counselors, and financial aid counselors in virtual environments. Social networking and text messaging changes student behavior, as many housing and residential life staff report mediating roommate conflicts in which the roommates never communicated face-to-face despite sharing living quarters. Academic advisors use data analytics to predict which students may not persist and attempt to customize information and interactions targeting at-risk students. These changes concern student affairs professionals, who fear losing opportunities to connect with students more intimately and thus endanger their ability to shape students' experiences toward positive growth (Smith & Blixt, 2015).

However, listening deeply to students' concerns and understanding how they experience the campus environment is increasingly critical for student affairs professionals, particularly as higher education moves into the next decade. Student affairs leaders predict the convergence of the critical social issues of race, class, and gender will ignite new waves of student activism and involvement (Cook, Marthers, & Fusch, 2017). As students seek to be part of the solution to local and global challenges, student affairs professionals have opportunities to help students develop their role in leadership and civic engagement. Student affairs professionals will need to make even stronger commitments to community and serve as leading voices on campuses for inclusivity and social justice, perhaps overshadowing other more traditional roles made easier or different by advances in technology (Cook, Marthers & Fusch, 2017).

CORE VALUES OF STUDENT AFFAIRS

Student affairs is a broad profession that comprises diverse functional areas that may appear far apart in purpose, such as financial aid and student health services. Yet the work of student affairs professionals is grounded and shaped by core values that bind the field cohesively. In order to address current challenges in higher education today, Porterfield and Whitt (2016) looked back at the seminal works of the profession, such as the *Student Personnel Point of View*, and at more recent guiding documents produced by the major professional associations. The following values form the foundation of student affairs practice today.

Educating the Whole Student

Student affairs professionals believe in a holistic view of education, which Sandeen (2004) calls educating the whole student. During their college years, students face new academic and social challenges and meet people with different perspectives from their own. These new experiences test students' perception of themselves and the world. As students interpret and make meaning of these experiences, their intellectual and emotional capacities grow. They develop a sense of identity and a set of values that will guide their perception of the world through adulthood. Student affairs professionals recognize this development is multifaceted and interdependent, including interpersonal, spiritual, vocational, and physical wellness components. Many of the experiences that challenge students toward growth will take place outside of the classroom. Consequently, student affairs professionals purposefully design services, programs, and environments that advance students' development in one or more dimensions.

Service

Young (2003) noted the fundamental mission of student affairs is to serve, yet the question of whom student affairs professionals serve has widened over time. Historically, the early student affairs professionals perceived service as *caring* for students, such as ensuring students were safe, well fed, and not running afoul of the rules and norms of the institutions. However, service as a core value has grown multilayered as the profession has evolved (Young, 2003). While student affairs professionals continue to place the well-being of students at the center of their work, their concept of service has extended to the betterment of the institution and of society. Helfgott (2005) provided evidence that student affairs professionals perceived the sharing of information about individual students with faculty members as service to faculty, so that they might be better informed about students' experiences outside the classroom that affect their academic performance. As student affairs professionals began to participate in campus initiatives, they provided service to the institutions by raising questions about campus climate and serving on task forces related to student development, recruitment and admissions, alumni relations, and campus partnerships with community and business organizations.

Community

Student affairs professionals appreciate the power of community development. Roberts (2011) attests to building community as the most complex and deliberative process for student affairs professionals. Students are more likely to persist to graduation if they are involved in a community that supports them and that they have helped shape. In particular, underrepresented and marginalized students need social groups to belong and succeed in college. Students build community through shared experiences, which in turn allow students to develop leadership, communication skills, and appreciation for individual differences. Ultimately, students see themselves as responsible for the communities they create. These communities may be as encompassing as the campus community or as small as certain floors of a residence hall.

Student affairs professionals play a particular role in designing healthy communities in which students can flourish. Using models of community building, student affairs professionals help students connect with other students who share a mutual interest, identity, or purpose. They identify students who demonstrate leadership skills, help students design programs that serve the students' intended goals, and coach students in negotiating conflicts with peers. To achieve healthy communities, student affairs professionals must be mindful of good internal communication among members, shared leadership and participation, and successful conflict management. Additionally, student affairs professionals must be attuned to the potential "dark sides" of community, such as racism and sexism, and be skilled in navigating student behaviors that harm others (Luter, 2007).

Social Justice

Student affairs professionals have long taken responsibility for advocating for equitable access to resources for all students, including fairness in the policies and practices of admissions, student discipline, residential living, and health services. However, the increasingly diverse demographics of students and more multidimensional understanding of identity have made advocacy more complex for student affairs professionals (Boss, Linder, Martin, Dean, and Fitzer, 2018). Recently, student affairs professionals have begun to perceive that the responsibility to advocate for more equitable campus environments now requires a more action-oriented approach using a social justice lens. ACPA and NASPA (2015) revised the profession's guiding documents to explicitly include social justice and defined it as ". . . seeking to meet the needs of all groups, equitably distributing resources, raising social consciousness, and repairing past and current harms on campus communities" (p. 30).

Furr (2018) noted that student affairs professionals wield a unique power to influence social change on campuses. Because of their positions as intermediaries between students and higher education institutions, they are able to challenge the dominant discourse in higher education on behalf of marginalized or underrepresented student groups. Student affairs professionals have led efforts to change campus climates by educating people from privileged groups on the lived experiences of underrepresented students and have provided models and training on allyship. They have advocated for structural and organizational changes such as the construction of all-gender restrooms and flexible housing assignments for transgender students, and for resources to break down socioeconomic barriers, such as the establishment of food pantries for students dealing with food affordability (Phillips, McDaniel, & Croft, 2018).

PARADIGMS OF STUDENT AFFAIRS

Like the library profession, paradigms shape the direction of student affairs. Ender, Newton, and Caple (1996) identify three paradigms that are prevalent in the student affairs profession: student services, student development, and integrated learning. However, these paradigms appear to operate differently than the paradigms in librarianship. The bibliographic and user-centered paradigms (and quite possibly the embedded librarianship paradigm) commingle, or even compete, at the same organization. Ender et al. (1996) suggest paradigms do not commingle nor compete in the student affairs profession. Instead, paradigms are shaped by institutional characteristics and frame the work of all student affairs professionals at a given institution. However, Ender et al. (1996) do not specifically identify these institutional characteristics.

Under the student services paradigm, student affairs is exclusively focused on student maintenance. According to Ender et al. (1996), student affairs functions under the paradigm are designed to meet the basic needs of the students that cannot be met by the faculty. Housing, admissions, financial aid, and health services tend to be the student affairs functions that are the most robust, with other functions less well supported or developed (Ender et al., 1996). The student affairs professional has little, if any, role in student learning. Kuh (1996) suggested student affairs professionals working in this paradigm are concerned with control over students and over procedures. Student affairs is extracurricular and does not work in tandem with institutions' curricula or faculty (Kuh, 1996). This paradigm hinges on a positivist framework, which emphasizes the efficiency of operations rather than the students' experiences, and a bureaucratic organization (Kuh, 1996).

The student development paradigm grew out of the student services paradigm and has effectively replaced it as the dominant paradigm in the student affairs profession (Ender et al., 1996). Student affairs professionals are active participants in student learning with faculty, but their focus is on cocurricular learning. Theories of student development guide student affairs professionals' work. The functional areas emphasized in the student services paradigm remain important in the student development paradigm, but other functions, such as minority student services and career services, are common and well developed (Ender et al., 1996). Programs and services are designed to emphasize the quality of the students' experiences on campus and are girded by pedagogical or psychological foundations. Guido, Chavez, and Lincoln (2010) suggest that an unintended consequence of the paradigm is that student affairs professionals are "often invisible" to students, as student affairs professionals rely on student experiences as vehicles for the students' development (p. 9).

Ender et al. (1996) acknowledged the emergence of a third paradigm that emphasizes student learning rather than merely development and referenced "seamless learning." Guido et al. (2010) coined the paradigm "shared learning," which is highly contextual and values the student's individual learning outcomes rather than aggregate student development. Student affairs professionals perceive their role as explicitly teachers rather than as educators. They design their practices to enhance students' content knowledge as well as cognitive and affective growth (Guido et al., 2010). Student affairs professionals working in the areas of residential life, counseling, advising, career services, and student activities assume greater responsibility for student learning than student affairs professionals working in "auxiliary" areas, such as housing and financial aid (Guido et al., 2010). Student affairs professionals and faculty work together to create learning experiences through co-teaching and curriculum design (Guido et al., 2010).

According to Whitchurch's (2008a) criteria for third-space professionals, academic librarians and student affairs professionals appear to occupy this third-space territory. Although academic librarians' traditional functions include the stewardship of collections, the provision of information services, and community development, they have clearly taken on an educational role through bibliographic instruction and information literacy. They see their role as educators as vitally important to their identity as academic librarians. Student affairs professionals, too, view themselves distinctly as educators, not only facilitating student success in higher education but also teaching students critical thinking and psychosocial skills. Both professions share certain core values, such as community development, service to others, and social justice, which are reflected in their work and care for students.

Academic librarians and student affairs professionals' respective roles in the educational mission of their institutions is evident. Librarians are employed in great numbers outside of higher education, and student affairs professionals may be employed more strictly as counselors, school administrators, and in other occupations outside of higher education. However, the professionals who work within higher education see themselves as distinctly infused with an educational purpose. Again, perhaps this should not be surprising given that Rubin (2010) claims academic libraries serve no purpose outside of the mission of the educational institution they serve. The scope of student affairs work is perhaps similarly dictated, especially when the higher education institution operates in a paradigm that values student development and integrated learning.

How are librarians and student affairs professionals uniquely situated to help one another through collaboration? The library and student affairs professions share service, community development, and social justice as core values. Collaborations designed with one of these values in mind appear to be appropriate foundations on which to begin. Librarians and student affairs professionals are very service-oriented. Collaborative activities that create a new service or strengthen an existing one should play well to librarians' and student affairs professionals' strengths as members of helping professions attuned to the success of their constituents and their institutions. This overlapping core value of service indicates that librarians and student affairs professionals should be natural partners in identifying and addressing systemic issues that impact their students' learning and success.

Both groups are also motivated by a desire to remove the barriers people face in achieving equity. While librarians may focus on reducing information barriers, student affairs professionals are addressing campus climate and other environmental barriers that reduce underrepresented students' likelihood to persist. Working together, librarians and student affairs professionals have the potential to significantly remedy social justice concerns on their campuses by sharing information about student populations and designing and marketing services that uniquely meet students' needs.

Community development is another core value shared by both librarians and student affairs professionals. This may be a particularly rewarding area on which to base potential collaborations. Librarians view the library as the intellectual heart of the campus but are increasingly offering programming to reshape the library as a social or cultural destination for students. Student affairs professionals are focused on ensuring students find ways to connect with each other in a variety of contexts. Together, librarians and student affairs professionals may find new ways of creating a student community that puts the library in the heart of student culture.

In short, librarians and student affairs professionals should have much philosophical common ground. Yet few examples of collaboration between librarians and student affairs professionals are detailed in scholarly and professional literature. In the next chapter, I review the literature that explores the concept of collaboration in higher education generally, examples of student affairs professionals' collaborations with other actors in higher education, examples of librarians' collaborative ventures with others, and the relatively few case studies of librarians and student affairs professionals working together on programming and improved student learning experiences.

Chapter Two

Review of the Literature

THE PHENOMENON OF COLLABORATION IN HIGHER EDUCATION

What does collaboration mean within the context of higher education? Schrage (1990) described collaboration as the process of shared creation, in which two or more people with complementary skills interact together to create a shared meaning that neither could have come to on their own. Montiel-Overall (2010) provided an excellent definition within the educational context: "collaboration is a process by which two or more individuals work together to integrate information in order to enhance student learning" (p. 8). John-Steiner (1998) suggested that collaborators not only plan, decide, and act jointly, but they also think together and combine independent conceptual schemes to create an original framework. They share resources, talent, and power, and their resulting work products reflect the blending of all participants' contributions.

Schrage (1990) claimed that collaborations in higher education are most ingrained in an institution's culture when those collaborations are formal and highly structured—essentially crafting a road map for successors to follow. Schrage (1990) said collaborations that are interdisciplinary must have at least two "passionate leaders," who are focused on solving a problem that each party sees as "real" and whose academic homes provide early support for such collaboration (p. 11). However, even formal, highly structured collaborations between people from different academic disciplines can fail when they do not recognize the road blocks of interdisciplinary work: the boundaries and norms that transcend participants and are systemic to their respective disciplines (Schrage, 1990).

The focus of this book is on collaborations between librarians and student affairs professionals that will ground a long-lived partnership. By "long-lived," it is meant that structures are in place to keep a program or relationship meaningful and productive even if the original people have moved on to other opportunities. John-Steiner's (1998) emphasis on collaborators' sharing of resources, talent, and power is intriguing because scholarship on educational organizations suggests that each of those elements is highly contested and likely the root of potential barriers. Indeed, Schrage (1990) warned that interdisciplinary work is "fraught with difficulties" (p. 17).

Kuh (1996) and Pascarella and Terenzini (2005) purported that student success is associated with seamless learning environments, in which comprehensive policies and practices are designed to complement cohesive educational missions and priorities. Pascarella and Terezini (2005) argued that engagement—the amount of time and effort students dedicate to their programs of study and other educational activities—is the primary vehicle by which students learn, develop, and persist to graduation. Pascarella and Terenzini (2005) claimed that

> [t]he greatest impact appears to stem from students' total level of campus engagement, particularly when academic, interpersonal, and extracurricular involvements are mutually reinforcing. Therefore, the holistic nature of learning suggests a clear need to rethink and restructure highly segmented departmental program configurations. (p. 647)

Whitt (2011) called the benefits of research on seamless learning environments "unequivocal" (p. 518) and noted higher education literature has extolled for years the benefits of collaborations between student affairs and academic affairs that reduce the fragmentation between curriculum and campus environments. Indeed, Blimling and Whitt (1999); Hamrick, Evans, and Schuh (2002); and Manning, Kinzie, and Schuh (2006) professed nearly identical arguments, although their works were largely exhortative rather than empirical. In the library literature, Bennett (2007); Raspa and Ward (2000); Gilchrist (2009); and Walter (2009) were similarly encouraging regarding the capacity of collaborations between libraries and academic affairs to enhance student success.

Despite the rather large body of literature devoted to the value of such collaborations, relatively little research has examined such collaborations and the conditions that make them fruitful or ineffectual. Kezar (2006) and Kezar and Lester (2009) examined collaborations in higher education broadly. Employing a multiple case study design, Kezar (2006) explored collaboration as a phenomenon and specifically the developmental process of collaboration. Among her research questions, Kezar asked how the context for collaboration emerges, grows, and becomes implemented; what the relative importance of learning is in the development of collaboration; what, if any, initial conditions are necessary for collaboration to develop; and if collaboration develops in stages. Kezar interviewed faculty and staff to discern their perceptions, analyzed documents related to the collaboration and to the institutional missions, and observed various activities related to collaboration, such as meetings, activities, and interdisciplinary research symposia. Kezar collected and interpreted her data at four non-elite higher education institutions that are geographically dispersed across regions of the United States, that serve large numbers of commuting students, and that have an overall population of approximately thirty thousand undergraduate students.

Using her findings, Kezar (2006) identified eight core elements that are necessary to create a context that enables collaboration: mission, integrating structures, campus networks, rewards, sense of priority from senior administrators, external pressure, values, and learning. Additionally, Kezar constructed a three-stage developmental model for collaboration. In the first stage of *building commitment*, Kezar described the institutions' senior administrators synthesizing ideas and information from a variety of sources to persuade faculty and staff of the need to conduct collaborative work. Senior administrators crafted their arguments using the institution's underlying values to make a case while also relying on external pressure from funding agencies and disciplinary professional associations to require faculty to seek out interdisciplinary partners for practical applications of their work. In *commitment*, the second stage of the model, Kezar claimed that senior administrators revised the institutional mission to better support collaboration and demonstrated through leadership that collaborative efforts were high institutional priorities. In *sustaining*, the third stage of the model, Kezar noted that collaborations are formalized by integrating networks to support collaboration, such as opening meetings to more individuals or using nonacademic spaces for meetings, and modifying reward systems—such as tenure standards—to recognize interdisciplinary work.

Kezar (2006) emphasized the importance of formal processes to enable collaboration, such as discussions within the context of academic senates and task forces to study and revise mission statements. Kezar did acknowledge informal processes, such as faculty members inviting like-minded colleagues to coffee to discuss collaborative ideas, as important to the success of collaboration, but she did not probe these informal moments deeply. Kezar speculated these moments might be as powerful or more powerful in reorienting a campus culture toward collaboration, but she simultaneously downplayed these as "micro-changes" (p. 858) that fell outside the focus of her study.

Although Kezar's (2006) three-stage developmental model for collaboration in higher education is compelling because it considers the phenomenon on an institutional scale, there is scant attention to people as actors in collaboration. Montiel-Overall (2010) claimed that successful collaboration requires interpersonal skills as much as it does synergy between functional areas. John-Steiner (1998) studied collaborations between artists and scientists inside and outside of higher education. Her observations and interviews suggested that individuals must possess a set of relational dynamics, such as intellectual ownership, trust, autonomy, and creativity. These dynamics must be present in order for participants to express both the desire and the capacity to engage in collaborative works with people outside their discipline (John-Steiner, 1998).

In a subsequent study, Kezar and Lester (2009) investigated the work lives of Harvard University faculty who participated in collaborative efforts, such as team-teaching with student affairs professionals in learning communities or working on curricular reform issues. In multiple interviews with participants and analyses of documents, Kezar and Lester (2009) found that faculty who participated in collaborative work with student affairs professionals or with faculty outside of their respective disciplines were highly discouraged and reported that the institution penalized their collaborative work while explicitly encouraging said work.

Kezar and Lester (2009) blamed responsibility-based budgeting, the "fiscal system in which various units or schools are responsible for their own revenue developments and covering costs" (p. 33), as a primary barrier to collaboration. A common application of responsibility-based budgeting in units with heavy teaching loads is the expectation for significant production of credit-bearing courses. One of the disadvantages of responsibility-based budgeting is that units compete for the same students to enroll in their courses and increase the revenue stream (Kezar & Lester, 2009). Similarly, team or interdisciplinary teaching is unintentionally discouraged because the instructors' salaries are paid out of their home unit's budget, while the revenue generated by the credit-bearing course will go to the unit associated with the course (Kezar & Lester, 2009). Additionally, Kezar and Lester found that faculty are often not awarded course releases, and collaborative efforts are then often above and beyond normal work expectations. Additionally, merit salary increases for student affairs professionals are typically allocated based on individual performance, as are evaluations for institutional service awards (Kezar & Lester, 2009).

Interestingly, the participants in Kezar and Lester's (2009) study often described their collaborative work with student affairs professionals as interdisciplinary whereas the student affairs professionals referred to their work simply as collaborations or partnerships. Given the paucity of research on the persons involved in collaboration, as well as Schrage's (1990) warning that interdisciplinary work is "fraught with difficulties" regarding disciplinary boundaries and norms (p. 21), it is worth examining collaborations between student affairs and academic affairs in the context of disciplinary cultures. Becher and Trowler (2001) suggested that faculty and other academic professionals are socialized into cultural patterns of behavior, which they called "academic tribes" (p. 2).

Disciplinary identity, according to Becher and Trowler (2001), is preserved through the distinction between "us" and "them," which often takes shape in the need to speak the same language, to participate in the social life of the discipline, and to share the same beliefs about teaching, research, and service. Distinctive cultural features of the discipline make it easy for the "in" group to identify outsiders and make it difficult for outsiders to join the group. Becher and Trowler suggested that outsiders are often treated with suspicion, which makes interdisciplinary work difficult, if not impossible:

> Men of the sociological tribe rarely visit the lands of the physicists and have little idea of what they do over there. If the sociologists were to step into the building occupied by the English department, they would encounter the cold stares if not the slingshots of the hostile natives. (p. 45)

Becher and Trowler (2001) asserted that academic tribes develop to protect knowledge. If knowledge were easily understandable and available, specialists would lose their authority and influence. Applying Becher and Trowler's definition of an academic discipline, student affairs and librarianship are academic disciplines in their own right. They have distinct objects of research (i.e., the information-seeking process and organization of information for librarians, and student development for student affairs professionals). Each has a body of accumulated knowledge organized by specific theories and principles. Each applies specific research methods and epistemologies to validate their knowledge, uses specific language adjusted to their knowledge, and reproduces its ways of knowing, working, and communicating through a process of institutionalization, which includes scholarly literature, professional bodies, and preprofessional training.

Becher and Trowler (2001) explained that academic tribalism does not make relationships between academic tribes impossible: Tribes with comparable values and technical language are more likely to reach a consensus. Collaboration between academic disciplines is most successful when each discipline shares a common vision of learning, a common language, a common perspective on students, and the ability to foster mutually satisfying dialog. Becher and Trowler acknowledged interdisciplinary work is less challenging between disciplines when the respective disciplines are malleable, at least partially, by their institutional mission.

Walter's (2009) perspective reinforces Becher and Trowler's (2001) argument. Walter (2009) claimed the library and student affairs professions are each "value-relational" disciplines, in which the members are "committed to, and find meaning in, specific ideologies" (p. 8). In other words, they must be attentive to their campus culture. If their institution values student development and learning outside of the classroom, then so too should the librarians and student affairs professionals employed at the institution.

Becher and Trowler's (2001) work illustrated that disciplinary differences can be a barrier to collaboration because librarians and student affairs professionals each have distinctive languages and ways of knowing that impede interdisciplinary work. Nonetheless, Becher and Trowler cautioned that their study was limited to interdisciplinary work between faculty of different disciplines. Their work omits higher education's professional staff entirely. Becher and Trowler (2001) confessed, "There is an almost total neglect of the professions in terms of documentation of their cultures. This may be connected with the fact that their academic embodiment is far from easy to demarcate" (p. 53). Trowler (2012) more recently reviewed the literature on disciplinary differences and academic identity and suggested that in the intervening decade few studies had examined whether interdisciplinary work involving professional staff would be stymied by disciplinary differences comparable to those of faculty (p. 38). Cownie (2012) argued that an ethnography of professional staff, such as student affairs professionals, is needed for "disciplines torn between the academic and the vocational," which "sit uncomfortably on the sidelines of the academy" (p. 60).

STUDENT AFFAIRS PROFESSIONALS AND OTHER ACTORS IN COLLABORATION

Collaboration between student affairs and academic affairs has received at least some attention in the higher education literature in recent years. Similar to collaborations between librarians and faculty members, many of these collaboration between student affairs and academic affairs seek to improve student learning and student experiences with the close involvement of faculty. These case studies focus on a variety of collaborations, including the design of living–learning communities in residence halls, diversity initiatives, and study abroad programs. Other studies examined the nature of the collaborations themselves rather than the intended outcomes of the collaborations.

Arguably one of the best known and widely emulated collaborations between student affairs professionals and faculty are living–learning communities (LLCs) established for the purpose of creating seamless learning environments between students' classroom and residence hall experiences (Borst, 2011). Laufgraben and Shapiro (2004) suggested that LLCs "represent a scholarly community, emphasize deep learning for an engaged and diverse community with a high level of faculty participation, and integrate the academic and social experiences of college life" (p. 156). Borst (2011) investigated the effect of faculty interaction on first-year students' cognitive development when those faculty and students participated in the LLCs at 19 institutions with cohorts in the 2006, 2007, and 2008 Wabash National Study of Liberal Arts Education. Among the LLCs included in the study, student affairs professionals tended to the students' living conditions and social and recreational programs, and met with faculty regularly to discuss the LLC's intended learning outcomes and student progress. The faculty members drove the LLC's educational goals, selected curriculum, and created learning experiences. The student affairs professionals were responsible for the LLC's continuity, recruiting both faculty and students when these groups moved on.

Borst (2011) did not specifically examine the partnerships between faculty and student affairs professionals themselves but instead evaluated the quality of these collaborations. In a longitudinal investigation of pre-test and post-test scores of the students, Borst (2011) determined that the correlation between students' cognitive development and academic performance was lower for LLC students than for students who did not participate in LLCs. Borst questioned why the collaborative efforts were not more effective and noted that in the subset of participants who did have a more powerful correlation between academic performance and cognitive development, the faculty and student affairs professionals reported an equitable share of responsibility for program administration and frequent, high-quality communication.

Barr (2013) explored partnerships between student affairs professionals and faculty in faculty-led study abroad programs. Barr interviewed participants at three higher education institutions where faculty created and coordinated study abroad programs and subsequently reached out to student affairs professionals for help with solving student problems, such as strategies for combating homesickness or counseling in the event of student death. Although student affairs professionals played a consultative role initially, faculty coordinators found that problems could be mitigated early by involving student affairs professionals more closely in the conception of new study abroad programs, in site selection, and in orientation and acculturation processes. Student affairs professionals enhanced student experiences by counseling students prior to departure, reached out to students at various points during their time abroad, and aided students with reflective thinking once they returned to their home institutions. Faculty members themselves reported less stress and burnout associated with the study abroad programs and indicated student affairs professionals aided students with "sense-making" and applying the lessons learned during their experiences abroad to enriching their domestic experiences (p. 145).

LePeau (2012) examined faculty and student affairs collaborations in the context of the American Commitments Project, a national project launched by the Association of American Colleges and Universities in the 1990s to integrate diversity initiatives within the curriculum and cocurricular activities. LePeau interviewed 18 faculty and student affairs professionals at four higher education institutions to identify how collaborators created partnerships built around diversity and inclusion. The findings suggest that three types of collaborations existed between faculty and student affairs professionals: complementary, coordinated, and pervasive (LePeau, 2012). Complementary partnerships were rigid and compartmentalized, but they were the most common type of collaboration, particularly among those who were new participants to working together. LePeau explained complementary partnerships as the student affairs professionals taught about those areas over which they had most authority, such as civic engagement or service learning, whereas the faculty members taught about those areas on which they were the most knowledgeable, such as the history of civil rights movements and the theoretical foundations of civic engagement.

Coordinated partnerships were defined by a blurring of the lines between student affairs and the faculty. The collaborators enjoyed productive, frequent collaboration and discussed wide-ranging topics. They felt entirely comfortable with either student affairs or faculty collaborators able to step in and teach any component of the activity. These collaborators tended to have relationships that were deep, personal, many years in the making, and often built on mutual respect (LePeau, 2012). The pervasive partnerships tended to be the most rare, and the participants perceived the blurring of student affairs and academic affairs as the "standard operation of the entire campus" (p. 222). These participants saw seamless learning as the ideal to which the institution should aspire to align all curricular and cocurricular programs, and they were comfortable challenging the barriers and contradictions that existed, especially in governance bodies. These participants rethought pedagogy inside and outside the classroom and were more likely to be campus leaders or faculty and student affairs professionals with highly established reputations at their respective institutions (LePeau, 2012). However, LePeau offered little guidance on how student affairs professionals and faculty might cultivate collaborations that yield coordinated or pervasive partnerships. Rather, these collaborations appeared to result because of the serendipitous meeting of like-minded individuals.

Stolz (2010) explored ways collaborations between student affairs professionals and faculty developed at a Midwestern university to promote seamless learning for students with disabilities. Stolz interviewed two campus leaders, three student affairs professionals, and nine faculty members to identify how, why, and when collaborations take place. The context of disability presented unique characteristics in collaborative efforts, but themes emerged from the participant interviews that described barriers to collaboration in regard to position, identity, and space. Stolz found that collaborators who created seamless learning for students with disabilities navigated these boundaries best by persistently demonstrating how the collaborations met the institution's stated values for inclusivity, success, and independence.

In addition to the case studies that recount best practices, a number of original research studies have emerged in recent years that investigate the perceptions, experiences, or conditions of collaborations between academic affairs and student affairs professionals. Most of these studies examine collaborations from an organizational or structural perspective. In a phenomenological study, O'Connor (2012) explored the factors that support or inhibit academic affairs and student affairs from working collaboratively to support holistic student experiences. O'Connor held focus groups consisting of faculty members and student affairs professionals who had participated in collaborations for at least three years at several public universities in the mid-Atlantic region. O'Connor found the factors that support collaboration include a common mission and values, support from senior administrators, and a shared understanding of student learning. However, participants noted a "siloing" effect between academic affairs and student affairs, which played an incredibly powerfully role in the inhibition of collaboration (O'Connor, 2012). Interestingly, the study suggested the siloing effect was blamed for disconnects in communication between collaborators, lack of resources to support collaboration such as marketing and flyers to stimulate student interest, and diminished student support in the collaborative ventures (O'Connor, 2012).

O'Connor's (2012) findings support Arcelus's (2008) study on the cultures of academic affairs and student affairs. In an ethnographic survey of a residential liberal arts college, Arcelus (2008) probed in nearly 100 interviews and in observation of over 250 meetings how faculty and student affairs professionals perceived their own and each other's roles as educators and how these perceptions influenced the potential for collaboration between the academic affairs and student affairs divisions to optimally benefit students. Arcelus concluded that the ethos for crafting a campus culture that emphasizes educating the whole student is often stymied by the "widening gap" between academic affairs and student affairs divisions that include structural differences, but is also the result of disciplinary and professional cultures that define the role of educators quite differently (p. 124). Indeed, Arcelus found that student affairs professionals perceived faculty as self-centered and little concerned with students' experiences outside of those students' performances in the faculty members' own courses—a strong indication that faculty were solely concerned with "the life of the mind" and not the whole student (p. 144). Similarly, faculty members were skeptical of student affairs professionals' attempts to collaborate, often perceiving overtures as attempts to diminish the "academic primacy" held by the faculty (p. 167). However, it is difficult to generalize Arcelus's findings since the study took place at a single institution.

Rodem's (2011) study appears to be one of the few that have examined interpersonal relationships between student affairs professionals and faculty in the context of collaborative activities. Rodem conducted multiple interviews with faculty and student affairs professionals who co-taught a first-year seminar course at Bowling Green State University. Most participants found collaborations beneficial for students, and they believed they were able to achieve more in partnership than they would have been able to accomplish individually (Rodem, 2011). While participants rated trust, comfort, and effective communication as essential factors in successful collaborations, they reported too that roles were far more complex and situational than they expected. Participants' satisfaction with the collaboration and the measurable effects on student learning increased with the passage of time, during which participants saw each other increasingly as friends, mentors, and confidantes. Rodem concluded that informal personal connections are vital for collaborations between faculty and student affairs professionals, and those responsible for fostering collaborations should intentionally develop and support opportunities for personal connection.

Lastly, Peltier (2014) examined the perceptions of student affairs professionals held by faculty who participated in collaborative work at a private, four-year liberal arts college located in the southeastern United States with a student enrollment of approximately two thousand undergraduates. The college's mission statement indicated that it created a "student-centered culture built upon openness and collaboration between faculty, staff, students, and alumni," and the college had been recognized for its excellence in integrative learning by the Commission on Colleges of the Southern Association of Colleges and Schools (p. 40). Peltier conducted interviews, analyzed documents, and observed people and places associated with the college. The purpose of the study was to probe the relationship between faculty and student affairs professionals from the perspective of the faculty, with a particular focus on the challenges to collaboration. The participants included faculty from the disciplines of history, biology, English, public affairs, art history, Spanish, and business administration; all of the participants had collaboration with student affairs professionals in service-learning programs, LLCs, or new student orientations.

Largely, the faculty identified lack of time as the most profound barrier to collaborations with student affairs professionals. Time spent on course preparation, teaching, research, and service to disciplinary associations left the faculty with what they perceived to be little time for being more committed to working with student affairs professionals. Although most of the faculty saw the benefits of working with student affairs professionals and recognized the difference seamless learning environments could make on students' success and academic performance, many faculty were less certain of the roles of student affairs professionals. One participant remarked:

> Even after several years at [the college] and understanding that student affairs staff work long hours, hold advanced degrees . . . I only vaguely know what they do beyond the briefest description of managing student issues outside the classroom—and that's *after* I've collaborated with several staff on new student orientation for three years in a row! (p. 80)

Other faculty observed that they had difficulty bonding with student affairs professionals because many tended to be young, not far removed from the students in terms of age and life experiences, and prone to leaving after only a few years at the college. Others perceived collaborations with student affairs professionals as unable to accomplish what the faculty members had hoped to achieve by collaborating—markedly advancing students' cognitive skills.

One faculty member claimed that

> [t]he student affairs staff only talked of social dimensions, whereas I was most concerned with helping students think. I understand how cognitive, psychosocial, and ethical development are interconnected—but I didn't see how I could contribute to those other areas as much as I could in shaping students' thinking. (p. 90)

Although Peltier's (2014) study is constrained in its generalizability as a single-site case study, it is nonetheless informative. While the argument for seamless learning is persuasive to many faculty, faculty may still perceive their influence on cognitive development as their primary contribution to student learning. Student affairs professionals may need to revise their message to emphasize the import and efficacy of cognitive development on co-curricular activities in order to forge successful and lasting partnerships with faculty. Additionally, student affairs professionals' roles and responsibilities may be poorly understood by faculty, despite past interactions that suggest successful relationships. Student affairs professionals may need to find ways to explain the myriad roles they fulfill, especially those at liberal arts colleges where they might wear many hats.

LIBRARIANS AND OTHER ACTORS IN COLLABORATION

Library literature is abundant with case studies exemplifying librarians who are working closely with teaching faculty to improve students' information literacy skills or to ensure the relevancy of library collections to research endeavors. Arguably, collaboration between librarians and faculty is essential for librarians to teach information literacy skills effectively to students. Yousef (2010) claimed that "[faculty] are the key to influencing student acceptance of information literacy. Therefore, librarians need to concentrate on academic partnerships and interest in information literacy" (p. 4).

Raspa, a professor of interdisciplinary studies, and Ward, a librarian, wrote one of the recent seminal works on librarian and faculty collaboration to promote students' information literacy. Raspa and Ward (2000) shared mutual interest in the ways students learn the research process. Together, Raspa and Ward tossed out the conventional methods of library instruction: faculty bringing students to the library as part of a course and assuming a nonparticipatory role while the librarian orients the students to the library and demonstrates how to find and search databases for topics pertinent to the course's assignments. Instead, Raspa and Ward created a new curriculum for UGE 1000, Wayne State University's freshman orientation course, by making students responsible for crafting their own strategies for finding and analyzing information. Raspa and Ward consulted with each student to revise and refine the strategies and interjected challenges to students' critical thinking in efforts to develop their information literacy skills.

As another example, the librarians at the University of Nevada–Las Vegas collaborated with faculty on student learning on a grand scale: They created the Faculty Institutes, a series of workshops in which librarians work with new faculty to investigate research-based learning activities that integrate library resources and course learning outcomes (Bowles-Terry, 2014). To this end, the participants discuss how research-based learning supports student learning and articulate goals and learning outcomes for research assignments. The librarians help faculty discover technology options that support research-based learning, such as data clearinghouses and cloud-based storage; the faculty help the librarians communicate the expectations of assignments to students and identify resources that best support the intended learning outcomes.

Faculty members are not the only actors within higher education with whom librarians collaborate to advance research and student learning. Wainwright and Davidson (2017) surveyed librarians at 180 higher education institutions to identify whether librarians partnered with nonacademic departments on outreach, instruction, and programming. They found that library collaborations with writing centers were the most common, but some unique partnerships included working with groundskeeping staff to maintain community gardens on library grounds (Wainwright & Davidson, 2017). Gibson, Morris, and Cleeve (2008) explored collaborations between academic librarians and university galleries and museum curators. Participants were interviewed at 12 higher education institutions whose campus leaders responded affirmatively to a survey that collaborations had taken place between the institution's library and its gallery or museum. Three themes to collaboration emerged: shared programming, in which librarians and curators jointly recruited and hosted visiting artists or exhibits; shared space, in which gallery and museum artifacts were exhibited temporarily at the library; and shared educational programs, in which curators taught workshop participants about the historic purpose and aesthetic values of artifacts, such as daguerreotypes, and librarians demonstrated conservation practices that restored the daguerreotypes (Gibson et al., 2008).

Librarians have often collaborated with information technology professionals in order to provide robust technologies that advance research and learning or improve workplace efficiencies. Melling (2013) described the "super-convergence" of libraries and information technology at higher education institutions in the 1990s and 2000s, in which libraries and information infrastructures were jointly administered by chief information officers. In Melling's (2013) study, librarians and technologists collaborated on the teaching of technology skills to adult students returning to U.K. higher education institutions; the technologists provided training during specialized new student orientation for adult students, while the librarians provided training during individualized consultations at the students' request. Melling noted that librarians and information technologists collaborated on the design and delivery of learning management systems, with librarians often responsible for the creation of new course modules and training for faculty while the information technologist supported and coded the back-end systems.

Interestingly, Melling (2013) found collaborations between librarians and information technologists to be "difficult" and "uneasy," particularly from the librarians' perspective (p. 156). The librarian participants claimed information technologists often lacked effective communication and interpersonal skills and were skeptical of the information technologists' commitment to supporting student learning or faculty research. Information technologists reported similar frustrations with the librarians, noting librarians sometimes lacked mastery of the technology they supported and seemed resistant or hostile to working alongside the technologists. Raspa and Ward (2000) found "similar beliefs about the importance of engaging students, meaningful discussion, humor, and a passion for [personal growth]" were essential elements to successful collaborations between librarians and faculty (p. 13). In contrast, Melling (2013) found these qualities to be distinctly lacking in librarian and information technologist collaborations and speculated that higher education institutions that converged libraries and information technology would one day split these entities as "too dissimilar" to achieve the desired outcomes (p. 153). This speculation suggests that collaborations may not work or may not be long-lived unless the actors share common values and belief systems.

Not all collaborations between librarians and technology professionals appear to be as vexing as Melling (2013) reported. Lightman and Ryan (2017) described a collaboration between librarians and university technologists at Northwestern University to create and implement a new geographic information system (GIS). The research services librarians noted the years-long demand from faculty and students for spatial thinking tools. The librarians were uniquely situated on campus to collect and share feedback for such a need. With backing from faculty, they and university technologists implemented a GIS site license for the campus. Together, they also created workshops for faculty and students they often taught together. Lightman and Ryan (2017) attributed their success in working with university technologists to having built a shared vision and common goals, and the desire to make a difference in the services the university offered to its employees and students.

Similarly, Wittenberg and Elings (2017) discussed the collaboration between the library and the office of research information technologies to offer a research data management program at the University of California, Berkeley. The collaboration grew out of a prior project that benchmarked existing technology services at their university's peer institutions. Recognizing that support for research activities at Berkeley was highly distributed across campus, the technology staff approached the librarians to help plan and deliver a new service model. Wittenberg and Elings (2017) said neither group could accomplish a coordinated effort alone; the technology staff brought highly technical expertise and capabilities in data security and storage whereas the librarians brought pedagogical expertise. The librarians taught faculty how to use technology solutions for managing research data. In both Lightman and Ryan's (2017) and Wittenberg and Elings' (2017) collaborations, the librarians were clearly recognized as valuable partners for their liaison skills and teaching abilities.

Perhaps surprisingly, few recent studies have examined faculty perceptions of their collaborations with librarians. Noting that qualitative descriptions of faculty–librarian collaborations in the library literature are largely positive portrayals but that none explore what collaboration with librarians means to the faculty, Schulte and Sherwill-Navarro (2009) surveyed 112 nursing faculty at 74 nursing schools in the Midwest and Southeast. Schulte and Sherwill-Navarro's study operated on the assumption that nursing faculty and librarians should have much common ground, as both groups belong to helping professions and as the rise of evidence-based nursing practice demands nurses become "information literate and appreciate the role of research in daily practice" (p. 57). Respondents defined their perspective of collaboration and described their perceptions of librarians, their experiences working with librarians, and their thoughts on how the work of librarians might or might not intersect with their roles as nursing educators.

Schulte and Sherwill-Navarro (2009) found nursing educators strongly perceived librarians to be experts at searching for information but little else. While many of the respondents replied that collaboration was the creation of something new that neither party could achieve alone—and offered examples of such collaboration—their ideas of collaboration with librarians were strictly limited to dedicating a portion of an instructional session to the demonstration of library resources. Moreover, the respondents believed that such collaboration was essential for student learning but did not feel that this collaboration should extend to their own classroom teaching. Schulte and Sherwill-Navarro concluded that librarians' skills are poorly understood by nursing faculty, and overcoming the traditional notions of librarians is a significant barrier to collaboration.

Nilsen (2012) explored teaching faculty members' perceptions of librarians generally and of their role in curriculum development and instruction at postsecondary institutions in Canada. Of the 106 respondents to Nilsen's survey, more than half rated information literacy as very important to undergraduate students' critical thinking skills and to their academic performance. Many of the respondents also reported that they did not regularly work with librarians and attempted instead to teach information literacy skills to students themselves. When asked why they did not collaborate with librarians, many respondents said the role of librarians is simply too different from what faculty members do and that librarians could not be taken seriously as educators. Instead, many respondents reported librarians were more like administrators and chiefly concerned with the business of running a library rather than with teaching or venturing outside the library, while others said they doubted librarians' effectiveness at teaching due to librarians' lack of doctoral degrees. A few respondents expressed surprise that librarians should instruct students in any way at all, as faculty members were perfectly capable of doing so.

Although Nilsen's (2012) findings were similar to Schulte and Sherwill-Navarro's (2009) findings, Nilsen's study probed more deeply into faculty members' perceptions of librarians in an instructional role. The results were more varied, and Nilsen articulated that faculty ambivalence toward librarians is complex and multilayered. Nilsen's findings indicate that faculty create their perceptions of librarians against the lens of their own roles and credentials as educators. The generalizability of the findings of both studies is questionable. Schulte and Sherwill-Navarro recruited their participants by asking librarians at different institutions to forward their recruitment message to nursing faculty. It seems likely that nursing faculty who respond to surveys brought to their attention by librarian colleagues might have different perceptions of collaboration with librarians than those who do not have a relationship with their institutions' librarians. While Nilsen's survey did not involve librarians as intermediaries and reached participants from a variety of academic disciplines, Nilsen herself noted a surprisingly high number of responses came from institutions in her province of British Columbia and were progressively fewer the farther the members of the sample population were from British Columbia. This casts some doubt on the generalizability of her findings to regions outside western Canada.

Nonetheless, Nilsen's (2012) findings suggest that librarians might find greater acceptance from student affairs professionals as collaborators in student learning than from faculty. Student affairs professionals share some similarities with librarians—namely that their teaching is not tied to academic coursework, they typically do not hold doctoral degrees, and they hold similar dual administrative and educational roles. There is a significant gap in the library and higher education literature regarding librarians' and student affairs professionals' perceptions of each other and of their collaborative prospects.

LIBRARIANS AND STUDENT AFFAIRS PROFESSIONALS IN COLLABORATION

Although descriptions or studies of collaborations between librarians and teaching faculty are plentiful in scholarly literature, few articles address collaborations between librarians and student affairs professionals (Hinchliffe & Wong, 2012; Swartz, Carlisle, and Uyeki, 2007). In perhaps the earliest argument for collaboration, Forrest (2005), a librarian, recognized that student affairs professionals support students by providing critical information for building plans of study, persisting with or departing higher education, and exploring careers. Despite the advocacy for librarians to cultivate relationships with student affairs professionals, Forrest was shortsighted in not recognizing the potential of these collaborations to enrich student learning. Instead, Forrest questioned student affairs professionals' technology skills and familiarity with electronic information and argued librarians should teach their colleagues how to find electronic information and how to use technology more effectively.

Forrest (2005) postulated that if librarians teach student affairs professionals the skills librarians also teach students, then student affairs professionals would increase their productivity and pass higher-quality information along to students. Certainly, Forrest's call for collaboration smacks of hubris and casts student affairs professionals in a poor light—even referring to educating student affairs professionals on technology use as librarians' "ethical responsibility to higher education" (p. 11). Nonetheless, Forrest asked an important question regarding collaborations between librarians and student affairs professionals: "Do they even exist?" (p. 12).

Gatten's (2005) perception of student affairs professionals was far more positive; he acknowledged student affairs professionals are experts in student development theories and suggested they have much to teach librarians about students. Gatten argued librarians should explore theories of students' psychosocial and cognitive development to better understand the context for students' information-seeking behavior. If bibliographic instruction and information literacy programs were adapted within the framework of these theories, the practice of librarianship would be improved (Gatten, 2005). Regrettably, Gatten's claims appear to have largely fallen on deaf ears in academic librarianship, with only a few subsequent studies on information literacy citing his work.

A few years later, Walter and Eodice (2007) noted that library instruction had evolved from merely demonstrating library resources to teaching information literacy, a critical analysis of information that emphasizes a student-centered, problem-solving approach. Walter and Eodice said:

> If we are to realize the potential, the establishment of strategic relationships with campus partners is essential. Although instructional collaboration with members of the classroom faculty has been a subject of study for over a decade . . . collaboration with student services and other co-curricular programs remains largely unexplored. (p. 219)

In the intervening years, a few case studies have emerged exploring librarians and student affairs professionals in collaboration, mostly thanks to Hinchliffe and Wong's (2012) edited collection. The subsequent studies discuss librarian and student affairs professionals' collaborations concerning students' pre-entry to higher education, the first-year experience, on-course study, and career preparation. These studies are organized differently than the preceding sections of the literature review. Perhaps the farthest ranging, the studies included showcase the intersections of librarianship and student affairs despite the breadth of their respective functions in higher education and diversity of roles. Consequently, Weaver's (2013) student journey lifecycle is employed in this section as a conceptual framework for organizing the studies into a coherent flow. Weaver argued:

> [Higher education professionals] need to understand a lot more about the entirety of the student experience, from a student's pre-entry into university, during their subsequent induction and first year experience, while on course, and beyond the [degree] into employment . . . or further study. Each stage of the journey places differing demands on academic and administrative processes. (p. 104)

Weaver (2013) developed the student journey lifecycle as a four-stage model spanning the stages of studentship. Weaver (2013) recommended that planning for services and programs, especially in libraries, commence from a student perspective with the four stages of studentship in mind. Consequently, services and educational experiences would be holistic, student-centered, and target the critical junctures of students' journeys through higher education. This framework is appropriate, given that many of the studies concern student-facing activities, such as marketing the library or teaching information literacy skills, in contexts that largely fall outside the students' formal courses of study.

Pre-Entry

Marines and Venegas (2012) examined a distinctive collaboration between instruction librarians and the Office of Educational Opportunities Programs (EOP), a student affairs unit, at the University of California–Santa Cruz. The EOP "ensures the recruitment, retention, and academic success of first-generation college students from low-income, educationally disadvantaged backgrounds" (Marines & Venegas, 2012, p. 221). The purpose of the collaboration was to specifically prepare racially and ethnically underrepresented high school juniors and seniors for study in the arts, humanities, and social sciences. The EOP recruited cohorts of 15–20 academically talented high school students to work on a research project for a semester under the mentorship of a faculty member. An instruction librarian met with students for one-on-one sessions during the research proposal, annotated bibliography, and writing stages of the projects. During the sessions, librarians taught students the "secret secrets" (Marines & Venegas, 2012, p. 222) of research, including familiarity with library resources and physical layout, understanding peer-reviewed journals, reading the discourse of the discipline, and writing logic statements for why students included specific sources in their bibliographies.

The collaboration between the librarians and the student affairs professionals associated with the EOP appeared strong. Although the student affairs professionals left responsibility for instruction with faculty members from the arts, social sciences, and humanities, they were ultimately responsible for developing the curricula. Marines and Venegas (2012) noted the program had been in place since the 1980s, with the librarians' roles growing over time from consultation to developing elements of the program together with the student affairs professionals. However, Marines and Venegas observed that librarians and student affairs professionals had considerably different expectations of students' academic performance, with student affairs professionals encouraging librarians to expect higher standards from students' writing.

Hamrick, Evans, and Schuh (2002) echo the student affairs professionals' insistence that students are capable of meeting higher academic standards than the librarians anticipated. Student affairs professionals shape students' cognitive development by helping students think through complex situations, and they observe students rise successfully to extramural challenges that require project management, financial, and consensus-building skills (Hamrick et al., 2002). Hamrick et al. speculated that faculty have a narrow understanding of students' cognitive ability and too often create assignments that emphasize content acquisition and writing over complex problem-solving. The librarians in Marines and Venegas's (2012) case study appear to share with the teaching faculty the lack of deeper understanding of students' learning capability. Unfortunately, Marines and Venegas did not explain if or how the librarians responded to the student affairs professionals' concern; rather they noted only the long-standing program was in danger of losing the librarians' participation due to the increasing need to provide the core services of reference desk coverage, bibliographic instruction, and collection development coinciding with declining numbers of librarians.

In direct response to Oakfleaf's (2010) entreaty for librarians to demonstrate greater value to higher education institutions, Miller (2012) sought a partnership with the office of admissions to enhance prospective students' and parents' tours of the campus at Miami University. Miller (2012) recognized university administrators were assessing the "golden walk," (p. 586) or the student-led campus tour, which is one of the strongest influences on prospective students' decisions to apply and to enroll. Miller (2012) viewed this assessment as an opportunity for the librarians to build awareness of the library before students engaged in coursework.

With the guidance of the admissions director, several librarians created web pages featuring library services embedded on the Office of Admissions' website and corresponded via e-mail with prospective students and parents to welcome them and answer questions. Miller (2012) herself researched information conveyed by student tour guides, revised the tour script, and participated in the guides' training. The admissions director also influenced the library by recommending "a few cosmetic changes" (p. 588) to the library's facilities prior to campus tours. However, Miller did not clearly describe what sorts of interactions emerged between librarians and prospective students and parents or if the library or the Office of Admissions changed the nature of tours in a meaningful way; she noted merely that the office of admissions staff were grateful for the librarians' assistance.

First-Year Experience

While librarian/student affairs collaborations focused on students prior to their entry to higher education are rare, those focused on the students' first-year experience have received greater attention in the literature. The "first-year experience" is sometimes associated with solely a seminar course or a "University 101" course, in which students are aided in the transition to higher education. In her student journey lifecycle framework, Weaver (2013) adopted a much broader perspective. The first-year experience is a constellation of student-centered programs, services, and activities that together create a cohesive learning environment, increase student persistence, ease student transition to higher education, facilitate a sense of community and institutional loyalty, and spark personal growth.

Weaver (2013) postulated that much, if not the majority, of student learning during the first year of higher education takes place outside of the classroom; therefore collaborations between librarians and student affairs professionals designed to support the first-year experience should engage students largely outside of the established curriculum. Specifically, Weaver claimed student housing, counseling and tutoring programs, student unions, and learning and media commons were the most promising grounds for collaborations. It is important to note that Weaver wrote with European systems of higher education, principally British, in mind.

Cummings's (2007) article does not concern the first-year experience per se but is the most appropriate study to preface this stage of the student journey lifecycle because she emphasized that student affairs professionals offer the most promise in helping librarians connect with students outside of the library, especially very early in students' experiences on campus. Cummings was focused on marketing Washington State University's library to students and recounted librarians' efforts at staffing tables with pamphlets advertising the library at transfer student orientations and at events coordinated by the Office of New Student Programs. When these activities attracted little interest from students, the residence life staff suggested librarians create door hangers advertising the library that the residence life staff would then post on freshmen's doors in the residence halls. The librarians ceased publishing the door hangers after two years due to fiscal restraints and uncertainty about their effectiveness, but Cummings noted the residence life staff taught the librarians more about student culture and the importance of timing when marketing the right message to first-year students. Despite this, Cummings did not imply that a new program or service developed together would subsequently commence.

Long (2011), Riehle and Witt (2009), and Strothman and Antell (2010) provided case studies of librarians entering traditional student spaces—the undergraduate residence halls—to market the library or to directly provide research and information support. Long (2011) described his role as a librarian who worked entirely outside of the university library and was embedded fully into the residence halls, managing several small branch libraries whose collections supported the living–learning communities at the University of Illinois at Urbana-Champaign. Long (2011) shared some responsibilities with residential life staff, such as training resident assistants, mediating student conflicts, and creating hall programming that integrated research skills and library resources. This unique position itself was borne out of a collaboration between the university library and the university housing division to bridge students' information needs not met by the research focus of the library (Long, 2011). The library initially funded the salary and provided a book budget to support first-year curricula, and the housing division provided space and infrastructure support. However, Long acknowledged his role was difficult to navigate, often marginalized by librarians at the university library, and poorly understood by residential life staff.

Strothman and Antell (2010) were inspired to bring library services into residence halls after participating in the University of Oklahoma's faculty-in-residence program and living among undergraduate students for three years. Based on their observations of students studying together in hall lounges and consulting each other for information guidance, Strothman and Antell concluded librarians could use these opportunities to teach students about research skills and information literacy at students' point-of-need. They established a program called Research Rescue, for which they provided refreshments at a set time in the lounges and made themselves available for research assistance. Additionally, they founded a book discussion group and held educational programs jointly with residential life staff, such as a popular program on censorship. Ultimately, student participation in these activities was low, leading Strothman and Antell to observe that "students guard their free time closely and are unwilling to give [it] up unless that an event is worth their while" (p. 53). Nonetheless, they found their involvement affirming because they believed they were able to reduce students' library anxiety and reach students who might not have otherwise benefitted from librarians' expertise (Strothman & Antell, 2010).

Riehle and Witt (2009) attempted to teach information literacy sessions in the lounges of residence halls at Purdue University. Their sessions were not tailored to individual students or to educational programs devised by residential life staff. Instead, they partnered with residential life to sponsor a traditional library instruction session as a regular hall program because the housing division's mission called for a specific number of academic programs in the halls. Residential life marketed the program and encouraged students to attend through food incentives, and the librarians oriented students to the library's website and services through laptop computers. Riehle and Witt believed their sessions would have proven successful with more time to become established as a regular program, but the librarians were unable to continue the programs due to a more urgent need to cover service points and activities at the library.

Otto, Meade, Stafford, and Wahler (2016) took a different approach and brought students residing in residence halls into the library for an overnight event. The librarians partnered with housing and residential life staff at Eastern Washington University to organize a program called "Lights Out," in which students residing in the undergraduate residence halls spent the night in the library. The students participated in team-building activities and various programs, including a scavenger hunt focused on library resources. While the authors found the learning outcomes limited, they acknowledged this was a flipped version of library outreach where first-year students were exposed to a different and emerging role of the library—that of an active agent in students' sense of community and belonging on campus.

Like residence hall staff, librarians have brought library services to students associated with cultural centers. Love and Edwards (2009) described their experiences approaching the student affairs professionals who managed the Latino/a and Asian American cultural centers at the University of Illinois at Urbana-Champaign. Much like Strothman and Antell (2010), Love and Edwards hosted programs at the cultural centers that oriented students to the library and held personal research consultations for students. The staff at the cultural centers provided space, introductions to students, and assistance with food incentives for the programs. Although Love and Edwards speculated they would be unable to forge long-lasting relationships with many students because of their commitments at the library, they noted the purpose of their outreach was partly to demystify the university library for underrepresented students, whose persistence was lower than their white counterparts. Consequently, Love and Edwards found their time and efforts to be well spent and beneficial.

Aguilar and Keating (2009) created a similar opportunity at the University of New Mexico after Native American students reported in a survey that the university's libraries were overwhelming and intimidating, and that the students therefore felt discouraged from using them. Supported by a grant from the Indigenous Nations Library Program, Aguilar and Keating provided wireless access networks and mobile equipment for the Native American cultural house and for the Women's Resource Center. Subsequently, three librarians spent an average of 12–20 hours per week at the cultural house and resource center. Aguilar and Keating reported significant success, suggesting the librarians answer primarily directional questions or provide referrals to student services offices at first, but held numerous research consultations as the academic year unfolded. Aguilar and Keating attributed their success to establishing personal relationships with students that segued into professional mentoring, but the librarians noted they shared Native American identities with the students they served and observed that some of their white colleagues were unable to establish rapport and became frustrated with the students' lack of interest in their presence.

Librarians at California State University, Northridge partnered with student affairs professionals to meet the information literacy needs of students in fraternities and sororities (Lampert, Dabbour, & Solis, 2007). Inspired to reach out to the Office of Greek Life by the character Elle's speech extolling the virtues of sorority life in the film *Legally Blonde*, the librarians learned fraternity and sorority chapters held members to certain academic standards, and that some members struggled to maintain their grade point average (Lampert et al., 2007). Through the Office of Greek Life, Lampert et al.

reached out to individual Greek chapters and offered library orientation and information literacy sessions for chapter members in their houses. Interestingly, Lampert et al. observed that the sessions were effective at reaching students, despite students appearing disinterested and bored at the sessions. Lampert et al. reported many of the same students visited them later at the library for consultations, explaining that they were too embarrassed to ask questions in front of their Greek brothers or sisters.

Librarians have also partnered with student affairs professionals to meet the unique information needs of first-year athletes. As health sciences librarians at James Madison University, Sapp and Vaughan (2017) provided visual tours of the library's website to freshmen football players in the athletics facilities. Additionally, they engaged football players in learning information about the libraries, including resources on kinesiology and sports injuries, by playing card games based on the popular game Apples to Apples. Sapp and Vaughan (2017) were able to build upon this engagement by offering dedicated study skills sessions to freshmen athletes throughout the year, noting that student athletes have high rates of college departure or transfer due to low academic performance during the first year of college. As with other case studies, the role of the student affairs professionals was not discussed beyond helping the librarians gain access to the freshmen athletes. Sapp and Vaughan (2017) reported satisfaction with and value in their approach, though they expressed concern about the library's capacity to continue their work, and they found the impact of their work on the students' performance difficult to assess.

Love and Edwards (2009), Aguilar and Keating (2009), Lampert et al. (2007), and Sapp and Vaughan (2017) demonstrated that librarians can reach new audiences when they enter student spaces. The students associated with the cultural houses and the women's resource center felt comfortable, protected, and at ease in those spaces. Consequently, Love and Edwards and Aguilar and Keating were reportedly successful at helping the students navigate the library, arrange research consultations, and improve their information literacy skills.

Lozano (2010) described the importance of spaces that support students' sense of identity and belonging, and noted that promoting spaces that enable students to feel psychologically secure will often positively influence students' academic performance. Long (2011), Strothman and Antell (2012), and Riehle and Witt (2009) appeared to have less success reaching students in undergraduate residence halls, perhaps because these spaces are not principally designed to support students' identities but to provide safe living spaces.

On-Course

Accardi, Garvey-Nix, and Meyer (2012) created a plagiarism prevention program as a partnership between instruction librarians, writing center staff, and the student conduct and judicial officers. The program was borne from a noted increase in plagiarism cases referred to the student conduct and judicial officers by faculty at Indiana University Southeast. The vice chancellor of student affairs approached the librarians and the writing center staff for assistance, and together the collaborators developed the curricula for a program designed for different stages of student development (Accardi et al., 2012). A staff member from each area is responsible for teaching a different element of the program: The librarians teach citing sources correctly, the writing center staff teach time management skills for writing assignments and developing original statements, and the student conduct and judicial affairs staff teach the consequences stemming from plagiarism. Accardi et al. (2012) planned to expand their program to include transfer student orientation and the living–learning programs in the residence halls so students did not associate the program purely with punitive measures. The plagiarism education program appears to be one of the few examples of a collaboration between librarians and student affairs professionals in which each party brought expertise and energy to create a new program or service that served the students in a way that neither party could achieve separately.

Arzola (2016) found an opportunity to collaborate with the Office of Student Disability Services, a unit of student affairs at Lehman College, City University of New York. In order to improve the accessibility of coursework for students with disabilities, librarians and disability resource specialists explored assistive technology features and options that could be easily implemented by students and faculty alike. Using focus groups of students, the librarians created outreach materials to create awareness of accessibility tools for faculty and taught workshops to students on how to use apps and other free software to translate or read documents necessary for their courses.

Dahl (2007) observed the traditional model of liaison librarianship, in which librarians perform subject-specific collection development, reference assistance, instruction, and outreach and communication to academic departments, which omits groups of library users. Dahl recommended that liaison librarianship should expand to include nonacademic units with unmet information or library needs. While Dahl did not specify which nonacademic units would benefit most from librarians' expanded liaison roles, she suggested librarians identify service providers on their campuses whose information sharing and programming goals overlap with libraries' goals. Crowe (2010) recounted a successful liaison program at the University of North Carolina at Greensboro, where the librarians established a program called the Student Affairs Connection. The program comprised a liaison program that provided programming and instruction for students associated with different student affairs programs. The librarians expanded their traditional liaison roles to include the living–learning communities in the residence halls, student government association, Greek societies, the writing and speaking center, service learning, the office of the dean of students, and athletics. Crowe (2010) reported the librarians' efforts have yielded positive changes, including student feedback for making the library itself more user-centered. The librarians reported enhanced collaborations on programs and activities with student affairs colleagues and a greater understanding of how to promote the library's resources and services more effectively to students.

Career Preparation

Much of the literature emphasizes collaborations between student affairs professionals and a subset of librarians—those whose responsibilities include providing direct service to patrons, such as reference, instruction, and outreach librarians. However, approximately half of academic librarians are principally engaged in other responsibilities related to library operations, such as acquiring and cataloging collections, preserving fragile or damaged materials, and administering electronic resource systems (Griffiths & King, 2009). Elguindi and Sandler (2013) described a collaboration between several of these librarians and the staff at the career center and the Gay, Lesbian, Bisexual, and Transgender (GLBT) Resource Center at American University.

Elguindi and Sandler (2013) recognized that the career center and the GLBT Resource Center managed sizable book collections related to both career exploration and GLBT fiction. The student affairs professionals desired to circulate the materials to students but found managing their inventory and loans to be too cumbersome to continue without better organization and technology. The catalog librarians and a technology services librarian helped the student affairs professionals determine that an automated catalog and circulation system would best suit their purposes. Consequently, they adopted a technological solution and taught the student affairs professionals how to organize and manage their collections. Elguindi and Sandler explained that all librarians are capable of outreach and collaboration and should consider what skills they have to offer that resolve unmet needs on campus; librarians should not look toward developing students' cognitive or information literary skills as the sole way they could contribute to student success.

The career services staff at the University at Buffalo maintained a book collection on job-seeking strategies and interview tips for students (Hollister, 2005). After meeting the career services staff by teaching a University 101 course with them, Hollister, a librarian at the University at Buffalo's undergraduate library, assessed the career center's book collection and found it "unwieldy, unattractive, and access-prohibitive" (p. 108). Hollister helped the student affairs professionals replace some materials with electronic counterparts, identify obsolete media, and craft a book donation policy. After Hollister helped the student affairs professionals curate their book collection, they found the opportunity to discuss the career center's goals and the ways they help students prepare for the job market. Hollister was then able to teach the career center staff about resources the undergraduate library held that helped the career center staff remain current on trends in career counseling in higher education.

GAP ANALYSIS

For nearly 20 years, studies have shown that student persistence, development, and academic performance are greatly enhanced when faculty and student affairs professionals adopt a collaborative approach to learning (Kuh, 1996; Pascarella & Terenzini, 2005). For higher education institutions to support a seamless or holistic approach to student learning, academic affairs and student affairs divisions must reconceptualize their roles in learning and in their relationships with each other. Librarians and student affairs professionals would appear to be successful prospective partners in such collaborations. However, relatively few case studies of collaborations between the two disciplines exist.

Librarians and student affairs professionals shape student learning and development outside of the traditional classroom environment. The core values of both disciplines suggest areas in which librarians and student affairs professionals might overlap in their work, such as developing students' citizenship skills, advocating for equity and social justice in the educational process, and simply serving students' needs so they are able to successfully navigate their educational experiences. Some examples of possible collaborations could include librarians and academic advisors participating together in intrusive advising to help exploratory students remain engaged in their studies. Librarians could also be embedded in career centers and TRIO programs in order to help students attain postcollege employment aligned with their value systems and orient at-risk students more deeply into the academic environment.

Forrest (2005) asked of collaborations between librarians and student affairs professionals, "Do they even exist?" (p. 12). A few notable case studies on collaborations between librarians and student affairs professionals are available in the scholarly literature, but these case studies present significant shortcomings. All of the case studies are written by and for librarians and intended to provide best practices or showcase a set of circumstances that "worked." However, whether these case studies truly embody collaboration is questionable. John-Steiner (1998) suggested that true collaborators not only plan, decide, and act jointly, they also think together and combine independent conceptual schemes to create an original framework. They share resources, talent, and power, and their resulting work products reflect the blending of all participants' contributions and endure long after the original collaborators have departed (John-Steiner, 1998).

Each of the collaborations appeared somewhat ephemeral: Lampert, Dabbour, and Solis (2007), Riehle and Witt (2009), Strothman and Antell (2010), Marines and Venegas (2012), and Sapp and Vaughan (2017) offered no evidence that their collaborations would survive long after the individual actors moved into different roles. Rather, their collaborations appeared to take shape because of common interests and unique, temporary circumstances. For example, Strothman and Antell taught information literacy to students through programs offered in residence hall lounges because those collaborators resided within the residence halls. Because her spouse's participation in the faculty-in-residence program was for only a year, the librarian collaborator noted that her residency was only temporary. Riehle and Witt concluded that their case study on research workshops in residence halls was successful in regard to student interest and attendance, but was constrained too significantly by budgets, staffing, and diverse institutional priorities to continue. Rather, they intended to move their content to self-directed online tutorials and to train resident directors and resident assistants in research expertise as much as possible (Riehle & Witt, 2009).

Perhaps more troubling is the lack of perspectives shared by the student affairs professionals in these collaborations. None of the case studies explained the stakes, benefits, or desired outcomes from the student affairs professionals' perspectives. In most of the case studies, they were invisible collaborators and were barely mentioned at all. Their contributions to the collaborations appeared relegated merely to the provision of space, supplies, or permission. Their roles were largely those of gatekeeping, helping the librarians gain access to students in spaces where librarians did not typically venture such as residence halls and cultural houses. Where were the voices of the student affairs professionals?

If librarians and student affairs professionals have yet to collaborate extensively, what are the reasons for their lack of involvement? Becher and Trowler (2001) suggested collaboration between academic disciplines is most successful when each discipline shares a common vision of learning, a common language, a common perspective on students, and the ability to foster mutually satisfying dialog. Yet higher education literature on collaborations between student affairs and academic affairs has focused primarily on the structural, cultural, human resource, and political barriers that exist to impede collaborations (Kezar, 2006; Kezar & Lester, 2009; Becher & Trowler, 2001). More research is needed to enable successful collaborations between librarians and student affairs professionals, including exploring their perceptions of each other's roles in student learning.

Swartz, Carlisle, and Uyeki (2007) acknowledged librarians and student affairs professionals have very different ideas regarding effective student learning. Kezar (2006) claimed that competing ideas as to what constitutes learning are one of the major impediments to collaboration generally, indicating that epistemological differences create conflict. Although librarians value citizenship and other forms of student development, librarians are most interested in developing students cognitively. Student affairs professionals have broader assumptions about student learning and might grow frustrated with librarians' rather limited view of the scope of their work. Consequently, librarians' and student affairs professionals' ideas about what constitutes student learning and success and the way they see themselves able to make contributions are crucial to developing successful collaborations.

Schulte and Sherwill-Navarro's (2009), Nilsen's (2012), and Peltier's (2014) studies conveyed the importance of perceptions to collaborations. If one actor has unfavorable or inaccurate ideas about the other actor, collaborations will not develop easily; personality differences, interpersonal skills, and broad perspectives of campus environments matter (Peltier, 2014). The extant literature provides little to no indication what student affairs collaborators might have thought about their librarian collaborators. Similarly, the librarians' portrayals of the student affairs collaborators were fleeting, marginal, or outright absent.

Accordingly, I attempted to address the gaps in the literature regarding how librarians and student affairs professionals perceive their respective roles in student learning and success. Additionally, I identified how librarians perceive student affairs professionals and vice versa, and decided upon the following questions: How do librarians and student affairs professionals describe student learning and student success? How do librarians and student affairs professionals perceive their own and each other's roles in student learning and student success? Where do they see the work of librarians intersect, if at all, with the work of student affairs professionals? How might they approach collaborations in these intersecting areas? How might the work and identities of librarians and student affairs professionals change because of these collaborations?

Chapter Three

The Research Methodology

The purpose of my book is to explore librarians' and student affairs professionals' perceptions of each other's roles in student learning and success, identify opportunities for prospective collaborations, and identify the conditions that impede or facilitate prospective collaboration. To collect my data, I employed focus group interviews with librarians and student affairs professionals at five universities in the U.S. Midwest region. The following questions guided my research:

1. How do librarians and student affairs professionals describe student learning and student success?
2. How do librarians and student affairs professionals perceive their own and each other's roles in student learning and student success?
3. Where do they see the work of librarians intersect, if at all, with the work of student affairs professionals?
4. How might they approach collaborations in these intersecting areas?
5. How might the work and identities of librarians and student affairs professionals change because of these collaborations?

I concluded focus groups were the most appropriate tool for collecting data for this book. Focus groups are a form of in-depth interviewing in a group setting (Krueger, 1998; Morgan, 2002; Stewart & Shamdasani, 2015). The purpose of focus groups is to collect rich, detailed data and to explore topics about which little is known from a group of people simultaneously.

Focus group interviews typically involve five to eight participants, who discuss a particular topic under the direction of a moderator who promotes group interaction, and will generally last between one and two hours (Morgan, 2002). Stewart and Shamdasani (2015) claimed personality traits are factors to consider in assembling focus groups, with extroversion likely to have the most common and greatest effect on group interaction:

> In a mixed group of extroverts and introverts, a moderator will need to work very hard indeed to keep the extroverts from dominating the discussion while drawing out the introverts. The bottom line with respect to personality factors in focus group research is that it is important to recognize them and in [some] cases make them the basis for selecting participants in specific groups. (pp. 22–23)

This is an especially important point in light of the two professional groups involved in this book. Cutler (2003) described the professional identity development of student affairs professionals and emphasized the great numbers of extroverted personalities in the student affairs profession. She speculated the student affairs profession strongly desires extroversion as a personality trait because student affairs professionals spend so much time working with students directly (often in informal environments, such as residential life). Student affairs professionals must build relationships with peers and students and be fully engaged during traditional work hours for meetings and nontraditional hours for face time with students. Extroverted personalities are typically able to meet these demands more easily than introverted personalities (Cutler, 2003). Although introverted personalities are present and necessary in student affairs, the profession has a tendency to screen out introverted applicants during the hiring process (Cutler, 2003).

In librarianship, the socialization process tends the other direction. Historically, the nature of librarianship has favored solitary work. Arguably, it is not strictly necessary for librarians to build relationships with peers and students in order to be successful at acquiring the right resources for a strong collection, demonstrating databases, or answering reference questions accurately—although this may be changing in light of librarian's increasing emphasis on working more closely with faculty and students (Maxwell, 2006). Maxwell (2006) claimed that librarians adopt passive student outreach practices, too, such as investing time and effort into exhibits and guest speakers rather than engaging students directly, and that librarians wait at service points for students to initiate contact rather than seeking out students for reference consultations. Maxwell (2006) speculated that libraries' traditional quiet atmospheres tend to attract introverted personalities who desire to work alone.

Although the high numbers of extroverted personalities in student affairs and introverted personalities in librarianship do not preclude collaboration, the differences in personalities must be acknowledged as a possible barrier to the way each group manages its work and relates to others. Accordingly, I employed separate focus groups for librarians and for student affairs professionals.

I conducted my research in two phases. First, I moderated seven focus groups at four higher education institutions in late 2015 and early 2016, which formed the basis of my dissertation study. In late 2017 and early 2018, I expanded upon my original research for this book. I recruited additional participants from a fifth institution and moderated two more focus groups there. I also returned to one of the original four institutions in my dissertation study to complete a focus group of the student affairs professionals, which had not been possible at the time I held a focus group with that institution's librarians in 2016. Of the 10 focus groups I held, five consisted of librarians and five consisted of student affairs professionals. All the focus groups had between four and seven participants. After I conducted the focus groups and analyzed my data, I held three webinars for all of the participants. In the webinars, I explained my findings and asked the participants if the findings made sense. Subsequently, my participants and I engaged in a discussion of the findings' implications.

SAMPLING

I sampled librarians and student affairs professionals from a specific set of higher education institutions. Because I selected the institutions before I sampled the librarians and student affairs professionals employed there, I will describe my selection method of the institutions before addressing my selection of the participants. This book concerns collaborations designed to benefit traditional-aged, residential undergraduate students. Consequently, I recruited participants from higher education institutions with an undergraduate profile defined by the National Center for Education Statistics as predominately four-year and residential in character with an enrollment of at least five thousand undergraduates.

Higher education institutions with enrollments of at least five thousand undergraduate students were more likely to employ library and student affairs staff of sufficient size to enable me to recruit at least six to eight persons from each profession for focus groups. Because my ability to travel was limited due to the constraints of my employment, I wanted these higher education institutions to be no more than two hundred miles, or approximately a half day's drive, from my home city.

Using the National Center for Education Statistics' College Navigator (https://nces.ed.gov/collegenavigator/), I identified 43 higher education institutions that met these criteria. Of these colleges and universities, I targeted 23 that represented a cross section of institutions in terms of control (public and private), enrollment size, and focus (liberal arts and comprehensive curricula.) The diversity of the higher education institutions strengthened the study's trustworthiness.

I wanted approximately half of the recruited participants to be employed as academic librarians and approximately half to be employed as student affairs professionals. I did not target participants of a particular age or length of employment, but I used the following criteria to determine eligibility for participation in my research:

1. The participant was at least 18 years of age.
2. The participant possessed a degree in either library and information science or in a field that commonly places persons into student affairs positions, such as higher education administration, college student personnel administration, educational leadership, college student affairs, etc.
3. The participant was employed at the time of recruitment as either a librarian or as a student affairs professional and had been so employed—at either the participant's current higher education institution or elsewhere—for at least three years. Those with less than three years of professional experience might not have had sufficient time to formulate perspectives on their roles in student learning and success and on the collaborative efforts that might be undertaken between librarians and student affairs professionals.
4. The participant was engaged in activities that brought the participant into significant or daily contact with undergraduate students, such as teaching, advising, counseling, providing library reference or instructional services, etc.

RECRUITMENT

Participant recruitment occurred in two stages. First, I sought permission from chief library officers and chief student affairs officers at the 23 higher education institutions to undertake my research with the librarians and student affairs professionals in their respective employ. I pursued the second stage of my recruitment only if both the chief library officer and the chief student affairs officer at the same institution consented. After both chief officers provided their consent, I pursued the second stage of recruitment by seeking librarians and student affairs professionals to participate in the focus groups.

Stage 1: Securing Permission from Chief Library and Student Affairs Officers

Morgan (1998) cautioned that focus groups that occur in the workplace must, by necessity, involve approved time off from participants' normal duties. Therefore, participants' supervisors must provide permission in order to gain access to participants. Morgan (1998) recommended seeking permission from the highest possible person in the hierarchy, who could then assure lower-level supervisors that prospective participants' time away from their normal duties was permissible. Since both libraries and student affairs divisions are often hierarchical organizations with many supervisors in the chain of command, I sought the permission of the chief library officers and chief student affairs officers.

I examined the websites and publicly available staff directories at the higher education institutions to identify the chief library officers and chief student affairs officers. I sent e-mail messages to those officers, in which I explained the purpose of my research, requested their permission to contact and solicit the participation of librarians and student affairs professionals employed at their institutions, and—if I recruited a sufficient number of participants to conduct focus groups—sought their agreement to help me secure a private location for the focus group meetings. The chief library officers and chief student affairs officers were to have no other involvement in the research in order to diminish the likelihood of coercion of participants. In my e-mail messages, I also included copies of the recruitment letters and the informed consent forms I intended to send to prospective participants. I sent a follow-up e-mail if I had not received a reply within four weeks of my initial message. In no case did I send more than two queries.

Because I wanted to recruit librarians and student affairs professionals employed at the same institutions for site triangulation purposes, my plan was to proceed with the second stage of my recruitment only if I was able to secure the consent of both the chief library officer and chief student affairs officer. Of the 23 institutions I targeted, I received affirmative responses from the chief library officers and chief student affairs officers at five higher education institutions.

Stage 2: Recruiting Focus Group Participants

Targeting librarians and student affairs professionals at these five institutions (table 3.1), I proceeded with the second stage of my recruitment. To minimize the risk of coercion from chief library officers or chief student affairs officers, I contacted librarians and student affairs professionals myself after obtaining their names and e-mail addresses from institutional websites and publicly available staff directories. In my e-mail message, I explained the purpose of my research, what the study required of participants, and anticipated risks and benefits of participation and my anticipated timelines for the focus groups and webinars. I also provided a copy of an informed consent form as an attachment they could return via e-mail, fax, or postal mail. Again, I sent a follow-up e-mail if I had not heard from participants within four weeks of my initial message. Again, in no case did I send more than two queries.

All together, I sent recruitment messages to 82 librarians and 91 student affairs professionals. Of these, 30 librarians and 28 student affairs professionals agreed to participate. I screened their eligibility in a subsequent message, and all participants but one of the student affairs professionals met my criteria. I excluded that participant from my research, leaving me with 27 student affairs professionals who were viable participants. (In the end, two student affairs professionals failed to turn up for the focus groups, leaving me with 25 student affairs participants.) These numbers were well within the number of participants I had anticipated interviewing, and each focus group appeared as if it would have no fewer than five and no more than eight participants.

Once I confirmed a minimum of five participants for each focus group, I sent the participants links to a survey I created using Doodle, an online scheduling tool, to identify the best date and time for the participants to meet.

Table 3.1. Characteristics of the Five Participating Higher Education Institutions

Institution	Undergraduate Enrollment and Profile	Basic Carnegie Classification	Size and Setting
University A	13,306 High undergraduate, selective, higher transfer-in	Public, research university with high research activity	Large four-year, primarily residential
University B	5,830 Very high undergraduate, more selective, higher transfer-in	Private, master's colleges and universities with balanced arts & sciences/ professions	Medium four-year, highly residential
University C	32,695 Majority undergraduate, selective, lower transfer-in	Public, research university with very high research activity	Large four-year, primarily residential
University D	15,814 Very high undergraduate, inclusive, higher transfer-in	Public, doctoral/ research university	Large four-year, primarily residential
University E	17,052 Majority undergraduate, more selective, higher transfer-in	Private, doctoral/ research university with higher research activity	Large four-year, highly residential

Often, I created more than one survey before I was able to secure a mutually convenient date and time. Then I contacted the chief library officers and chief student affairs officers again to secure a location for the focus groups, which in all cases were private conference rooms in either the library or student union building. A week prior to the focus groups, I sent each participant a reminder via e-mail.

PARTICIPANTS

Altogether, I held ten focus groups at five higher education institutions (table 3.2). All the focus groups with librarians took place at a conference room located in the library whereas all the focus groups with student affairs professionals took place in rooms associated with the student union. The doors were able to be closed to ensure the confidentiality of the discussions. I provided light refreshments such as coffee, bottled water, and bagels for participants at most focus groups, but a few of the libraries had policies against food and drink.

FOCUS GROUP PROCEDURES

I employed separate interview protocols to guide the focus group discussions with librarians and student affairs professionals. The interview protocol for librarians consisted of the following questions:

1. What do you perceive to be the role of librarians at this institution?

Table 3.2. Focus Group Participants

Institution	Profession Type	Number of Participants	Female	Male
University A	Librarians	6	5	1
University A	Student Affairs	4	2	2
University B	Librarians	4	1	3
University B	Student Affairs	4	3	1
University C	Librarians	6	6	0
University C	Student Affairs	6	4	2
University D	Librarians	7	6	1
University D	Student Affairs	5	3	2
University E	Librarians	7	6	1
University E	Student Affairs	6	3	3

2. Tell me about your interaction with undergraduate students. How do librarians here interact with students and for what purposes?
3. Let's turn our discussion to student affairs professionals. What do you perceive to be the role of student affairs professionals at this institution?
4. Do librarians at this institution interact with or collaborate with student affairs professionals? If so, tell me about those interactions or collaborations.
5. What other observations or insights about our discussion today might you wish to share?

The interview protocol for student affairs professionals was nearly identical but transposed *student affairs professionals* for *librarians*. I intended for the focus group discussions to be semi-structured, so often I asked follow-up questions based on something a participant had just said, or I asked for clarification or elaboration on certain points. Occasionally I redirected the discussions back to the interview protocol when discussion veered too far off topic for too long, but mostly I allowed participants to respond to each other's comments without further moderation.

Each focus group lasted approximately 90 minutes. I recorded the entirety of the focus group discussions with a 1800PC digital voice recorder, but I also jotted notes in a field notebook. This helped me give additional context to the transcripts.

DATA ANALYSIS

The recordings and the transcriptions of the focus group interviews served as the primary forms of my data. Transcripts do not reflect the way group members use words or the tone with which words are used, which are important sources of information and can radically alter the interpretation of a statement (Gee, 2011). Consequently, I transcribed the interviews myself so that I was able to note the nuances of the discussions that might otherwise be filtered out by a transcription service. Additionally, I listened to the recordings multiple times, often in conjunction with reviewing the transcripts. During transcription, I assigned pseudonyms to each of the participants and removed any personal identifying information they revealed during the focus groups. When using quotes from particular participants throughout this book, I have used the pseudonyms I assigned to the participants.

Discourse analysis served as the framework for my analysis of the group interviews. Discourse analysis is the study of "language-in-use" and how people use language to create meaning in social, cultural, and political terms (Gee, 2011, p. 3). Although the constant comparison analysis, in which the researcher labels smaller, similar parts of multiple interviews with a coding scheme, is a popular method of analysis for group interviews, it is arguably insufficient for capturing the interactive nature of group interviews and answering such questions as "[W]hy was this said just then[?]" (Myers & Macnaghten, 1999, p. 173). Indeed, Myers and Macnaghten (1999) claim that identities are negotiated in discourse, so researchers should examine how participants set up and work out roles in focus group; that discussion is sequenced, so researchers must consider each response in terms of what came before and after; and that participants reorganize discussions moment to moment, so researchers must examine how participants define sections rather than researchers defining sections. Consequently, discourse analysis is an appropriate framework for analyzing the transcripts of the group interviews.

Specifically, I used Gee's (2011) theory of discourse analysis to analyze the group interviews. Gee developed 27 tools for discourse analysis, and each tool represents a specific question to ask of data. Each tool makes the researcher look closely at the details of language and tie these details to what the speakers mean, intend, and seek to accomplish by the way in which they have used language (Gee, 2011). Of the 27 tools, some will yield more illumination from the data than others, and the researcher must determine which tools will be the most appropriate (Gee, 2011). For this book, I found the deixis, vocabulary, intonation, "why this way and not that way," and the intertexuality tools to be the most critical.

The Deixis Tool

Deictics, or "pointing words," are words whose reference must be understood from the context of the larger speech (Gee, 2011). Speakers make assumptions about listeners' knowledge and experiences and drop from speech words that convey preciseness or explicitness, and deictics help listeners create the appropriate meaning. Common deictic words include "I", "you," "we," "them," "this," "there," and "that." These words often suggest how speakers position their sense of self and sense of belonging in larger groups (Gee, 2011). The deixis tool helped me interpret the situated meaning in participants' discussions by asking "How are pointing words being used to tie what is said to context and make assumptions about what listeners already know or can figure out?" (Gee, 2011, p. 10). For example, two participants at University D said to each other:

> A lot of our students from over there, they're just not ready. (Dorothy)

> And it's our job to help them navigate here, build them up, and help them be successful here. (Peter)

Yes, that is absolutely why we're here. (Dorothy)

In the exchange, Dorothy used the pointing words "over there" to indicate a lot of students come from a specific economically disadvantaged area, and "ready" to indicate those students were not prepared for college-level work. Yet Peter employed the deictic word "our" to position himself as part of a collective identity of student affairs professionals charged with helping students become capable of meeting the realities they faced as college students.

The Vocabulary Tool

With the vocabulary tool, I examined the specific words people used in their discourse. Gee (2011) claimed people employ a hierarchy of vocabularies depending on their social contexts, and formal words signify academic or professional domains. This tool helped me understand how participants' word choices contributed to the shaping of multiple identities. For example, a librarian shifted her vocabulary as she recounted her transition from a student employee in a library to a member of the library's professional staff; she replaced "day-to-day stuff" with "daily operations" and "jobs" with "positions," she changed from an identity grounded in her student experiences to an identity grounded in the specialization of her professional identity. In essence, she was performing: As she progressed through her career, she embraced language that invokes technical expertise, polish, and experience.

The Intonation Tool

Gee's (2011) intonation tool highlights the saliency of a speaker's messages by focusing on how they emphasize or modify words. This helped me understand the ways participants designed their messages indirectly for others. For example, the participants emphasized certain words in the group interviews by changing their tone. For example, Greta, a student affairs professional, said, "I've *learned* to work *with* faculty and deans," and "I share ideas *with* them at meetings." Her intonation contributed to my understanding of the importance she placed on collaboration in order to enhance student learning, but that working with faculty and administrators required her to approach those colleagues differently than she might have approached her student affairs colleagues. Her consistent emphasis of the word "with" in connection with both her student affairs colleagues and also with faculty and administrators emphasized that she considered collaboration a core value of her work.

The "Why This Way and Not That Way" Tool

Gee (2011) recommends examining participants' grammar and word choices for explanations as to why participants answered questions in a certain way and not in another way; what message are they truly conveying? The "why this way and not that way" tool helped me recognize tension in participants' identities. For example, two librarians discussed their interactions with undergraduate students:

> Interestingly, I talked with some students this week. (Sabrina)

> This is such a busy time of year, isn't it? I can barely keep my head above water, but I actually have spent a few hours with students this week. (Yolanda)

The "why this way and not that way" tool showed me that these librarians were preoccupied with the day-to-day business of running their library, and they found these responsibilities took them away from their work with students.

The Intertextuality Tool

Lastly, the intertexuality tool brought to light the layers of multiple contexts from which people constructed dimensions of their identities. Gee (2011) suggests intertextuality exists when people's phrases or text refer to other literary or cultural sources; their use of quotes or allusions have certain functions, such as establishing credibility or reinforcing worldviews. For example, the student affairs professionals threaded references to other sources throughout one of the group interviews. When speaking of her work as a student affairs professional, Dorothy referenced the *Student Personnel Point of View*—"That's what the *SPPV* says"—when she explained how she had to learn about all dimensions of a student's life in order to resolve a student's problem, indicating its centrality to her professional identity.

TRUSTWORTHINESS

The trustworthiness of qualitative research is often questioned because the concepts of validity and reliability cannot be addressed the same way in quantitative research (Shenton, 2004). However, Guba (1981) proposed four criteria that respond to the issues of validity and reliability and that should be considered by qualitative researchers. Additionally, Guba (1981) proposed qualitative researchers adopt different terminology in order to distance themselves from the paradigm associated with quantitative studies. These criteria include transferability (in preference to external validity), dependability (in preference to reliability), confirmability (in preference to objectivity), and credibility (in preference to internal validity) (Guba, 1981).

Transferability

Shenton (2004) suggested the researcher demonstrates transferability by explaining the boundaries of the study and assessing the extent to which the findings may be true of people in other settings. This could be accomplished by the researcher describing the characteristics and qualities of the higher education institutions where participants are employed; the number of participants involved in the study; any restrictions in the type of participants; the number and length of the data collection sessions; and the time period over which the data was collected. I accomplished this by sharing anonymous descriptions of the higher education institutions and of the focus groups themselves.

Dependability

Lincoln and Guba (1985) suggest the study's procedures should be reported in detail, thereby enabling future researchers to repeat the work. Dependability can be accomplished by descriptions of the study's research design, addressing the "minutiae" of what actions the researcher took to complete the study, and by the researcher's appraisal of the research design's effectiveness (Shenton, 2004, p. 72). I accomplished this by detailing the planning and administration of the focus groups.

Confirmability

Lincoln and Guba (1985) suggested the researcher must take steps to ensure the study's findings are the result of the experiences and ideas of the participants rather than the result of the researcher's preferences. Beliefs regarding the study's methods should be acknowledged. I accomplished confirmability by explaining the strengths and limitations of focus groups as a research method, by recording my research activities in a research log, and by reflecting upon my experiences with focus groups as a research method in a journal. I shared copies of my transcripts with participants who agreed to be contacted after the focus groups to confirm my transcription represented accurate portrayals of the group interviews. Finally, I confirmed my findings with the participants of the two webinars.

Credibility

Credibility addresses whether the study's findings are congruent with reality (Shenton, 2004). A number of different provisions could aid a study's credibility, including testing the interview protocol, triangulating the sites of data collection, checking transcripts and interpretations with members, and including a description of the researcher's background and positionality (Shenton, 2004). I tested the interview protocols for credibility by moderating two test focus groups with three librarians and three student affairs professionals, respectively, who were neither participants in the study nor employed at the universities where the participants were recruited. The purpose of the test focus groups was to ensure the interview questions were pertinent to the research questions and that the interview questions were written in natural language and easily understood by participants.

Additionally, Shenton (2004) recommends site triangulation as a means "to reduce the effect on the study of particular local factors peculiar to one institution" (p. 66). Site triangulation lends credibility to a focus group study and underpins Dervin's (2003) concept of "circling reality," or "the necessity of obtaining a variety of perspectives in order to get a better, more stable view of reality based on a wide spectrum of observations from a wide base of points in time-space" (p. 124). Consequently, I held focus groups at several higher education institutions. This reduced the likelihood that participants were influenced by one higher education institution's particular set of beliefs, culture, or dynamics. I also employed member-checking by sharing the transcripts and my interpretations of the data with the participants who agreed to be contacted following the focus groups' conclusions. Their verification of the transcripts and of my interpretations lend credibility to my analysis and conclusions. Additionally, I offer a reflection of my subjectivity and positionality as the researcher.

Researcher's Subjectivity and Positionality

As an academic librarian, I see higher education through the lens of librarianship. Weiner (2008) noted librarians tend toward a library-centric view of higher education, in which the library is the "intellectual focal point or 'heart'" (p. 4) of the institution. This tendency has deep historical roots; Johnson (1939) noted that academic libraries were principally the domain of faculty members and graduate students, and were disconnected from undergraduate students and the curriculum through the 1930s. Fearing this characteristic of libraries appeared permanent, Johnson advocated a "radical readjustment in the scope and character of library services" that included the convergence of scattered, departmental libraries into newly constructed central libraries that were the "intellectual and geographic heart of the college or university" (p. 15). Johnson (1939) proposed that the purpose of the library should be to provide formal instruction on library resources to undergraduate students, to correlate library instruction with classroom pedagogy and the curricula, and to promote social issues, democracy, and "reading for pleasure" (p. 237).

Johnson (1939) commented:

> The library is the great common denominator of the college, the real democracy where all meet together to gratify their intellectual curiosity. It is a world in epitome to be exploited for the scholar's enrichment, to be the generating station for permanent life interests, to develop an individuality and personality in students, to furnish cultural preparedness for the leisure which modern industry will afford, and is the only real orientation course. (p. 6)

Although many domains of higher education lay claim to the aspects of student development embedded in Johnson's (1939) vision of libraries, I must note libraries have played formative roles in the development of my own identity. As an undergraduate student, the college library was my sanctuary. I grew up with parents who valued libraries. They took me to the public library often, and some of my earliest memories are of the children's reading room.

Despite my parents' encouragement of reading, I was underprepared for college. I was not an enthusiastic student in high school. I struggled with some subjects and doubted my ability to be successful academically. My family's socioeconomic status and our community's blue-collar values did not make higher education a part of my everyday conversation. I surprised myself and my family by enrolling at my local community college after I graduated high school. I placed into remedial education because of my low test scores, and I quickly questioned whether I would succeed in college. I sought solace at the college library, where a concerned librarian noticed me and asked if I was all right. She offered me a position as a student assistant, and I began employment in the library's media department during my second week on campus. I continued to work in academic libraries even after I had transferred to a liberal arts college to finish my baccalaureate degree and still later when I started law school. Clearly, the libraries provided the continuity and stability I craved during my educational experiences. I decided to earn a master's degree in library and information science when I realized I was more interested in the tools of legal research than I was in the law itself. Thus, I became a librarian rather than an attorney.

I came to the world of student affairs when I accepted a position as the residential life librarian at a research-intensive university, reporting to the division of student affairs. My libraries were located in the undergraduate residence halls and brought me into daily contact with the student affairs professionals employed in university housing, judicial affairs, and minority student services. Intrigued by the work of my student affairs colleagues and determined to better understand their work, I took a course first in student affairs administration and then in theories of college student development. Eventually, I earned a second master's degree in higher education with a specialization in student affairs.

Despite my admiration for my former student affairs colleagues, I consider those four years embedded in the residence halls a brief—if highly informative—diversion from my "real" work as a librarian. I was never entirely comfortable working in student affairs. Student affairs professionals' extroversion, confidence, and willingness to share their lives and reflections makes me uneasy at times. As an introvert, I can be exhausted by prolonged interactions with others. I was also taught to not express my feelings to others, so reflecting and sharing can also be challenging for me. The long hours and teachable moments with first-year students wore me out. I returned to a more traditional librarian role in a central library, which feels more like "me."

I will probably spend the rest of my working years in the library community, but I think frequently about applying the lessons I learned in student affairs to the library context: How do I make the library more welcoming and inclusive for students of differing identities? How do I teach information literacy skills to students who aren't cognitively ready for the lesson? Do librarians have roles to play in civic engagement or service learning? So, I'm approaching this study first and foremost as beneficial to the betterment of libraries and of librarians. Hopefully student affairs professionals will benefit, too, but I must acknowledge my interests favor librarianship and librarians.

I must also note that I am male, and that I am also an associate dean at my library. Currently, male librarians comprise only about 17% of the library profession but hold 48% of the upper management and executive positions (Davis & Hall, 2012). The student affairs profession is somewhat better balanced between the genders at 32% male, but men still hold the lion's share of executive leadership positions (Calhoun & Taub, 2014). Accordingly, the demographics suggested a strong likelihood that the majority of my participants would be both female and not in leadership positions, especially among the librarian groups. So it is possible that my participants see me not only as a man, but as a man who occupies a position of power within my own organization.

Kosygina (2005) suggests that women's interviews with male researchers are shorter in length, less reflective, and consist of question/answer dialogs rather than of monologues. Women are more likely to be enthusiastic and reflective on their professional experiences when interviewed by female researchers. Kosygina (2005) claims male researchers should avoid question/answer patterns with female participants and structure interviews conversationally to reduce the significance of power associated with gender in communication. Listening carefully and understanding how women make meaning out of their roles and experiences might be challenges for me, as my natural inclination is to let my attention waver when my question is not directly answered. Ensuring that my participants are not exclusively responding to me as a man, or especially as a male administrator, would be challenging too.

Additionally, I have served on state and national committees related to libraries for more than a decade and have published regularly in library literature. I was also not intending to recruit participants from higher educations institutions that were more than a few hundred miles from my home. Consequently, some of my participants in the librarian groups might know me well, and others might know me by name or by sight. I was likely not a bona fide stranger to at least some of the participants in the librarian groups. However, I was likely a stranger to many of the participants in the student affairs groups, as I have not participated in any student affairs committees at the state or national level. Morgan (2002) noted that a known identity is a double-edged sword to focus group moderators: On the one hand, participants are more likely to engage in protracted, open, and honest discussions when they know the moderator, and on the other hand some participants may be more likely to try to please the moderator by editing their discussion to suit the moderator's interests.

Unlike me, not all of my participants would hold faculty rank and status. The student affairs professionals would be highly likely to not hold faculty rank and status. Only approximately half of librarians hold faculty rank and status (Bolin, 2008). Faculty members wield greater power and authority than academic staff at many campuses, so communication between academic staff and faculty might be less frank and less open than communication between academic staff or between faculty. However, I suspected that my participants would not know my faculty rank and status unless I disclosed it. Certainly I intended to do so if I were asked, as no part of this study was deceptive, but no one asked.

In short, privilege and power are threaded throughout the context of this study. To mitigate this, I adopted a less structured approach to moderating the focus groups. Morgan (2002) and Kosygina (2005) suggested researchers should enable conversation among participants by allowing participants' interests, rather than the researcher's interest, to dominate the discussion. Consequently, I enabled this by asking more general questions rather than larger numbers of specific questions; by allowing participants to explore new directions in discussions rather than always refocusing off-topic remarks; by being flexible in the allocation of time per question rather than setting specific amounts of time; and by ensuring that participants addressed each other rather than addressing me as the moderator.

Lastly, I attempted to reduce bias in how I interpreted the participants' responses and how the participants responded to my questions. Onwuegbuzie, Leech, and Collins (2008) developed a framework to help researchers reduce bias by reflecting on key research concepts: the researcher's interview experience, the researcher's perceptions of the participants, the researcher's perceptions of nonverbal behavior, the researcher's interpretations of interview findings, the researcher's perceptions of how the study might have affected the researcher, and the researcher's identification of and response to unexpected issues or dilemmas that emerged during the focus group planning and interviews. I reflected on these six key concepts.

To address Onwuegbuzie, Leech, and Collins's (2008) six concepts, I used journaling as a means to record my thoughts, feelings, and reactions as I moved through the research process. The journaling process consisted of two instruments—a research diary and a research log. My research log was a trusty notebook, where I jotted notes impulsively and spontaneously as I moved through the process and where I recorded times, places, and other details of meetings and communiqués. I recorded the journal entries in a Word document on my home desktop computer when I had the time and the opportunity to reflect.

To help me understand the purpose of journaling, I reviewed Ortlipp's (2008) and Newbury's (2001) works. Ortlipp (2008) described her journaling as a place for writing as a method of inquiry. Ortlipp used her journal to clarify her research aims and approach, and it is where she asked and answered her own ontological, epistemological, and methodological questions about what she knew, her relationship to what could be known, and how she might come to know it. "Reflective journal writing," Ortlipp (2008) claimed, "enabled me to articulate my ideas about conceptual frameworks for analysis of the data and led me eventually to reject an interpretist-constructivist framework" (p. 700).

Following Newbury's (2009) perspective on journaling, I resolved to scrutinize my own journal entries for three distinct types of notes: observational, in which "statements [bear] upon events experienced principally through watching and listening" and contain as little interpretation as possible; theoretical, in which I reflected about what I experieneed and derived meaning from one or more of the observational notes; and methodological, in which I critiqued my own operations, processes or tactics (p. 3). I hope that I lived up to Ortlipp's (2008) and Newbury's (2009) advice as I reflected on the nature of my journal entries.

CONCLUSION

In order to best address the qualitative purposes of this book, I moderated ten focus groups at five higher education institutions to better understand the participants' perceptions of librarians' and students affairs professionals' roles in student learning and student success. In this chapter, I presented the rationale for employing focus groups within a phenomenological methodology. I described how I recruited participants, conducted the focus groups, and analyzed the data once the focus groups were completed. Additionally, I discussed issues related to the book's trustworthiness.

In the following two chapters, I share the themes that emerged from the librarians' and student affairs professionals' focused discussions. Because I want the participants' perspectives and stories to resonate with readers, I have interwoven participants' exchanges from the focus groups to illustrate the themes.

Chapter Four

The Librarians' Stories

The librarians who participated in my focus groups were mostly subject or instruction librarians, but a few had responsibilities in other areas of librarianship too, usually overseeing another public services area of the library. First, I am compelled to note the atmosphere and energy of the librarians' focus groups were largely similar to each other but contrasted sharply with those of the students affairs professionals. The librarians warmed quite slowly to the group discussions. Often, they replied to my probing questions with several moments of silence and then a tenuous "I've never thought of that before. . . ." They asked me many clarifying questions, such as what I meant by student persistence or which areas of their university comprised student affairs. While their responses were thoughtful, their sentences were often left incomplete and trailing, leaving me with the impression that they lacked confidence in their own perceptions or that they found formulating responses to be challenging. This is not surprising given the preponderance of librarians with introverted personalities (Maxwell, 2006). Morgan (1998) noted that introverted focus group participants tend to struggle with formulating responses due to introverts' need to consider the questions carefully, sometimes leading the moderator to falsely assume the participants are ill-informed. I counteracted my own initial assumptions by reviewing my research journal, where I recorded my own feelings toward the focus groups.

    The librarians checked with each other frequently, seeking confirmation of their perceptions and opinions. Often they expressed surprise at not knowing the stories shared by other participants, many of whom were presumably close colleagues, suggesting the librarians worked rather autonomously and did not regularly communicate their experiences with each other. In fact, many of the librarians were not entirely familiar with the scope of each other's responsibilities despite working together for some time. As introductions were made at University D, a brief exchange between Howard and Deanna encapsulated this lack of familiarity well:

> I have to do this [liaison to departments]—economics, political science, and philosophy. (Howard)
>
> What about religion? Do you still do religion? (Deanna)
>
> No. But . . . Ahhh . . . I guess we just don't talk about it. You're behind. (Howard)

Not until quite near the end of the allotted 90 minutes together did the librarians seem comfortable and did the discussions flow fluidly and with bits of laughter. Still, an air of uncertainty hung over all the focus groups, which I felt was finally given voice by Sabrina at University D at the very end of the group interview:

> We are all so looking forward to the results of your research and learning about all the collaborations the other libraries are doing. I'm not sure that we could really offer you much ourselves but hopefully we can put a good many of those [into] practice here!

Tables 4.1 through 4.5 provide brief descriptions of the participants at each institution.

LIBRARIANS' ROLES

Initially, I asked the participants "What do you perceive to be the role of librarians at this institution?" The librarians were remarkably consistent with their responses across the five institutions despite the institutions' differences in mission and character. Their perceptions of the role of librarians are cate-

Table 4.1. Librarians at University A

Name	Sex	Years of Service
Jeanette	Female	3
Crystal	Female	3
John	Male	6
Beverly	Female	10
Amy	Female	7
Jodie	Female	3

Table 4.2. Librarians at University B

Name	Sex	Years of Service
Joe	Male	12
Paul	Male	17
Alan	Male	9
Margaret	Female	23

gorized into three broad themes: information purveyor, teaching, and community development.

Information Purveyor

The librarians' primary role appeared to be what I call the "information purveyor." In this role, the librarians acquired and organized information sources—such as monographs, databases, journals, datasets, etc.—and evangelized the resources to faculty, staff, and students. I note the distinction, if subtle, between what I am labeling "information purveyor" and what one student affairs professional called "information provider." Ther term information provider implies a passive role—the librarians make resources readily available for use by the library's clientele but do not proactively inform clientele of these resources; rather, the clientele must actively seek out these resources. However, the term purveyor implies the librarians' role is active, deliberately promoting the resources' existence and usefulness.

I purport the librarians have adopted an evangelical orientation because they employed a vocabulary suggestive of persuasion. When the librarians spoke of alerting their constituents to the existence of resources they thought would be helpful, they chose action words such as "promoting," "outreach," "building awareness," and "connecting." These action words indicate a thoughtful deliberativeness and professionalism that more casual phrases of speech such as "letting them know" or "telling them about" do not suggest. They did sometimes use casual phrases such as "letting them know" when referring to informing students about library hours, policies, and the fact that student ID cards doubled as library cards. However, the librarians adopted the more formal or sophisticated words, such as "promoting" when they spoke specifically of the monographs, databases, and other information resources they thought were helpful for research and curricular work.

Furthermore, their other choices of vocabulary suggested they considered their interactions with constituents to be a form of marketing when speaking of information sources. Lucy at University C noted her library had "sharpened its communication" regarding its collection. Jeanette at University A described brochures—surely a common marketing tool—she had designed

Table 4.3. Librarians at University C

Name	Sex	Years of Service
Lauren	Female	22
Wendy	Female	24
Lucy	Female	12
Jennifer	Female	5
Alison	Female	5
Molly	Female	15

with the 3-D printers the library had recently acquired. Rebecca at University D also spoke of distributing brochures that advertised the library's government documents during her visits to classes and at a student health fair, although she was dubious if the brochures made the library a trusted and relevant organization to students given that she noted with a sardonic tone the brochure's dated age and students' marginal interest. She said:

> They're horrible. Dated pictures of people and ugly fonts. No one takes them or even glances at them for half a second. Well, a few do, the ones who talk to me for a bit. They feel bad, probably. But then I just see them in the trash can outside the door when I leave the event. What does it say about the library's relevance to their lives when our materials look like they were printed in the 1980s?

John "delivered presentations" to faculty and to classes on the information resources best suited to courses' topics. He believed his presentations "demonstrated value":

> Instruction has been my main avenue towards, toward outreach. That, ah, you get into someone's class, you give a good presentation, deliver a good lesson plan, essentially demonstrate value. "Hi, I'm helpful, I'm not a scary monster," and "here's what I can do for you." And then the faculty say to each other "Oh yeah, this worked, this worked really well," and then you have your foot in the door with more faculty and thus more students.

This specialized language, coupled with the use of traditional marketing tools such as brochures, indicates marketing is an integral aspect of the information purveyor role. Additionally, I argue this role appears to be the librarians' primary role because the participants described this role first and foremost and emphasized it more frequently than other broad themes I identified.

Table 4.4. Librarians at University D

Name	Sex	Years of Service
Rebecca	Female	3
Deanna	Female	10
Howard	Male	21
Sabrina	Female	10
Ellen	Female	7
Jessica	Female	3
Yolanda	Female	5

Much of their purveyor role is exercised through their formal relationships with disciplinary faculty and the students who major in those fields of study. At all of the institutions, the librarians specialized in subject areas that corresponded to the fields of study taught by the disciplinary faculty. For example, Beverly at University A; Alan at University B; and Ellen at University D specialized in music. They were responsible for ensuring their libraries provided print and electronic resources related to music that were current and appropriate to the curriculum. As the "experts" in resources related to music, they also taught music students when and how to use these resources. While one might think a librarian is only as good as the collection he or she curates, several librarians noted their emphasis on building robust collections has dwindled; more resources are no longer better. Instead, the librarians invest great energy attempting to connect students with the information resources, as evidenced by these quotations from librarians at different institutions:

> We don't do that [building collections] anymore, now, so much. We've done collection assessment, and they're [information resources] so little used and yet so expensive. We've changed our philosophy so that we are not collecting everything but, uh, trying to direct the students to those that are most appropriate. (Lauren, University C)

> [Chuckling] Oh, when I think about all the hours I pored over reference guides, reading reviews, comparing what other libraries like us owned that we did not . . . oh, all those hours I wasted! Then we ran out of time to do all that because—I'm not just the music librarian but also the communication librarian after *that* librarian retired—we started using jobbers to just automatically send us the new books in our subject areas. But then we looked at how much this stuff is actually used, and it's not really a lot. Like a certain database will have a half dozen searches on it but the annual subscription is like $10,000. So now I spend a lot more time trying

Table 4.5. Librarians at University E

Name	Sex	Years of Service
Hilary	Female	16
Janet	Female	22
Sarah	Female	7
Courtney	Female	5
Kyra	Female	5
Gabriel	Male	8
Gina	Female	15

> to tell students that resources actually exist and why they'd want to use them. (Alan, University B)

However, not all the librarians exercised their purveyor role through their relationships with disciplines. Jodie and Crystal at University A and Wendy at University C evangelized information resources to undergraduate students by participating in activities in traditional student spaces, such as the residence halls and at meetings of student organizations. Jodie and Crystal attended programs associated with living–learning communities in the undergraduate residence halls. Sometimes they chose to eat dinner with these students in the dining halls. Wendy spent time with student organizations focused on gender, racial, and ethnic identities. All three librarians attempted to get to know students personally and then informed students of information resources pertinent to the topics the students were researching in their coursework, as demonstrated by the subsequent exchange between Jodie and Crystal:

> I go eat in the residence halls and talk to the students. It's easy for me, because, well, I look young so they don't look at me like I shouldn't be there. And I talk to them, really, ask them about their majors, what they hope to do, how they're doing in classes. (Jodie)

> Yeah, and then you just . . . slip it in . . . about how you know a really great resource that will help them out a lot . . . in the library [laughter] (Crystal)

Some of the librarians were uncertain if their efforts led to students' increased usage of information resources. Jennifer at University C was primarily engaged in assessing the library's effectiveness, which included analyzing the usage of information resources. She was able to share with Wendy the usage of databases Wendy had promoted to students associated with her student organizations, but still they did not know whether any increased usage was directly attributable to those students' increased awareness of those databases. Crystal at University A said: "Yeah, one of the things I discovered about this institution when I came here . . . those promotional messages don't really work."

John at University A speculated that increasing students' awareness of information resources required a more consistent strategy over the academic year than the effort many librarians actually put in. He said:

> Yeah . . . one of our ongoing concerns since I have gotten here is that the majority of our outreach efforts . . . all take place within, say, the first four months of a student arriving here. And then, they then drop off precipitously. So, it's sort of like, it's "you're really important when you are new . . ."

John's sentence trailed off in such a way as to imply that students receive the impression that they are less valued after being on campus for a longer period of time. Later, John asked "Are we pissing in the wind?" suggesting he was completely uncertain if the investment of his time produced any gainful returns. Although John asked the question somewhat flippantly, I should note the participants at University A fell silent for a few moments after John's question and did not really respond to a probing question I asked subsequently. When discussion began again, the participants changed topics entirely, coloring my interpretation that John's rhetorical question was particularly poignant.

Teaching

I purport that the participants perceived teaching to be a significant role of librarians because they spoke of teaching activities in many different contexts and vocabularies. Many of the participants said teaching was one of the principal responsibilities on which their performance as librarians was evaluated. Despite that claim, the participants themselves rarely used the word teaching to describe their role except in the narrow context of formal classroom instruction. However, they used words like "coaching," "facilitating," and "creating experiences" to convey teaching moments outside the classroom in which they introduced new information to students or helped students gain new understandings.

Formal Instruction

While none of the participants said they taught credit-generating courses, virtually all of the participants taught what they called "instruction sessions." Through their liaison work with academic departments, librarians worked with faculty to identify the information resources most relevant to the intended learning outcomes of specific courses. Faculty brought their students to classrooms housed in the library, and the librarians taught students searching strategies appropriate to the information resources and how to analyze information for appropriateness and credibility. These instruction sessions were often no more than a single class period, but librarians felt instruction sessions were singularly important to students' ability to locate and synthesize information. The following exchanges between librarians at University A and between librarians at University B demonstrate this. The librarians at University A said:

> This is the single most important thing the students should get from us. This is really the only way they're learning how to recognize good information from bad. (Beverly)

> The faculty complain all the time the students don't use good information in their papers. "Wikipedia!" they [faculty] moan. Well, bring 'em here. They need an instruction session, and I can change that. (Jeanette)

> It is really the only time they get that kind of teaching. No one is else is doing it, and it's so critically important. And these sessions seem like the only format in which we can offer the students that sort of instruction. (Amy)

At University B, the librarians said:

> I hate that we usually only get the students once, for a single session. This is vitally important, maybe the most important we offer. (Joe)

> Sometimes, if we're lucky, we can get them for two sessions. The same class, that is. (Alan)

> I don't understand why faculty don't build instruction sessions with us into every single class. This is what we do, and the students can't really learn how to search for information effectively without it. They really do write better papers after our sessions. (Joe)

> They really need this, especially if this is an upper-division course, and the faculty are expecting students will be familiar with certain journals or databases by the end of it. You really need to know *PsychInfo* if you're a psychology major. You'll be writing so many papers by the time you're in your 300s. It's a very writing-intensive major. And, of course, the faculty can tell students about *PsychInfo*, but they really don't spend the time showing students how to search it, or maybe even not why *PsychInfo* is

the source to find credible information and not, say, *Psychology Today*. That's what we do in instruction sessions. (Alan)

Many participants worked hard to convince faculty members to bring their classes for instruction sessions, yet—interestingly—the librarians evinced skepticism about the value of providing formal instruction. John at University A said instruction was the librarians' "bugbear" when they had so little formal face time with students and librarians had difficulty demonstrating their sessions increased students' information literacy. He implied formal instruction represented a problem for librarians because it was the established way of teaching students information literacy skills and he questioned the efficacy of this style of teaching. The following exchange between the participants at University A suggested this skepticism:

> In effect, that, that's been kind of one of the big bugbears of instruction programs, especially at the undergraduate level, is determining to what degree we are able to support those, those students in their learning. Uh, or to what degree are we, we really being successful? And, we don't always know. (John)

> But, we have to put in some assessment measures to test, like the card swipe machines, so we can see later on [if] those who attend our sessions are actually going to graduate on time. Or just graduate. (Jodie)

> Yeah, those efforts are just being implemented. And so, we hope in, in the coming, oh, 40 years, that the data will be used to correlate our activities with student success. There has to be a better way. (John)

> No one pays attention in instruction sessions. They're a waste of everyone's time, except for like two or three students who are really paying attention. Maybe we can teach those two or three some other way. But instruction is . . . well, it's just the way it's done. All librarians teach instruction. It's how librarians teach. So we do it. (Beverly)

Some of the librarians at University D were similarly skeptical:

> Well, I feel bad for [name of another librarian]. We just hired her, so she gets the heaviest instruction sessions. (Rebecca)

> She gets the burn-out stuff like English 101 where there are dozens of sections, mostly freshman, and no one wants to be there and no one pays attention. The rest of us put in our time, so she gets that stuff and we get the upper-level courses. (Howard)

I mean, I guess it's important. It's the best way we demonstrate to the rest of the university that we're teachers too. But, frankly, we just really can't tell if any of it makes a difference. (Rebecca)

Don't you use pre-tests and post-tests to see if the students get it? (Sabrina)

Well, we tried. But that only works if you see the students at the beginning and at the end of the semester for separate sessions. But most faculty want to pare it down to just a single class session. So, great in theory, hard to put into practice. I think we're actually more effective at teaching students when we're one-on-one, like they have an appointment with us. (Yolanda)

Coaching

The provision of reference services is also a teaching activity for participants, although less formal than instruction sessions. While answering reference questions in person at a desk or virtually through a chat service could be transactional in nature, many of the participants interviewed students about the circumstances that led them to seek assistance. Often, these interviews revealed to the librarians how students perceived their assignments and information on the students' information-seeking behaviors. Rather than locating multiple sources of information for students, librarians demonstrated to students how to search the library's catalog or explained how to use databases to locate the information students needed. While some participants did think of this as formal teaching, several other participants noted that these experiences lacked depth. The librarians persistently referred to "coaching" or "guiding" students in this setting by asking probing questions about the students' information needs and challenging the students to conduct their own searches.

Joe at University B noted that many students seemed dissatisfied, believing that students perceived interactions at the reference desk to be more like a customer service experience rather than an educational experience. In fact, Joe speculated that some students resisted this learning moment so significantly that they were subsequently discouraged from interacting with librarians at the reference desk. Margaret at University B built on Joe's speculation and postulated that librarians sitting passively at a reference desk awaiting student interaction conveys an image of customer service to students. She said this image is reinforced by students' prior exposures to librarians at public libraries, where she believed librarians have a less developed educator identity. Margaret argued students' image of librarians as part of a helping profession first and foremost represents a disconnect from academic librarians' emphasis on teaching information literacy concepts and skills. Paul at

University B contributed that librarians themselves are not effective teachers despite the educator identity, as few librarians formally learn pedagogical strategies and techniques. Rather, Paul said librarians are "magically expected to inspire, engage, and challenge" students "by virtue of having earned a master's degree" when most librarians are more likely expert demonstrators rather than teachers. Indeed, many of the participants across the focus groups used words like "demonstrating" or "instructing" rather than "teaching"—formal words that suggest a more mechanical process and a distance from students, whereas teaching implies a more intimate relationship with students. Interestingly, many participants referred to disciplinary faculty as "the teaching faculty" when making distinctions between the disciplinary faculty and the library faculty—an interesting distinction when the same participants claimed that their own predominant role was also teaching.

Creating Experiences

Many participants perceived the library as a vehicle for students to make sense of new information. Lauren at University C called the library a "laboratory for learning," and Joe at University B said "the entire library is a classroom." Participants varied in how they perceived this. Margaret at University B said librarians' creation of exhibits that captured students' attention and provided students with new perspectives represented a way that librarians teach. Alan called this passive programming, and the participants at each of the institutions shared stories about creating displays, art installations, or bulletin boards:

> We stimulate their curiosity by creating exhibits. We just had one up for a while on graphic novels. I wrote a small grant that helped us get a traveling exhibit here, with illustrated pages from graphic novels. The artists shared their stories, their lives, and how that translated into visual storytelling. We put them up around the walls and brought in a guest speaker from the art department. That's a vital thing we do, to introduce them to new perspectives, it's part of teaching. (Margaret)

> Well, I don't call it teaching per se. It's passive programming. But certainly we're engaging students this way, through the exhibits we create, through our guest speakers. We don't really have a great space in the library, though. We've thought about moving our speakers to the student center where they have actual space designed for that purpose. (Alan)

> Oh but we don't want to. We think it's really important to have this in the library. It's part of our mission, I guess. (Margaret)

> I think we don't want to give it because, really, the library's the intellectual heart of campus. I think we're threatened in so many different ways, Google and lack of funding, and what not. Letting go of our programming to the student center—well, no way, that's one more knife in our heart. (Paul)

Jeanette at University A managed a 3-D printer station at her library. She encouraged students to create objects both as a way to engage students' sense of innovation and creativity and to enable their familiarity with new technologies they might later encounter in their careers. Although she promoted the 3-D printer primarily to students in engineering and the sciences, she was considering ways to promote the 3-D printer to students in other disciplines as well. Jeanette said her primary role was to demonstrate to students how to use the 3-D printer, make supplies available, and troubleshoot technical problems. She was adamant that she was creating a learning environment that taught students creativity.

Community Development

Many of the librarians emphasized the role they—and, by extension, the library—played in crafting a relationship between the students and the campus and creating a sense of community. The librarians played a role in community development both by fashioning the library into a premier social destination for students and by participating directly in significant campus events, as suggested by the following exchange between librarians at University A:

> We have Friday night live . . . I think that's what it's called. We do music in the library after our regular hours end. Sometimes it's jazz, but usually we have student bands who play all sorts of things. We really want the students to see the library as something more than, well, a library. (Jeanette)

> Oh, more importantly, this is their building. I mean, really, everything we do here is designed to serve students' needs. We play an important role, or should, in student engagement and bringing students together, and helping them see this place differently, like this place being essential in making them feel like they belong here, on this campus. We even had the mascot rappel off the top of the library at the beginning of the semester. (Beverly)

> That was weird, but the students all gathered around. They were really excited. It was kinda cool, really, although I did wonder if that was exactly safe. (John)

The librarians at University B seemed to be the exception, as they did not offer any evidence that they participated in campus life; rather the small size of the library staff and the complications of administering the library drove them to devote nearly all their attention to activities within the library itself.

Library as Student Hub

Nearly all the librarians envisioned the library as a hub of student activity—a destination where students congregated not only to study together, engage in research, and interact with librarians but also to socialize, use technology, or appreciate cultural or aesthetic experiences. The degree to which the libraries had accomplished this varied. Many of the librarians noted this was a significant cultural shift that brought new colleagues who weren't librarians into the library and created tension for space when book stacks, offices, or classrooms were reallocated for use by these new partners. Additionally, the presence of new services and staff in the library led to students asking the librarians questions about areas outside the librarians' expertise. The librarians at University A and C embraced this evolving role for the library and librarians, while the librarians' reactions at University B and D ranged from ambivalent to tentative.

At University A, the reimagining of the library as a student hub was a concerted effort encouraged by the dean of the library and the university administration. Jeanette explained:

> There has been a recent push not just, um, to promote the research side, side of things, but also to build community on campus. And so, I'm sure we'll talk about this eventually, but we've, ah, partnered with the residence halls and we talk about the library as a place, as well, to come together.

John noted that student success is a cornerstone of the university's strategic plan, and that community development was an aspect of this. Amy followed John's comment with an assertion that student success as a university priority was ill-defined, but she took this to mean the university needed to improve student retention, timely graduation, and academic performance. However, she said the librarians hadn't "figured out how we target that—we mostly just focus on student learning objectives through the teaching we do."

However, Jodie and Beverly at University A noted the librarians were heavily involved in "Set Up for Success," a week intended for first-year and transfer students to receive the logistical help they need to be successful students. Student technology services was now located at the library, and both librarians and technology specialists helped students activate their various accounts and passwords. Additionally, the librarians passed out a limited number of electronic tablets for students to use for free for the semester, which seemed so popular a service that most tablets were claimed within days. They explained they also arranged to bring puppies into the library several times a year, which served as a popular stress-reliever for students eager to take a break from their studies to interact with the dogs. The librarians also baked cookies and placed these out for students. They believed they were successful at creating a library that was comfortable and inviting to students, as the library was often filled to capacity with students engaged in studying and socializing.

John said:

> Well, I think by, by providing a common areas for study and socializing, uh, the library, uh, as I think of community is this common place where people can come and get together, especially with classes being in, all over the place, online classes taking away from a sense of place. That the library is this sort of beating heart of campus where you just . . . people from all different areas will have common ground.

Jodie seemed to have worked directly to sell the library as a space where students could come together to work or share mutual interests. She said:

> Yeah, um, as far as the different student organizations, that, that being here is really nice. I've been approached by, uh, the Greeks to, to meet here and also start working with us. I haven't pursued that yet but I'd like to. But, they always meet here, as do Athletics and the RSOs. And, I love it when I'm at the gym or something when I hear people say "Do you want to meet at the library later?" Like "Yeah, let's go there." Well, wow! So, it's really nice but then I've noticed that there are many different faculty groups that actually choose to meet here and have, um, communities of interest like within the space as well.

Comparing distinctions between institutions, the participants approached their roles as actors in community development quite differently. Jennifer at University C noted that the academic library doesn't serve the same purpose as public libraries, but that her library was working toward creating a sense of community for students by subtly sending messages that reinforce the concept:

> But, then, compared to a public library, we don't necessarily have a sense of community in the library sometimes. Our wall is blank. You know, that the community of a public library would have pictures of historic buildings or, uh, an ice cream shop or something like that. That's why they [librarians] go into the archives and find photos that do present our life here. So I think that is another thing about library or librarians, it's part of building a community for the students. That's what campus community

really means, or what a particular small library—it imparts something to you, and you'll use it. What that community is supposed to be about, isn't it?

The librarians at University C believed the library should be a place where students are inspired by the creativity and accomplishments of their peers. Remarking on Jennifer's comment about "blank walls," Lauren said:

> I want to touch on the facilities piece with student learning because, again, at the library we do a lot of these little surveys and such. . . . Um, part of it was trying to find out from the students what of [the] student learning experience they would want in the facility approach, and, uh, as a result we've redesigned and put, uh, certain services together. But the thing they wanted was to have some signs, some posters, some images around of other successful leaders—students—rather than just looking at blank walls. To really have things so when they are studying, they can look up and say "Oh, what an inspiration!" So that's one of the initiatives that we're working on . . . to develop some of our, uh, images that students can see and be immersed in a successful learning environment.

Additionally, Lauren indicated the library served as a cultural and aesthetic space for students. The librarians had deliberately chosen to replace their little-used reference collection for exhibits of student artwork that they believed would showcase student talent:

> We're developing a student exhibit area, um, in part where we used to have the reference books that no longer exist. David's working with the fine arts and design program to develop that [space] and then we'll have rotating student exhibits. (Lauren, University C)

It was clear from my discussions with the librarians at Universities A and C that other factors played a strong role in the librarians' movement toward redesigning the library as a student hub. At both institutions, the librarians seemed knowledgeable of trends in student learning and development. Like the librarians at University A, the librarians at University C found ways to provide stress relievers to students. Lucy implied that librarians' discussions about meeting the needs of the whole student—cognitive, psychosocial, and emotional—and their knowledge of theories of wellness led the librarians to create experiences and spaces that allowed students to decompress while studying. Lucy also implied that she made decisions about building collections based on her knowledge of student development theories and considered whether the complexity of the information resource matched the students' reasoning abilities.

Additionally, library and university leadership seemed to serve as a genesis for the librarians' initiatives in redesigning their library spaces and services. The librarians at Universities A and C indicated their respective deans of the libraries were quite clear in developing priorities that enabled the librarians to craft student-centered learning environments. The librarians understood the reasoning of their deans' messages, and they recognized these messages' connections to greater university priorities. Both groups referenced the difficulty students had navigating their large campus environments, and the libraries played a role in helping students integrate their academic and social experiences. The following discussion between librarians at University C illustrates this point:

I actually think that even in academic libraries, especially when you're working with students from a variety of backgrounds . . . (Wendy)

We have a lot of international students who aren't used to American customs. And lots of students from rural communities where this campus is larger than their entire towns. That can be really intimidating. (Lucy)

Right. As I was saying, we have a role to help them in personal situations, in their personal lives. And, um, you know, a lot of the students, especially the LGBT [Lesbian, Gay, Bisexual, and Transgender] students have issues with coming out, talking about, about the whole issue of coming out to their family and friends. You know, there's all kinds of eating disorders and sexual assault. You know, I think we have a role in helping these students, you know, with issues that they're struggling with, not, not just academic issues but their own personal issues. And I think that's really good connection. (Wendy)

We've seen that need, and also for connection, we do our bathrooms, bathroom stall flyers with these types of issues. Resources to help them. And [the health center] does a great job of providing us with those top things that they see concerning students. (Alison)

I [can] completely affirm that sort of the, um, direct work with the students as far as our role relative to them. Um, and, one thing I think a lot of the discussion here is sort of focused on, um, this sort of formal instructional role that we have. But, um, I think it's also that we have, we spend a lot of time whether one-on-one or in larger settings sort of providing immediate assessment of where a student is at. And so how far we can take them in the given moment or setting, so I agree with [Molly] in that we tend to take an instructional approach but at the same time we are always mediating that with the student's level of anxiety, the skills that they have for coping. I think where [academic librarians] differ from . . .

is . . . at the public library, if a user resists going into a learning role, then they go without learning. Where our job is to help them lean into that resistance, just to sort of help them find their way through that resistance. (Lucy)

I'm not sure how successful we are. We could do better at integrating students' social experiences on campus with their academic work. I think that there's a lot more that we could do, and I think our own literature and our own training actually lacks the theory that would help us do some of this better because we tend to privilege things which are important in our profession, like more information is always better, but which may not actually match what we know about student learning and development. The other piece, and here I don't want to go on too long so I'll just say this: I think that we have a huge role to play by creating the campus learning environment, and how students relate to the curriculum. (Lauren)

Changes were afoot at the library of University D. The librarians noted the writing center and a coffeehouse had recently occupied space at the library but several librarians interpreted this as a threat to the library's importance and suggested these changes were imposed upon them by university administrators who had little firsthand knowledge of the library itself or the librarians' work. Howard thought the changes were likely necessary because "nobody knocks on our door, we have to invite them," meaning the students. At the same time, he implied the university administrators didn't see the library as important, noting the library appears in university literature and strategic plans less and less often and suggesting the librarians emulate the strategies of other libraries: "The university is saying 'no, no, no, not good enough, not good enough, so we'll take these spaces from you. *These* libraries are thriving." When I asked whether he or others were actively developing their own ideas to present to the university administrators, he fell silent.

Howard and Deanna noted the library is much busier with students than it was five years ago, and the library did have more varied and comfortable seating, longer hours, and a greater tolerance for noise. However, they were uncertain as to why the students now found the library a more desirable place than they used to. In fact, Deanna's tone indicated she was mystified as to what the librarians should even be doing now with the students. She said:

. . . there's a lot of people. I don't know what they're doing. A lot of them are just hanging out. They're not doing anything. They're just here, um, which you know . . . Just get the bodies in the door . . . once, maybe, they're asking you for a pencil today, but in a few weeks, maybe, they'll be asking you for help later.

However, Sabrina believed community development was essential for the library—and the university—to thrive. She said enrollment had declined precipitously, and she perceived the lack of activities to keep the students engaged partly led to a high attrition rate during students' second year. Yet Sabrina did not feel empowered to advance any ideas on how to solve the problem. Nor did Yolanda or Rebecca, who both expressed shock and dismay that the librarians make little to no attempt to engage students outside the library—something that both said was a regular, expected part of their jobs at their previous institutions.

The librarians at University D agreed that library leadership proved problematic for them in reaching out to other areas of campus. The dean had not—in their opinion—ever articulated a compelling vision or plan for the library, and all the library administrators were not particularly visible or communicative. Indeed, Deanna said the librarians' work had not been coordinated for some years and any sustained efforts came about because of librarians' individual ambitions and passions. Jessica agreed, saying everything was due to "scrappy librarians." Despite the lack of coordination, it did not seem the librarians felt particularly empowered. Even seemingly simple tasks, such as designing updated brochures for Rebecca to pass out at the student health fair, seemed to lack ownership.

I noted, too, the mixed signals the librarians at University D appeared to send to students regarding the library as a community place. Despite the presence of a coffeehouse on the library's lowest level, a few of the librarians discouraged me from sampling the coffee there. "It's terrible," said Ellen. She wondered aloud why on earth the students chose to spend time there. A nearby exhibit case served as a seemingly contradictory message regarding the permissiveness of food and drink: It displayed books in various states of disrepair or damage caused by foods and liquids.

The librarians at University B were experiencing discomfort, too, with the concept of the library as a student hub, as evidenced by this brief exchange between Paul and Alan:

> I think we're getting a coffeehouse or something. And we got rid of the long library tables and most of the study carrels. And there is a lot of talking now. I guess it's good, the students seem to prefer that way now. I'm just not really sure how I feel about it yet. It just seems . . . wrong somehow. What are we giving up about ourselves? (Paul)

> Well, the library is changing. Change happens. But I don't know that we're really changing right along with it. Do I need to? I'm not sure. No one is suggesting that I do anything differently, so I'm just not really sure what this all means for me yet, but it is vaguely alarming when the library used to be as quiet as [a] tomb, and we were expected to keep it that way,

and—wow—and now that students want to practice presentations here. (Alan)

Margaret said the library's director had encouraged the librarians to proactively consider ways to enhance the students' experiences at the library. However, Margaret was perplexed as to why the librarians should make the effort, noting the student union was only across the parking lot and was filled with students at all hours. However, she conceded the library may not be as welcoming to students as it could be, given the age and worn conditions of the library's furnishings and the lack of adequate seating and wireless connectivity.

Many of the librarians asserted that libraries were once the physical and intellectual hearts of campuses, but both Amy at University A and Deanna at University D lamented recent changes that challenged that notion. Amy observed their four-year-old central library where we held our focus group was on the periphery of campus while the old, no longer used library at the heart of campus had an uncertain future ahead of it. Amy's tone evoked a wistfulness and sense of loss at the librarians' relocation—but whether this was for the old library building itself or for the old library's location on the campus quad was impossible to discern. While University D did not boast a new library, Deanna said the increasingly westward expansion of the campus placed the library further from the new buildings that attracted students, such as residence halls and the recreation center. Therefore it was more incumbent on the librarians to make the library a more welcoming space for the students.

INTERACTIONS WITH UNDERGRADUATE STUDENTS

Next, I nudged the focused discussions toward the librarians' direct interactions with students. I asked, "How do librarians here interact with students and for what purposes?" This question generated the least amount of discussion among the participants. John at University A summarized neatly the librarians' responses across all the institutions: "I think we have like five basic areas in which we interact with students. Ah, and that would be in an employment capacity, in an outreach capacity, at the desk, in the classroom, and, uh, one-on-one consultations." I distilled these capacities—to use John's word—into three broad themes that ran through the participants' stories: managing student employees, limited social presence in students' cocurricular activities, and transactions with students.

Managing Student Employees

Several of the participants claimed the undergraduate students they interact with the most, and consequently know the best, are students they employ at the library. Paul at University B and Sabrina at University D manage their libraries' circulation desks and interlibrary loan operations. They said they employ the greatest number of students compared to other librarians at their libraries. Although they hired and train students to perform specific tasks necessary to the libraries' operations, both Paul and Sabrina emphasized that they are teaching students to be part of the workforce and what it means to be an employee:

> These are their first jobs, most of them. They have no idea what it means to show up for work on time and how being late affects the student workers they're relieving. I'm teaching them customer service, how to listen, how to make eye contact, how to make referrals to others. . . . Whether they realize it or not, these are skills, skills that must be learned and mastered. (Sabrina, University D)

However, other participants also managed student employees. Jessica at University D is responsible for collecting works by the scholars at her university and depositing these in the library's institutional repository as well as advising the library's patrons on digital publishing. Initially, she employed students to handle mundane tasks associated with these responsibilities, but she is recasting the student employee positions as internships and focusing more on preparing students with transferable skills for when they enter the job market. She said, "I want them to have a really good cache of resumes when they, when they walk away from, from my fold."

It was clear that these librarians found managing student employees to be highly rewarding. Sabrina and Paul said they have remained in contact with many former student assistants over the years, providing references occasionally but also simply maintaining a social connection. Paul felt that he had clearly had an impact on these students' maturity and development. A few former student employees had even gone on to choose careers in librarianship, partly based on their rich experiences working in libraries during college.

Limited Presence in Students' Cocurricular Activities

Many of the participants acknowledged that they interact with undergraduate students very little outside of the confines of the library or outside the context of library work; the library's student employees were often the only students they knew by name. Nonetheless, several of the participants said they sought out undergraduate students in the context of their cocurricular activities.

Rebecca at University D volunteered as the faculty/staff advisor for a fraternity, which initially perplexed her because she had requested to advise a sorority. Although fascinated by the complexities of fraternal life, Rebecca conceded that she struggled to know how to advise the men appropriately, particularly on conduct. She relegated herself to more bureaucratic activities, such as signing paperwork, and admitted that she was "not much use" and should be asking the dean of students for training or help.

In contrast, Wendy at University C was highly involved with students who belonged to underrepresented identity groups, particularly Latina/Latino students and LGBT students. Wendy attended the programs sponsored by the offices and student organizations that focused on those students. She wanted to be visible in those student communities as a way to humanize the librarians for students whom she believed could benefit from librarians' expertise in ways that aren't strictly related to coursework. For example, Wendy said she buys literature related to the coming out process for LGBT students and makes connections with the parents of Latina/o students at Latino Family Day in order to help those families understand how the library could help the students acclimate to the campus.

At University A, Crystal and Jodie attended programs at the residence halls in order to develop personal connections with undergraduate students. Crystal said she often attended guest lectures held in the residence halls, went to movies in the lounges, and ate dinner with the students in the dining centers. Crystal said she thought the students were often confused and bemused by the presence of a librarian. She believed making these personal connections would inspire students to ultimately seek her out when needing research help. Crystal said she also better understood student culture because of her involvement.

Jodie was less certain of these potential benefits. In fact, she was pulling back on her efforts because she felt these connections were not rewarded by the library's tenure and promotion system. She felt she could argue that her involvement with students in the residence halls is a form of outreach, and therefore a dimension of her librarianship, but her position description didn't include this as one of her librarianship responsibilities. Instead, she felt the tenure and promotion system rewarded the personal connections she cultivated with faculty. Consequently, she was currently making more of an effort to get to know the faculty in the college of business on a personal level rather than getting to know the students.

Transactional Interactions

In returning to John's response that librarians at University A interact with students "at the desk" and "in class," I am classifying these types of interactions as transactional, or need-based, in nature. When many of the librarians referred to "at the desk" or "desk time," they meant their time spent at either the reference desk or the circulation desk, during which they waited passively for students to approach and ask a question. These questions were often directional in nature, (i.e., "Where is the restroom?"), sometimes technological (i.e., "How do I print to this printer?"), and less frequently instructional (i.e., "How do I find sources for my paper on X topic?") These interactions tended to be relatively brief, impersonal, and need-based. Often, the librarians did not learn the students' names and did not encounter the students again after meeting the students' immediate need. If the librarian interviewed the student in a desk setting about their information need, the interview was not focused on the student's thoughts or beliefs so much as on the assignment. Generally, the librarians desired to know if the question was related to a particular assignment and which faculty member had created the assignment. The most successful of these interviews, suggested the librarians at University A, yielded a copy of the assignment the librarians could retain at the desk for future reference.

The librarians at University B offered a unique example of a need-based interaction with undergraduate students: They had "door duty," in which they were posted to stand just inside the library's entrance and greet each person who entered. Ostensibly, they were engaged in proactive assistance by asking students what the librarians could help the student with that day and then referring the student to the appropriate person or desk. However, the librarians were also supposed to ask visitors to display a valid university ID; if the visitor was unable to produce one, the librarian disallowed entry. Several of the librarians stated the purpose of door duty was less about customer service than it was about heightening the library's security by barring outsiders. Their director had mandated door duty only this past year, and the librarians found it terribly distasteful and could not understand why they, the librarians, were expected to undertake the responsibility when security guards or support staff could carry it out just as well. In Alan's words, "We have many other, and better, things to do."

Even without door duty to worry about, the librarians at University B found transactional interactions with undergraduate students tough to navigate. Student employees handled nearly all the lending of library materials and answered most reference questions, referring only difficult questions to the librarians. On the whole, most of the librarians' interactions with undergraduate students took place within the context of teaching students how to use library resources and understand concepts of information literacy in classroom settings. While their focus group tended to lack enthusiasm for the questions on the whole, I could not help but detect a tone of exhaustion that colored their responses. Joe said, "There is so much to do that I just run like a chicken with my head cut off. . . ." Margaret invoked one of Raganathan's five laws of library science in a joking but put-upon way:

Raganathan said "save the time of the user," but what about the time of the librarian? I'm teaching, teaching, teaching . . . answering questions from faculty . . . committees . . . the director has some new idea every few weeks, and then there's a task force to study it . . . but there's only like seven or eight of us. That's like one librarian for every seven hundred students.

Librarians' workloads appeared to be problematic at all of the institutions. Jessica at University D noted the librarians classified as faculty at her library followed a formula for allocating their productivity. Librarianship occupied only 60% of their time, whereas a combination of scholarship and service demanded the remaining 40%. Consequently, they focused much of their librarianship time on what Yolanda called "high-impact practices" or work that reached the greatest number of students. Yolanda found creating how-to guides in the form of video for a potentially unlimited number of students to watch at their convenience more high-impact than teaching a face-to-face class of 27 students. However, she admitted she lost the personal connection she might have made with those 27 students.

Lauren at University C also emphasized the sheer demands on librarians' time rendered interactions with undergraduate students a lower priority. She said:

I want to be very clear that I am not saying that librarians do not care about undergraduate students. I am saying that the scope of their work, the priorities of the campus, and the way we have historically, um, conceptualized the way we see workload . . . it, it makes it virtually impossible in a number of areas for librarians to develop extensive . . . [trails off without finishing]

Despite the workload and sense of overwhelm that many of the librarians suggested, there still appeared to be room for reimagining the library and their work as librarians as student-centered concepts. This was most evident with the librarians at University C, who credited their dean with the genesis for moving away from what Lucy described as the concept of the library with the "Big L" and "very librarian focused" to "moving toward thinking about user with a capital 'U.'" She said, ". . . we're asking what is, what do our users need? And, I think, that is a big shift for us."

THE STUDENT AFFAIRS PROFESSIONALS' ROLES

When the focused discussions on the librarians' interactions with undergraduate students slowed, I asked the participants: "Let's turn our discussion to student affairs professionals. What do you perceive to be the role of student affairs professionals at this institution?" The participants answered this question with the briefest answers, and they engaged in considerable checking with each other to confirm their thoughts and impressions. Many of the participants switched to different tones than they had used previously, often sounding less certain of their perceptions.

Overall, the participants did not have well-developed impressions of the student affairs professionals at their institutions. Many participants said they were simply unfamiliar with the student affairs professionals, having rarely interacted—if at all—with these colleagues. Others perceived the primary role of student affairs professionals to be the provision of students' basic needs for survival, such as housing, meals, and health services. A much smaller number of participants speculated that student affairs professionals help students navigate the daily, if complicated, business of students, such as financial aid, advising, career services, and conflict resolution. Perhaps surprisingly, those participants who did express a more well-developed perception of student affairs professionals were often critical: They perceived student affairs professionals to be disorganized, to communicate poorly with academic affairs generally, and to seemingly inhabit a wholly separate reality of the campus.

Lack of Familiarity

The lack of familiarity with student affairs professionals hindered the participants' ability to probe and explore my question with each other. Overall, most of the participants demonstrated a lack of awareness of student affairs at all but University C. At University A, the librarians expressed considerable confusion as to who the student affairs professionals were. For instance, Amy asked me "Do you know on our campus what it [student affairs] includes?" The librarians then checked with each other to confirm their suspicions as to who constituted student affairs, naming the office of the dean of students, student programming, the career center, an office for nontraditional students. Jodie summarized their consensus: "Well, it sounds like they have all the life stuff other than like academic, like, everything they need in order to succeed so they can do their academic work on that foundation. Um . . . almost like a support system."

They remembered the associate dean of students had come to speak with the librarians in the past year or two. He provided the librarians with information about different areas of student affairs that could help students with different problems, and at least Beverly was impressed with a "who to call" flyer he distributed. She remarked that she had called one of the offices listed on behalf of a student who lacked anywhere to go on Thanksgiving Day.

At University B, the participants seemed completely at a loss. Their discussion focused on the student union building, which housed student dining, student programming, and the offices of housing and residential life. They recalled that the director of career services chaired the library's board of alumni advisors, but they weren't certain whether career services fit into the realm of student affairs. Ultimately, they concluded that it must because career services wasn't managed by any of the academic colleges. They confirmed that student affairs professionals must tend to students' basic needs, like housing, and entertainment. However, the librarians said their understanding of student affairs was based on their memories of their own undergraduate experiences rather than on their knowledge of their own institution.

Sabrina at University D said "I don't think about [student affairs] very much. I mean, the most I probably think about it is in terms of making sure students have their [ID] cards." Deanna offered that student affairs professionals support students' housing, dining, counseling, entertainment, and financial aid needs. She said that she had interacted with student affairs professionals primarily when students suffered breakdowns in the library due to stress, and she made calls to the counseling staff on the students' behalf. Crystal at University A had made an almost identical remark.

Throughout the focus group discussion at University D, Howard noted his institution suffered declining enrollment and high attrition, endangering the ability of academic affairs to function without stable revenue brought by tuition dollars. He acknowledged student affairs professionals were vital to the financial health of the university by successfully reducing students' barriers to persistence and by creating a campus environment that fostered students' interest in returning for subsequent years. However, he perceived student affairs as a threat to the primacy of the academic affairs side of the university. He noted the proliferation of student affairs positions corresponded to the decline of the number of faculty positions at University D. He expressed skepticism of student affairs: "We have an awful lot of vice presidents for a school of our size, so if you want to know what we think about student affairs . . ." The other participants met his unfinished statement with a chorus of laughter but they chose not to offer further discussion when I probed for greater explanation.

The Shuffle

The diversification of student affairs' functions appeared, according to the librarians, to erect unintended barriers for students and librarians alike. The librarians reported that often students did not know how or where to obtain the help they needed, for instance with financial aid. The students visited multiple different offices, with staff reportedly referring the students on to other offices before the students finally located the correct office or staff member. The librarians noted the students required tenacity and time in order to navigate the myriad student affairs offices successfully, and they did not believe most students showed this commitment. Instead, their problems often went unresolved. The librarians themselves had experienced this phenomenon when attempting to call various offices on behalf of students. Too often, Jessica said, student affairs staff proved unhelpful at directing the librarian to a specific person or office, offering only vague advice such as "call financial aid," suggesting to Jessica that student affairs professionals did not have any greater knowledge of other student affairs offices than did the librarians or students. Essentially, the diversification of functions created silos.

The problem of ongoing referrals was so pervasive and well known among the librarians at Universities A, C, D, and E that they had named the phenomenon the "[X] Shuffle," after the institution's mascot or nickname. The librarians at University B did not indicate they or their students experienced shuffles, but they did note their institution was physically small enough that most student services were concentrated in a single building. However, a single building for student services did not diminish the shuffle at University A, whose librarians noted the university had centralized student services recently to reduce students' frustration and enhance student retention. Organizationally, they claimed, various offices remained distinct and physically separated within the building. The "shuffle" persisted but was at least confined to a single building.

At University E, the librarians found the shuffle at their institution difficult to comprehend. Gina said "We're a faith-based university, and I think student affairs is somehow involved in the running of our campus ministry. Somehow that's tied up with admissions and new student orientation too, but I'm not really sure how." Sarah agreed and added "Student affairs feels very . . . diffuse to me. Whenever we have a complaint from a student—and we do get complaints from students about their experiences with other parts of the campus—I am never sure where to refer them. Even searching a staff directory doesn't help because the person you reach in admissions says 'I think that's counseling's job, so send them over there.' And then the student comes back to me and says 'Nope, they weren't the right people to help me either.'"

"Running a Different University"

Lucy at University C made a remark that I found particularly poignant. She said, "You asked what we perceive their role to be, and I . . . feel that student affairs is almost running a different university than the academics." She claimed that she could not adequately call the lack of cooperation between student affairs professionals and faculty a divide because a divide implied that she could see the other side. "There is really almost a separate, very separate things," she said. As an example, she explained the perceived struggle between academic affairs and student affairs over the teaching of leadership skills. Students could study theories of leadership through systematic coursework taught by an interdisciplinary group of faculty, or students could earn a certificate in leadership through coordinated cocurricular experiences managed by student affairs professionals. However, the program of study and the certificate were not linked. While Lucy initially perceived this disconnect to be the result of the university's decentralization, she decided later that student affairs professionals resisted efforts to be more closely tied to the academic mission. She believed student affairs professionals were attempting to cultivate their own niche in which they could actively teach and educate students but were likely hesitant to partner for fear the academic side of the university would subsume what they had built.

Molly agreed with Lucy, claiming student affairs professionals decide what they think is important in regard to crafting the ideal student experience. She was frustrated that student affairs professionals rarely responded to her invitations to share information or to discuss outreach opportunities at the libraries. She noted the autonomy student affairs professionals appear to enjoy, speculating that individual student affairs professionals pursue the opportunities they believe are worthwhile. When that person moves on, successors or other persons affiliated with the same office won't respond, indicating that the person's colleagues had come to different decisions about what was important for their work. Molly seemed to disapprove of this perceived autonomy, noting that librarians are greatly accountable to each other and "would be dinged" by their peers during their annual peer-conducted performance reviews for "going off the reservation."

Lucy considered whether faculty had unintentionally empowered student affairs professionals to devise their own sets of educational outcomes by abdicating teaching in favor of scholarly pursuits. She said:

> So many of our faculty on campus don't actually ever teach undergrads. They might never actually even teach, but they certainly do not teach undergrads. If the campus has, um, either intentionally or unintentionally essentially created a line of old-time instructional faculty who are not tenure-line faculty but full-time academic professionals—and that's what student affairs people are—especially for looking at undergraduate education. So, it just, it just allows a further distancing of faculty who are . . . further and further removed.

Alison at University C had contributed very little to the focus group thus far, but she surprised me with the revelation that she was herself a former student affairs professional. She had worked in career services before she had transitioned into a new career as a librarian at the same institution. Alison lamented that her former colleagues in career services had little interest in reaching out to her now. She imagined many ways career services could be well served by working with a librarian to ensure library collections contained current information on careers, certification programs, and job-searching strategies. Similarly, she felt that she could teach the career counselors better information-seeking and analysis skills in order to help them do their jobs better. As a pre-tenured librarian, she said she was unsure about how aggressively to market her skills to her former colleagues and had let her ideas remain idle. The other librarians in the focus group encouraged her but simultaneously affirmed that she had better focus on her core responsibilities until she earned tenure.

Alison did point out that student affairs professionals need to understand the academic affairs side of the university better. During her years in student affairs, she had the impression that only student affairs professionals provide career counseling, academic advising, and other traditional student services at the institution. After her transition to librarianship, she was surprised to learn many of the academic departments perform these responsibilities as well. She said, "Everyone is running a student affairs function. So you could argue there is duplication of effort. But, I really feel a huge, um, disconnect." Alison seemed to feel that student affairs wasn't laying claim to an educational realm that faculty had abandoned so much as they were remaking it in a form all of their own:

> Faculty are still advising students, still giving career advice, still reviewing applicants and making admissions decisions, but student affairs put their own spin on it and do things differently with those things. Because they have student development theories, and because they're a lot more in tune with the students themselves. So the same work begins to look and feel, well, different than when the faculty do it.

Alison felt that, at times, student affairs professionals forgot that they could have partners to enrich their work.

Lucy returned to her assertion that student affairs professionals inhabit a different university than the faculty. She pointed to governance, indicating that faculty participate directly in the university's strategic decisions. Although faculty from different disciplines may disagree with elements of the university's strategic plan, Lucy contended faculty are largely on the same page in regard to the university's mission and definitions of academic excellence. Student affairs professionals, however, do not play a role in university governance because they are not faculty. This lack of participation in university governance created distance between student affairs professionals and the faculty.

COLLABORATION WITH STUDENT AFFAIRS PROFESSIONALS

Next I asked the participants "Do librarians at this institution interact with or collaborate with student affairs professionals at this institution?" While this question elicited a wide range of responses, often tangential, the librarians were largely consistent across institutions in their assertion that collaboration had not transpired, or at least not with lasting success. However, the librarians' desire to collaborate differed greatly between institutions. At two of the institutions, the librarians were uncertain of the library's priorities or they perceived the library to be undervalued by the institution itself; they did not appear to have given much prior thought to the possibility of collaborations with student affairs professionals. At the other three institutions, the librarians felt the library administrators valued and encouraged collaboration with student affairs professionals, but the librarians themselves had not actively done so. Their reasons varied from feeling overwhelmed with the diverse demands on their time to low returns—or even threats—in their formal reward systems.

Mission Confusion

The librarians at University B expressed frank surprise at my question. After searching her colleague's faces for any sign that she might be wrong, Margaret answered for the group:

> We haven't thought really about it. I'm pretty sure we've never discussed it at all. I think . . . our director has certainly told us, encouraged us, that we should collaborate more with other people on campus but I'm not sure that we've really understood why we should do that. It doesn't really seem to be a priority either since we don't actually talk about it together as a group.

The library's director had not provided any further direction other than that the librarians should collaborate with student affairs professionals, but Joe and Paul claimed the director had not articulated her desired outcome—was it to improve direct service to students? To facilitate librarians' teaching of information literacy outside of the context of academic programs? Without further discussion, Joe and Paul felt they were being encouraged to collaborate with student affairs professionals for the sole sake of collaborating—which they believed to be a waste of time without clear goals and outcomes. However, none of the participants had asked the director for greater clarification or had attempted to begin a group discussion. Individually, the participants seemed to have concluded that collaboration with student affairs professionals didn't fit neatly with their library's overall mission to make information resources available for the purpose of teaching and student learning. Thus, group discussion had failed to take place.

The participants at University D offered a nearly identical discussion. However, they were sharply critical of their library administrators whereas the librarians at University B were not. At University D, the participants noted a distinct lack of coordination of the library's activities by the dean and associate deans. The administrators had encouraged the librarians to collaborate with student affairs professionals but had provided no clear desired outcomes or benefits for students, nor had they identified which student affairs functions would be conducive for collaboration. The lack of coordination appeared to be the norm, judging from the participants' open dismay that they are often left to decide among themselves how best to accomplish the library's stated goals. Howard and Deanna noted this way of working was counterproductive: Collective decision-making implied consensus was necessary in order to move in a new direction, but consensus rarely occurred and no change transpired.

Perceived Lack of Interest from Student Affairs Professionals

Unlike their counterparts at Universities B and D, the librarians at Universities A, C, and E reported they'd engaged in broad discussions about the library's role in student persistence, and they did see collaboration with other groups on campus as a way for librarians to play different roles. Each group of participants said their respective deans saw collaboration with student affairs professionals as a priority for the library and was quite clear on what that collaboration could look like. However, the groups reported unfavorable results in their past attempts to collaborate with student affairs professionals, and no current initiatives were underway. Jodie at University A reported her attempts at reaching out to the staff at career services had gone unanswered so often she had simply given up. Crystal said she had met with the residential life staff, who did want to collaborate, but no one could come up with any good ideas. Crystal and Jeanette said they received regular invitations from residential life staff to participate in programs or dinners at the residence halls in order to mingle with the students. While they appreciated the invitations, they felt confused and overwhelmed by the sheer volume of activities. They reported receiving at least one invitation per day for a different activity, and they were unable to discern which activities were important. Consequently, Jeanette attended none. Crystal said she had time for perhaps one activity per week but the inability to pick an activity meant she participated in few to none. Crystal believed individual student affairs professionals were interested but student affairs seemed to experience high turnover. When a staff member departed, no other colleagues continued the discussions.

At University C, the librarians felt stymied in their overtures to student affairs professionals as well. Molly remarked that she did not know who in student affairs she should contact, finding the websites unhelpful or confusing. Similar to the "shuffle" experienced by students, Molly said her e-mails or voicemails often went unreturned or were endlessly forwarded to other student affairs professionals. Many of the other participants agreed strenuously with Molly, suggesting they had similar experiences. Largely, these efforts to reach out to student affairs professionals centered on the librarians' offer for the student affairs professionals to use the library as a space for meeting with students. Lauren reported that, for a time, the career services and academic advisors held drop-in hours at the library at her suggestion. While students responded favorably to their presence at the library, the drop-in hours ended rather abruptly and without much explanation. Like Crystal at University A, the librarians believed the desire to collaborate was largely based on the individual preferences of student affairs professionals. When these people departed, the drop-in hours at the library ceased.

At University E, the librarians felt the faith-based character of their institution should have made discussions with colleagues outside the library easier. Kyra, Gabriel, and Hilary shared their frustrations:

> We should have similar expectations on what the student experience should look like at our [institution]. Our teaching and our services are guided by the tenets of our faith, and our president has led numerous discussions over the years about what a [faith-based] education looks like at our campus. (Kyra)

> Student affairs has part of those discussions, every time. I think our director has tried more than once to reach out to the leaders in student affairs. Everyone sounds pretty positive about working together in some way, but it just never seems to really take hold for some reason. (Gabriel)

> Yeah, but we [the librarians] haven't been the ones necessarily making the overtures, have we? It's always our library director and maybe . . . maybe [the head of reference]? So we can't really say why it doesn't get off the ground. I think maybe [the head of reference] once told me that she and the . . . the director of the student union, maybe . . . were going to get together to talk about ideas, and the other person canceled and it just never got rescheduled. Maybe they felt they didn't really have any ideas so it wasn't worth meeting. (Hilary)

"The Jenga Pile"

Many of the participants felt overwhelmed at the prospect of integrating collaboration with student affairs professionals into their current responsibilities. Joe at University B speculated the small size of the library staff and the daily business of running the library constrained their ability to step outside their traditional responsibilities. Joe and other participants at University B pointed out that they are already balancing multiple roles—liaising with faculty as subject matter experts for multiple academic departments, managing the support staff who perform circulation and interlibrary loan duties, and curating the library's website and access to subscription databases and journals. John at University A referred to this jumble of responsibilities as "the Jenga pile," in which individual librarians take on more and more responsibilities as departing librarians aren't replaced or as library operations grow in complexity. John referenced a game called Jenga, where the object of the game is to collaboratively construct a tower by removing blocks from the base and adding new layers to the ever-growing peak; the tower's collapse is always inevitable and the player who removes the ultimate block loses.

Jeanette at University A explained that she had little time to think deeply about student affairs professionals because her own position had gone unfilled for years before she was hired. Her predecessors had each lasted only a few years before leaving for other positions. She said the turnover and the library's slowness at filling her position had damaged the library's relationship with the faculty in her assigned subject areas. Initially, they were unwilling to develop a relationship with her for fear that she might leave. Jeanette felt that she had to concentrate her efforts to prove herself to the faculty, as she deemed her ability to search their research interests and those of their students to be what the library valued most from her. While she was still receptive to the invitations she received from residential life to attend programs in the residence halls, she only rarely accepted these invitations.

The librarians at University E were particularly struggling with the Jenga pile. Gabriel noted that their liaison responsibilities kept them busy, as University E had many graduate programs as well as a large undergraduate population. He said, "Our library's new strategic plan calls for greater student engagement, greater outreach, and liaison activities with cocurricular areas, like the residence halls. But I'm just not sure where to find the time." His colleague Courtney agreed, noting the librarians had expected staffing levels to increase to meet the new expectations of the university administration, but this had not happened. "Instead," Courtney said, "We're expected to make do, to carve out time from . . .what? Collection assessment, I'm not sure, in order to spend more time with student engagement."

Reward Systems

Many participants noted too that existing reward systems do not facilitate "going off the reservation," as Molly at University C said. At University A, John acknowledged that the reward system for librarians focuses largely on what he called the three core activities: teaching, publishing, and committee involvement. He implied collaboration with student affairs professionals would likely be considered something distinct from any of those core activities. He said the library employed a staff member whose work was principally outreach to students outside of the library but that her work fell so outside the paradigm for faculty librarians that she was not even classified as a librarian. John speculated that supervisors would not know how to evaluate a librarian's efforts at collaboration. He said there are so many factors that could derail the anticipated outcome of collaboration that are not within an individual's control—so would the librarian be evaluated for their effort or for the collaboration's success?

The librarians at University B were not faculty and did not have a tenure system. They were evaluated by their director based on the duties and responsibilities outlined in their individual position descriptions; none of their position descriptions reflected any language they thought resembled outreach or collaboration. They did feel that collaboration with other groups could be theoretically added to their position descriptions with their director's support, but they were uncertain as to what that work would look like.

At Universities A and D, the librarians did not explicitly perceive reward systems to be a barrier that prevented collaboration with student affairs professionals. Rather, they suggested the path to tenure was so rigid that little time and energy was left for fulfilling anything but their routine library responsibilities and their scholarly pursuits. The librarians at University C suggested from their simultaneous support and caution of Alison's desire to work more closely with the career services staff that stepping outside the traditional norms of librarianship was risky during the pre-tenure years but looked upon more favorably post-tenure.

CONCLUSION

The participants in the librarians' focus groups provided rather consistent responses despite the differences in the types of institutions to which they belonged. They perceived their principal roles to be collection purveyors, teachers, and agents of community development. In their collection purveyor role, they build awareness of information resources among their constituents in order to facilitate students' and disciplinary faculty members' learning and research endeavors. In their teaching role, the librarians perceived themselves as chiefly responsible for developing students' information-seeking and information literacy skills. As agents of community development, the librarians fashioned the physical and virtual spaces of the libraries to foster a sense of community between students and between students and the institutions.

The participants perceived their interactions with students to be relatively narrow in scope and often confined to the physical spaces of the library.

Their primary contact with students was with those employed as student assistants in the library and those the librarians taught in formal instruction sessions. While they valued their contact with students at the reference desks, these interactions were often impersonal and ephemeral. Some librarians interacted with students outside the library through their ventures as advisors of student organizations or as participants in programming hosted by the universities' residence halls.

When I turned discussion toward the role of student affairs professionals, the participants seemed uncertain. They were often confused as to which functional areas of the university belonged to the student affairs domain. Primarily, they saw student affairs professionals as responsible for meeting students' basic needs, such as housing, dining, and recreation. At most of the institutions, the librarians expressed concern that students were shuffled between different student affairs offices and did not receive the assistance they needed.

None of the participants reported significant collaboration between librarians and student affairs professionals. While some student services had entered the library, such as advising or writing assistance, some librarians perceived such collaboration as a threat to the library's historic importance. Other librarians reported attempts to explore collaborations with student affairs professionals that were met with disinterest. Many librarians also seemed concerned with the leadership provided by library administrators, who supported collaboration with student affairs professionals but failed to engage the librarians in meaningful discussions of how such collaborations could benefit students or be accomplished. Other librarians were reluctant to pursue collaborations for fear of stepping outside the norms of the library and preferred to postpone such plans until their positions were secured with tenure.

Chapter Five

The Student Affairs Professionals' Stories

The student affairs professionals who participated in my focus groups came from many different functional areas, including residential life, career centers, advising centers, student conduct, student union management, minority student services, and Greek affairs. Across all five of the focus groups, the student affairs professionals could not have differed more starkly from the librarians in their comportment. Three words summarize my impressions of the student affairs professionals: eloquent, confident, and lively.

Whereas the librarians often spoke in incomplete sentences, used garbled words, and often did not match tense to verbs, the student affairs professionals appeared to be masterful public speakers. With nearly flawless grammar, the student affairs professionals spoke clearly and coherently throughout the discussions. They evinced confidence; their replies came so swiftly and so fully formed after I had asked my questions that I felt almost dumbfounded at their nimbleness of thought. I noted, too, that they did not often turn toward each other or seek out each other's eyes while offering their initial opinions—they seemed completely at ease with their personal convictions and had little need for confirmation. They mostly engaged with each other when building off each other's replies, filling out what a previous speaker had said with a story of their own unique experiences or challenging or supporting each other. A portion of the dialog between Lorraine and Michelle at University C offers an example of this confidence built by mutual support:

> I had the opportunity to investigate the incident [a boyfriend/girlfriend dispute] a little further, talk with the students, and explore what would be fair and reasonable. So, I spent probably four hours to five hours with the different students involved in that incident. And, really, I hope and think

that I helped them gain some perspective. I think I made a real learning opportunity. . . . I was an authority figure, but I also became someone who offered some insight and advice. (Lorraine)

Oh, I know what you mean. You work in housing, and I'm in the student union, but our goals are so similar. . . . We want students to develop their identities, to be exposed to different perspectives, and we find a way to open a dialog about what those differences are. (Michelle)

Their passion for their work was quite evident, both through the vigor of their excited tones and their liberal use of phrases such as "Oh, I *know*!" to confirm something their peer had just said, along with emphatic body language such as nodding and hand gestures. They often shared laughter, but rarely did I have difficulty getting the discussions back on track. Rather, they remained quite focused.

Tables 5.1 through 5.5 provide brief descriptions of the participants at each institution.

STUDENT AFFAIRS PROFESSIONALS' ROLES

Initially, I asked the participants "What do you perceive to be the role of student affairs professionals at this institution?" The participants' responses were consistent between focus groups: educating the whole student and contributing to student success. The participants felt quite strongly that their predominant role as student affairs professionals was to spark growth in students' critical thinking and interpersonal skills and to create experiential learning that imbued students with marketable job skills. Many participants felt they as student affairs professionals were chiefly responsible for "adulting" students—as Lorraine at University C jokingly called it—or preparing students for entering postcollege life. They felt responsible because faculty members' roles were focused either on teaching students the content knowledge of their respective fields or on generating new knowledge through research activities. The participants were also focused on student success, or helping students attain their degrees by reducing the barriers that inhibited

Table 5.1. Student Affairs Professionals at University A

Name	Sex	Years of Service
Kate	Female	20
Daniel	Male	7
Peter	Male	12
Dorothy	Female	14

Table 5.2. Student Affairs Professionals at University B

Name	Sex	Years of Service
Jack	Male	17
Alice	Female	23
Megan	Female	12
Kimberly	Female	9

students' likelihood of doing so. The ways by which the participants accomplished this varied by institution and were dictated by the institutions' unique circumstances.

Holistic Student Development

All the student affairs professionals articulated a holistic definition of student development. Each student affairs professional spoke expansively on the particular dimensions of student development that their functional area influenced the most, such as interpersonal skills and managing emotions appropriately. Nonetheless, each student affairs professional described student development as how the college experience shapes students: their cognitive processes, leadership skills, career interests, sense of identity, interpersonal skills, and how they see themselves in the world. They described student success as how students move toward attaining a degree. The following exchange between Daniel and Kate at University A summarizes the participants' perspective of their roles:

> We have a journalism degree, and you want to be a news broadcaster. Student affairs provides housing, food, recreational opportunities, engagement opportunities, leadership opportunities, the television station where you can practice your things you learned in your courses, in the classroom. (Daniel)

> Learning how to navigate different identities and those types of things, getting the support services you need. We run a gamut basically from getting from major to career. (Kate)

> I think it all boils down to that. (Daniel)

> Employers are going to be looking for more than just a degree. There's going to be three thousand other students graduating with your degree. What sets you apart? What makes you different? What makes you the most qualified for that job? And what are employers looking for nowadays—"What did you do outside the classroom that's going to help you

Table 5.3. Student Affairs Professionals at University C

Name	Sex	Years of Service
Robert	Male	22
Greta	Female	24
Miguel	Male	5
Lorraine	Female	5
Michelle	Female	12
Louise	Female	15

succeed in this job here?" So, it's "What did you get involved in?" Planning an activity, getting a team together, show some leadership. . . . (Kate)

So, you know, so we have to encourage. I think everybody, regardless of what umbrella of student affairs you're under, is encouraging students to take the most, take advantage of the opportunities that are here. Um, be involved on campus, grow, change your thinking, change your perspective, meet people different than you, solve problems. (Daniel)

Be a functioning adult, really, with some perspective on life and able to work with people who don't always think like you. (Kate)

Institutional Differences in Participants' Interpretations of Roles

Despite their agreement on student success and educating the whole student, the participants interpreted the focus of their roles differently based on the student concerns that troubled their university administrators the most. Moreover, the participants within the same focus groups were in agreement as to their interpretations and were highly aware that their interpretation of their roles was distinctive to their institutions. They evinced a clear connection between the importance of their work and the goals of their institutions, indicating they perceived their roles to be simultaneously valued by their institutions and vital to their institutions' reputation or fiscal well-being.

At University A, the participants emphasized the high proportion of students from low-income families among the student body. Their presence caused the focus of the participants' work to be making the college experience more affordable for their students. Otherwise, they noted, student retention decreased. Kate, Daniel, and Peter felt student affairs professionals bore great responsibility for retention:

Table 5.4. Student Affairs Professionals at University D

Name	Sex	Years of Service
Tonya	Female	20
Toby	Male	9
Oliver	Male	11
Valerie	Female	13
Marcie	Female	8

You know, students are coming in and needing more, and what have you. And what do we do with this leftover work-study money and who are we going to give it to? How do you engage the students on campus? Because we know that engagement is important for their ultimate success on campus. (Kate)

I mean, it all boils down to that. Um, because the student comes here, and they attend some great parties, have great relationships while he is here, met some cool faculty, learn some stuff, but you didn't graduate. And now you are tens of thousands of dollars in debt with money folks knocking at your door. How successful were, uh, we at supporting and, um, moving that student through his . . .[trails off]. (Daniel)

What good are we, what kind of experiences are the students having, if they fail to graduate but still leave here with great amounts of debt? We have failed them. (Peter)

At University B, the participants noted student enrollment had declined, endangering their ability to fill vacant positions. Nonetheless, the institution enjoyed a reputation for placing students into their desired careers quickly after graduation, and the student affairs professionals were focused on helping students gain transferable skills. A discussion between Jack, Alice, and Kimberly summarized their position:

All of student affairs is very involved in creating situations where students can learn the skills they need in order to be good candidates for graduate school and for employers. (Jack)

Yeah, we do that really well as a group. (Alice)

I think we spend a lot of time helping students take what they are learning in the classrooms and apply them in real-world situations. We're very civic minded, so we encourage them toward the right community service opportunities, "right" meaning "is it giving back to the community in a

Table 5.5. Student Affairs Professionals at University E

Name	Sex	Years of Service
Stan	Male	17
Kristin	Female	16
Marta	Female	12
Barbara	Female	23
Don	Male	9
Matt	Male	6

> way that is also connected to their studies?" That gives them experience, gets their name out there too, but we do have to counsel them about quality versus quantity. (Kimberly)

At University C, the student affairs professionals observed the very large size of their campus is often a barrier for students, making students feel overwhelmed, lost, and anonymous. Consequently, the student affairs professionals perceive their role as helping students navigate the campus and finding a niche that still makes the college experience meaningful. In the following exchange, Miguel, Greta, and Michelle explained their roles in helping students make personal connections:

> Our first role is really is to [help students] know their community. I think student affairs is right in the middle of navigating this. (Miguel)

> Um, I think there's really less engagement from the faculty. The faculty are almost entirely focused on research here, and so many of the lower-division courses are actually taught by T.A.s, who are grad students, in very big lecture halls. Undergrads may not actually interact with anyone but their friends and classmates, well, maybe not until their junior- or senior-level classes even. The people who are their advisors are not faculty, and so I think they [students] get less engagement, and the academic side seems so much farther away, and the professors are way up here and they don't engage. So the student affairs staff seem more reachable, I would say. (Greta)

> I think it takes some time for you as an individual to reach out, you know, and to being involved. There's a lot of opportunities for them to be involved. But, um, I think, you know, it's knowing when to. (Miguel)

> We have to help guide them when they step outside of the classroom. Some of them just don't get that connection. (Michelle)

So we all offer opportunities for them to connect. Some get things from the housing, some things from the union. Our students, you know, some do feel isolated still but the majority . . . I think they do find their niche, you know, whether it's with the cultural houses or the union or their residence halls, and all that. There's a lot of entry points the students can find community, but we have to create those opportunities for community to develop. (Miguel)

The participants' perceptions of their contributions to student success contrast greatly with the librarians, whose perceptions of their roles varied little between institutions. The student affairs professionals' recognition that they must adjust their roles to correspond to the institution's values supports Walter's (2009) perspective that student affairs is a value-relational discipline, in which practitioners of a discipline are attentive to campus culture and find meaning for their work in what the campus values. However, the librarians' perceptions of their work varied little between institutions, which suggests the library profession may be less value-relational than thought. This may have negative implications for the feasibility of collaboration between librarians and student affairs professionals, as Becher and Trowler (2001) theorized that interdisciplinary work is less challenging when the collaborators belong to disciplines that are value-relational to their institutions' values.

INTERACTIONS WITH UNDERGRADUATE STUDENTS

Next, I nudged the focused discussions toward the student affairs professionals' direct interactions with students. I asked, "How do student affairs professionals here interact with students and for what purposes?" I noticed a profound change among nearly all of my participants with this question: They were more lively, leaned closer as they spoke to me, and clearly took pride and pleasure as they shared their favorite moments or relished what they love most about their respective positions. Student affairs professionals used many "helping" words and phrases to describe their work and their relationships with students such as "empathy," "care," "understanding," "advise," and "belonging." Clearly, the participants respected students as individuals who matter and are unique in their own personal experiences, circumstances, and needs. The predominant themes of the student affairs professionals' responses to my question centered on teaching moments with students and on advocating to the administrations of their respective universities on behalf of students.

I noted, too, that the participants' interactions with students did not appear bounded by spaces or locations, unlike the librarians' interactions. The librarians were aware that their interactions with students mostly took place at specific locations, such as at a service point or within a classroom. Although the librarians managed student employees at the library and occasionally conducted outreach to students outside the library, the librarians still emphasized that these interactions occurred because of the places where the interactions transpired; the librarians may not have had reason or circumstance to interact with students without those parameters of space. Additionally, some of the librarians seemed to have conflict with that awareness—was it constraining or enabling the nature and quality of their interactions?

I had expected the student affairs professionals would similarly reference specific places, such as residence halls or advising centers. They made few such references. In fact, the participants spoke of their interactions with students as if they were not bounded at all by physical spaces, suggesting instead that student affairs professionals feel a sense of autonomy in being able to work with students wherever students might be found.

Student Affairs Professionals as Teachers

The participants certainly saw their interactions with students as involving teaching, but they generally described these interactions as informal and relatively brief. Many participants used the phrase "teaching moment" to describe an interaction that was short-lived (often less than an hour), such as in a roommate mediation, but purposeful on the part of the participant. Greta and Louise at University C discussed applying transformative learning to their interactions with students:

> I would agree with that, and I would also say maybe learning some of the responsibility they don't get [to] learn in their classroom. For me, as an employer of students, means teaching them. I've had a lot of conversations about what it means to have a job and to have a supervisor and to understand what it means to provide good customer service. Those are skills that you do not learn in the classroom, and so . . . and so I think that is a majority of my, my job when it comes to the people, to the students, I employ. (Greta)

> We stimulate their curiosity. We help them learn outside of the classroom and connect that learning to what they are doing in the rest of their lives. Um, we help them become lifelong learners, and we help them develop their creativity and their critical thinking. We help them communicate well with their peers. Um, we help them learn how to make things happen within their sphere of influence, how to organize things, how to be leaders. (Louise)

All of those things. [laughter] I see this transformative piece as being, uh, a reframe opportunity. They have a chance to look at either old things in new ways or to, um, learn entirely new conceptualizations of the world around them, and to, I think the thing that we do in student affairs, we provide that practice ground to do that. (Greta)

Usually, the participant described guiding a student toward a particular outcome, such as a new understanding of a complex situation, through discussion. Some participants referred to this method as "challenge and support," in which they verbally challenged students' beliefs by asking many questions such as "Why do you think that way?" and supporting students' commitment to a possible new perspective. Barbara at University E recounted an interaction where she taught perspective-taking skills to a boyfriend and girlfriend engaged in a dispute:

I talked with each of them separately, and then again. I asked each of them questions like "Why do you think she responded like that?" and "How do you think he felt when you said that to him when you knew it wasn't true?" Then I bought them together, and I prompted them to say, to say to each other what they said to me. I'm not sure, I think I spent maybe three hours with them, all told. They seemed to really get it in the end, why their words and their actions to each other incited the other. They're only 18 . . . they have a hard time seeing anything from any angle but their own, at least at first. I think [I] offered them some insight.

Tonya and Toby at University D explained that student affairs professionals walk a fine line by teaching with the challenge-and-support concept. While it often worked for them, they felt it was successful only when they had developed trusted relationships with students. Otherwise, students less familiar with Tonya and Toby were not as open to being challenged.

I think that there is this natural tension between being helpful and being too helpful. You can't lift them over the bar, you've got to show them how to get, uh, up and it's okay to give them a hand every once in a while but you really have to sort of show, teach them to fish. (Toby)

I agree. You gotta make the student want to get there. (Tonya)

Show them . . . why it is important and turn [them] loose. (Toby)

It's always started with a relationship with the students. Taking the time, how much ever time that is, and meeting them on their level to develop a relationship. Now, there's a line though. I don't want too much of a personal relationship but there's got to be a relationship there to begin with. So, I always take time to build relationships with the students. Once a relationship is there, you can challenge them and, and they're going to be less resistant to it. I mean like "Who do you think you are?" You know. Well, if I know them, and they know me, then we can have an honest dialog. (Tonya)

Challenge-and-support doesn't always work. Sometimes they can't meet your expectations. Often they do, but sometimes they don't. I really don't like this method though. How many students do we reach? This is so dependent on the relationship you build, and you can only build so many. (Toby)

Yeah . . . You know, most students have no idea who we are. They don't interact with student affairs. Who interacts with us? The students who are really in trouble, in crisis, and they're tough to build a relationship with because maybe they're adversarial since they're in trouble. (Tonya)

Right. Or the students who want to be involved, so they seek us out. They want to be part of something, be leaders in the community here. So they gravitate toward us for those programming opportunities. Usually they start out as R.A.s in the halls or maybe as student workers in our offices. They're the ones we build a relationship with but I bet they're less than 10% of the kids here. (Toby)

We never see most. (Tonya)

So I don't think this is a very effective way of teaching, you know? But I'm not really sure what the alternatives are. How do we make a bigger impact? (Toby)

Moore and Marsh (2007) postulated that student affairs professionals teach students from "afar" by creating environments and experiences that stimulate personal exploration and growth (p. 7). The participants bear out Moore and Marsh's claim through their emphasis on creating opportunities, programs, and experiences, but they also appear to have a stronger teacher identity than Moore and Marsh suggest student affairs professionals have. Moore and Marsh claim student affairs professionals have an educator identity but have yet to intentionally structure interactions with students to lead to intended learning outcomes. The participants' focused discussions suggest that they are doing so but are frustrated by the limitations of their method, namely that interactions are dependent on forging personal connections with students and thus they are not able to reach as many students as they would like.

Student Affairs Professionals as Advocates

The participants perceived themselves as advocates on behalf of students and that advocacy played a vital role in student success by ensuring the universities remained responsive and flexible to meet students' needs. They educated university administrators and others on the needs of special populations of students in order to change policies or procedures that remedy disadvantages or unfair circumstances, such as in the stories Daniel and Kate at University A shared. Daniel recounted his experience working with the chancellor's office to address bias complaints minority students had brought to him; he believed his advocacy on behalf of the African American and Latino students had helped persuade the chancellor to establish a high-ranking position focused on diversity initiatives. Meanwhile, Kate observed that students who self-identified as transgender expressed concerns about restrooms, and she was working with the university's facilities managers to plan for gender-neutral restrooms in future renovation plans.

Robert and Louise at University C acknowledged that student affairs professionals walk a fine line between representing students' interests and serving an institution whose culture or goals may not coincide with those interests:

> I think that there's this other role that we are called upon to play in terms of the students. We impact the students but how do we make sure the students are impacting [the university] so that we are evolving along the way? And, um, so often there's this tension there that we're, uh, I think student affairs is right in the middle of navigating this. How do we take what students are bringing to us as concerns with the environment that they're in, and of ways that we can advocate for them, ways that we can encourage them to advocate for themselves, and build this structure so that they can navigate it themselves? (Robert)

> So it's this . . . this kind of dance where ultimately they want help, they want to help, help provide the best kind of space for students to have all these things. But we're part of an institution . . . the bureaucracy is thick [laughter] and um . . . I think many of us struggle with figuring out how to advocate for them best. (Louise)

LIBRARIANS' ROLES

Next I asked the participants: "Let's turn our discussion to librarians. What do you perceive to be the role of librarians at this institution?" I believe this question elicited the most uncertainty from the participants, judging from the lengthier pauses between their responses and the increased frequency of checking their responses with each other through direct eye contact. The participants' perceptions of librarians varied across focus groups and even among participants within the same focus groups. Some participants saw—and valued—librarians as educators, influencing students' cognitive development by teaching analytical skills and self-sufficiency, whereas other participants found librarians unresponsive to students' needs and consequently believed librarians were too removed from student learning to be taken seriously as educators. This mirrors the ambivalence that faculty members expressed in Nilsen's (2012) and Schulte and Sherwill-Navarro's (2009) studies, indicating that student affairs professionals' perceptions of librarians' instructional role is just as complicated and multilayered as their perceptions of faculty members.

Most participants agreed that librarians are principally resources for students, faculty, and staff by developing collections that enable their constituents to find the answers they seek. Several of the participants referred to this role as "silent partners in higher education" and valued this role. Other participants were disturbed by what they perceived as librarians' diminishing visibility, leading one participant to refer to librarians as "the invisible people."

Librarians as Educators

The student affairs professionals considered librarians critical for academic support but felt that their impact on student development was limited to critical thinking skills. Nonetheless, many participants saw critical thinking skills as vital to problem-solving and not important merely for classroom work. Kristin and Stan at University E illustrated the participants' assertion:

> What librarians do is really important. They teach students how to recognize good and bad information. What they're really teaching there is analytical skills. Students need analytical skills in all dimensions of their lives—as they select majors, internships, careers . . . (Kristin)

> I agree with [Kristin], I agree completely. Analytical problem-solving is essential for lifelong learning. But in addition to analytical skills, librarians are teaching students self-sufficiency. If they [students] can learn how to search for information themselves—search effectively, that is—then they [can] be self-reliant. They can be independent and autonomous adults. That's really what we're trying to accomplish, isn't it? So, yeah, I do hear students say they don't really need the librarians all that much, but I tend to think that's because the librarians have already done their job, providing a strong foundation for these students to find and use the information they need to be successful. (Stan)

Despite many participants perceiving librarians to have an important educator role, some participants seemed less convinced. These participants felt librarians were more interested in the organization of information rather than in students, which they believed was evidenced by the language librarians used:

> Librarians are concerned with information, which is detached and something external to the student—something to be found, to be analyzed, to be digested, whereas we [student affairs professionals] are more concerned with knowledge, which is a synthesis of information and experience, shaping it into how a student then sees the world or approaches a problem. (Louise, University C)

> It goes beyond what Louise said. I'm really confused by the language they use—what is "user services?" That is the phrase they are using now for the check-out desk, I think. What is a user, exactly? I mean, I know they're talking about the people who use the library—all of us, students, staff, faculty. . . . But, really, it's so impersonal, we're not interchangeable, and the language they use makes them seem very impersonal and unapproachable when I know they're trying to achieve the exact opposite. It's actually very off-putting. (Michelle, University C)

Alice and Megan at University B suggested librarians are not very responsive to students' needs:

> [Librarians] push things around—do they even know what students need? (Alice)

> Responsiveness needs to be in their work now. (Megan)

> You know very few of them teach students how to think about information. Most of them might spend a few minutes showing students how to make sense of a call number or how to build an effective search in a database, but all of that is "library literacy" in a way and not how to think about "information" in a critical way. I think they're so caught up in the tremendous amount of administration it takes to keep a library running that they dedicate three or so librarians to teaching students and the rest order books, catalog the books, check out the books, or maybe answer very specialized questions from faculty and graduate students. [pause] And actually I only know that much because I worked with the librarians to bring my University 101 class to the library, and there's a librarian I talk to in my water aerobics class. (Alice)

> Yeah . . . Younger students have less attachment to the library as a physical space because they interact with the library digitally. They don't see the space as a resource, and they only interact with the librarians if they are physically in the space. Although most students won't know it, I know the library assigns its graduate students to reply to reference questions asked by text message or by instant messaging—and really that's probably how most undergraduates prefer to ask their questions now. (Megan)

> They need to restructure their information literacy lessons because first-year students aren't ready to absorb the lessons. (Alice)

> Library 101 needs to be "where is it, what does it offer, and how do I get it," and a "level two" function needs to happen in students' third year when they're cognitively ready to critique sources and synthesize conflicting sources. (Megan)

Miguel at University C speculated the librarians are "trapped in the library" due to the amount of time and expertise that must be required to review books, journals, and databases and then make these resources available for faculty and students. Louise agreed with Miguel's speculation, but she and Greta believed the librarians make a decision to not be involved with matters outside the library:

> I see the librarians as a resource, not for myself but for the students. When I recognize a student is struggling academically, I always suggest they meet with their librarian even before I suggest meeting with their advisor. However, I'm not sure students today understand what a librarian does, especially if they came up through a K–12 system that didn't place librarians in their schools. So, I've thought about this, and I've tried to work programmatically with the librarians so they'll come to where the students are. That's been such a struggle. The librarians just won't do it. They say "Well, refer the student over to me," and I'm saying "No, they won't go see you. You need to come over here to where the students are," but then I don't hear from them again. They really seem to miss the whole point. (Louise)

> Well, I'll be negative. I'm an advisor for undeclared students, which means I'm in the student affairs division and came up to that from being a residence hall director. So I see the students when they're in crisis, usually right after their first tests or essays. I don't think they [students] really get the research help they need until they're taking upper-division courses, usually after they've declared a major. Then they're assigned a librarian who specializes in that particular major. So the librarians under-

serve these undeclared students. I've been trying to talk to them about that . . . and I'm telling you, it's taken five years. Five years for the librarians to remember that I exist. (Greta)

Oh, I know. I think my frustrations with the librarians is that they're coming from academic affairs but no one in academic affairs thinks all that much about the students. They're always talking about student learning—"we support it, we support it"—but very few of them can actually show how they support it. (Louise)

"The Invisible People"

Jack at University B said: "A great librarian is one that you don't even know is there because they've built relevant collections and libraries that are so easy for you to find what you're looking for that you take it all for granted." Many participants explained that librarians work principally behind the scenes in students' lives: Librarians select books, journals, and databases that students will use for their studies. Unlike student affairs professionals who worked in a variety of settings on campus, the participants associated the librarians with only the library. Their assumption was that librarians are engaged primarily in administrative duties—the "behind the scenes" work that must be necessary to keep the library operating smoothly. Many of the participants seemed somewhat surprised by this realization, which is illustrated by an exchange between Jack, Kimberly, and Megan at University B:

Come to think of it, I never see them outside the library. . . . That's the only place I see them, really. I do go to the library pretty often. I just took a new position here in a different part of the [student affairs] division, and the job is so different than anything I've done before . . . so I've been going to the library a lot to read up with the journals they have, just to try to give myself a stronger foundation in my new role. But, really, I only see them there at the library, and really once I found the journals I needed, I didn't even really interact with them again after that. I just go straight to what I need. (Jack)

Huh. I don't ever see them either, Jack, but I don't go to the library at all. I think they might be the only group of people on campus that I truly never see. . . . I see the faculty at programs, at committee meetings. I talk to the facilities staff and the technology folks all the time, of course. Even the directors of development sometimes. But I never see the librarians. I guess they are always busy running the library? It must take a lot of work to run a library. I've never really thought about this. (Kimberly)

> I think we don't see them outside the library because they need to be near the books. Those are the tools of their trade, and that's the whole reason they are here, isn't it? In one way, it doesn't make sense for them to be out of the library much, away from the books. On the other hand [long pause], the students are getting what they need from digital sources and probably aren't seeking help for finding things as much as they used to . . . so maybe the librarians do need to get out of the library more, just to now be a different kind of campus citizen. To contribute differently. (Megan)

While they did, in fact, recognize librarians as tied closely to the academic mission of the university in regard to helping students connect with information, most of the participants acknowledged that they'd had little to no significant contact with librarians since beginning their professional lives. Their interactions with librarians were largely in the past, during their years as undergraduate or graduate students. With a few exceptions, most of the student affairs professionals said their primary interactions with librarians were the result of referring students to the library or because of committee work. During all of the focus group discussions, most of the participants said they didn't need to use the library for assistance with solving problems in their daily professional lives; rather, their sources for trusted information were other colleagues across the student affairs profession. This revelation spurred many of the participants to ponder librarians' relative invisibility. Many participants speculated that librarians were simply too preoccupied with the administrative business of reviewing and selecting information sources to be well known as colleagues.

Robert at University C explained that "librarians honor traditions and preservation, whereas student affairs [professionals] are concerned about making an impact and about immediacy." He indicated student affairs is a broader discipline than librarianship, with highly diverse skill sets and talents found among the people employed in residential life, culture centers, student unions, Greek affairs, and counseling services. The skill sets and talents found among librarians are more uniform, he said:

> I think most outsiders looking in at student affairs can see a profound difference between the student affairs staff who manage a career center versus a cultural house for minority students. I think most outsiders looking in at a library can't tell the difference at all between the people who work in libraries.

At University A, the participants speculated that librarians were increasingly less visible because of the recent changes to library spaces and technologies. Daniel, Kate, and Peter marveled at the recent changes they'd observed at their university's library but wondered what the changes had meant for the librarians' roles:

> There are lot of things that happen behind the scenes, like interlibrary lending and maintaining computers and redesigning the building so it's modern. Uh, I would imagine that what makes the library have those books, and rooms, and computers, and all those things available. I don't think there's a lot of acknowledgement to the librarians of their library administration. Did you know they have music rooms now? Where you can practice an instrument—in a library! That's amazing. (Daniel)

> I didn't know that. Really? Wow. I have to imagine the world of a librarian has changed over the course of the last 20 years. Before the Internet, you had to go to the library to find anything. And now you just don't have to go to the library. You can Google something, and you'll get a million different things but chances are something on that first or second page is pretty close to what you need. And the students would much rather look at something online now. So, I bet the librarians at this point are wondering: "What am I doing here?" (Kate)

> The librarian used to be the person who hands you a book, stamped it, and told you when it would be late. They were the keeper of the knowledge and that, you know, they'll allow you to have it for short periods of time. But, yeah, [Kate] is right that students do everything online now. I have no idea what those librarians must be doing now instead, but the library is definitely a changed place with cafes and food, specialized software, and even self-check stations like you see at the grocery stores. They must be busy managing all of that, but they're very much out of the public eye. (Peter)

The student affairs professionals at University C purported that librarians are saddled with an image as people who sit behind reference desks, passively waiting for students to call upon them for help. However, they acknowledged the librarians at their institution are spending fewer hours at reference desks in favor of providing more specialized research services. Yet they felt the librarians' exploration resulted in greater invisibility:

> I think especially on this campus it is really hard for students to learn how to navigate the library. I've spoken with colleagues at the university library, and the librarians think students are there. They're "there" but they're not really there because they're only studying and not really making use of the library's resources. The librarians don't show them how to make a library account, how to request books. They assume the students

know how to use libraries because our students are typically from upper-class, upper-middle-class schools. (Greta)

They assume the students know [how] to use [libraries] but trust me, they don't even know how to use the catalog. I'd been sending students over but it's not that easy now. Like, you can't just say "go and see this librarian" anymore because a lot of the librarians changed their [reference desk] model, and you have to make an appointment now. That model assumes students are planful, but our undergrads haven't really learned those planning skills yet, haven't quite figured out they need to look at their assignments way ahead of time and think about what they might need. No, they're still starting papers pretty close to when the papers are due. (Lorraine)

Right. And the students can't talk to the librarians when they need them now. They have to talk to a graduate assistant instead. It's very few times when a librarian is actually there to help them. So, yeah, the librarians are getting pretty advanced with being able to help students with statistical modeling now and things like that, but who are they serving? Only a very small segment of the students who are ready for that. (Greta)

I think students' basic needs aren't being met well anymore. I'm not sure where the librarians are if they're not accessible at the library's service points. We don't see them outside the library, but we don't see them in the library either. The vanishing librarians—where are they? [laughter] (Robert)

COLLABORATION WITH LIBRARIANS

Next I asked the participants "Do student affairs professionals at this institution interact with or collaborate with librarians?" While none of them did and they were not aware of any such collaborations, they did have insight into the reasons why collaborations with librarians may not have been explored. Many of the participants simply lacked familiarity with the librarians at their institutions. The participants at University A drew their impressions almost entirely from the librarians they remembered from their own student days and confessed that they didn't know any of the librarians at their university personally. Other participants perceived librarians somewhat negatively and believed the librarians at their institutions were neither flexible nor persistent in their past attempts at collaboration. Curiously, only the participants at University C noted an organizational gulf between the student affairs and academic affairs division, whereas the participants in all of the librarians' focus groups remarked on the "otherness" of student affairs professionals.

Persistence and Flexibility

Several of the participants at different focus groups indicated the librarians had attempted to collaborate with student affairs professionals in the past, but the efforts had not been fruitful. The participants felt the librarians had given up too quickly. If the librarians had persisted by adapting their programs or workshops, they might have stood a greater chance of success. Greta and Michelle at University C discussed a failed venture:

> I think some libraries have tried to do that from what I heard, but it seems like everyone I know was "didn't work, not doing it again." So, um, that's a bad philosophy to have that it didn't work that time so it won't work this time. What can we evaluate and do a little differently and try again instead of giving up on the first time? Because, I know we had, we had the [name redacted] Library here in this building and no one [students] used them because no one knew they were actually there. So the librarians stopped coming. (Greta)
>
> Do you mean in our old building? (Michelle)
>
> No, this building. (Greta)
>
> Oh. Did I even know that? (Michelle)
>
> Like two years ago we had . . . the librarians would have hours twice a week for two hours each time, and nobody [students] came to them for research help or whatever. And they're [the librarians], like, "We're done, we're not going to come back." (Greta)
>
> Two hours isn't much time. (Michelle)
>
> No, and it was . . . right in the middle of the day. There aren't any students here because they're in class or working. I tried to explain, told them they should come back from seven to nine p.m., when the students are finishing dinner and coming back to the halls. Nope—they're strictly "business hours" people, I guess. Too bad. (Greta)

At University A, Kate remembered that other student affairs colleagues had developed programs with librarians to create awareness among the students of the resources the library offers. Students did not attend, and the collaborative programming was later abandoned. Kate and Dorothy shared their reflections but I could not help but detect a note of sadness, or perhaps futility, in their voices during this exchange:

> I don't know that students see [the usefulness], and I don't know, if I was a librarian, how you would get the message across. I don't know. I don't have a great answer to that question but I'd just say, you know, from my experiences in student affairs, it's, you know, trial and error and keep trying. And try different ways, and you know, even if it seems like a crazy idea, try it. What's it going to hurt at this point, you know? (Kate)

> And I'm just saying that collaboration, you know, we do so much collaboration, but as I think about it, we really don't collaborate much with the library. I mean, I used to promote the writers' workshops and things like that, and refer students to our learning support services, but it would be nice to have the librarians . . . maybe even in the summer, when it's a little slower . . . to come and really interact with student affairs folks and let us know what services they provide, so that we are better equipped too as we interact with students to say "Oh, you need to go see so-and-so." Or, "Did you know the library does this?" So come and better inform us and also allow us to inform as to what we do. (Dorothy)

Greta, Michelle, and Robert at University C observed that librarians' and student affairs professionals' concepts of programming are different, and this difference may prevent them from knowing how to work together. They perceived the librarians as heavily relying on passive programming, such as creating exhibits and displays to showcase library resources, whereas the student affairs professionals are used to designing experiences that make students interact with each other:

> I think it's a new concept for librarians thinking of programming. I don't think they know how to do programming or what they would program about. (Greta)

> They do more workshops, it seems, than programming. (Michelle)

> They do a big . . . I think I'd say it's a display . . . with banned books. It's an awesome display and really touches on freedom of speech. I think the archives does displays sometimes too. But I'm not really sure what my part in something like that would be. . . . I'd want to *talk* about something, get the students to talk. I think the librarians just put up their display, hope the students take something away from that, and they're done. Back into the woodwork. They need to try something different if their goal is student engagement. (Robert)

Perceptions of Librarians' Personality Traits

Perhaps one of the biggest barriers to potential collaboration between the participants and librarians is the participants' perception that librarians do not possess personality traits that student affairs professionals commonly believe are essential to working together successfully. One participant speculated their "high touch skills" were not sophisticated, such as empathic listening or making personal connections with students easily. Alice, Jack, and Megan at University B explained how the librarians' lack of communication skills reinforces their negative stereotype of librarians:

> Maybe this is just the stereotype . . . everyone has that image in their head of the biddy librarian with her hair in a bun. Very severe. Probably owns a lot of cats. [laughter] (Alice)

> But maybe it's also kind of true? (Jack)

> Yeah . . . I mean, when I think about our librarians here. Wow, they *are* kind of severe. They won't let you even come inside the library unless you present your ID first . . . and I've worked here for years and they haven't let me in. (Alice)

> I've gotten in without my ID plenty of times. (Megan)

> Well, this is such a barrier to using the library. I don't get why they started this. But they look . . . soooo sour and miserable when they're at the door. Not only can they not really explain why they have this policy . . . they just repeat over and over "You need to have your ID," without really seeming to listen to why you're asking . . . but they really don't look too pleasant about it either, so that doesn't really make me want to really work with them. I can only imagine what the students must think. (Alice)

At University C, Greta recounted a story of a student harassing the librarians at the reference desk. Greta had encountered the student before, and he was later found to be experiencing a serious mental health crisis. Greta reported the librarians lacked the confidence to handle the situation themselves:

> They were like, "Oh we'll talk to [Greta], and she'll tell her people to deal with it, and we'll just leave it at that." I took care of it but I was annoyed because they lack the confidence and skills to even approach a student who appears to be in crisis, much less know what to actually do when they learn what that crisis is or what the student is experiencing. It's scary at first, but then you do it and then . . . (Greta)

Surely the librarians have to deal with plenty of that . . . (Robert)

I am sure there are some real stressed out students in the library at two a.m. and three a.m. [laughter] And, are they trained in mental health or . . .? (Lorraine)

Nope. I think it's the [support staff] that handle those students. I don't necessarily know the librarians . . . I think they're not there at night. (Louise)

It would be helpful for them to have some kind of training. I reached out to them and approached them. Nope. Not interested. The head reference librarian seemed pretty mystified too that I even asked. She said "Well that would be a good thing but I guess it's easier for us to just call you?" (Greta)

If they really want to be partners in student success, they really need to step outside their box. They need to realize that we're all in this together, and they need to show a genuine commitment to students' well-being. I realize a lot of faculty would rather just call us too, but a lot don't. They ask for us to help them know when and how to refer a student. We teach them to actually walk a student over to the counseling center so they know the student actually goes to get the help they need. They seem really thankful for that. (Louise)

I guess I would expect the librarians would be more willing to do that than faculty. I'm surprised to hear that. I've always thought librarians had such a really strong service tradition. (Robert)

Focused on the "Here and Now"

Some of the participants noted that librarians tend to be very deliberate in the plans they make. Greta at University C observed that librarians at her institution wanted to schedule their outreach hours at the residence halls with her months in advance but she found that she didn't know that far ahead of time when her student organizations would be putting on programs that might compete with the librarians' programs. Understanding Greta's predicament, Miguel explained that student affairs professionals have difficulty planning because they work so closely with undergraduate students, who are still mastering time management and planning skills. He said this makes it difficult for student affairs professionals themselves to commit to plans when coaching students towards established schedules for programs and events—it is a constant work in progress.

Additionally, Miguel said student affairs professionals' lives are dominated by a sense of immediacy, which he suspected isn't the case with librarians' lives:

> There is always a crisis. A parent can't reach their child by phone, and you're sent to make contact with the student and make sure everything is okay. A student is talking about self-harm, and you're finding them counseling. Everything is disruptive, and everything needs an action from you right away. (Miguel)

> I think that's much worse in your area [residential life], but I do agree. I work in service learning and civic engagement, and I'm amazed how many things fall through at the last minute. The work site can't take as many volunteers as we have interested—like, they're telling you hours before you're supposed to load people on the bus to go there. And here I am calling other sites trying to make last-minute arrangements. Or . . . far more students show up than had registered, and now I need to find a second bus and drive. Like, now. (Louise)

> So, we don't, because of time. We don't plan ahead, and we don't think ahead, and how can we pool the resources together in, uh, a timely fashion, and that's not because we're slacking, just because there's so many other things that are interrupting. Um, some of the things that are more secondary to . . . (Miguel)

> We're dealing with roommate conflicts, and then students who are in crisis and then "Oh, I have to do this too now . . ." We're really living in the here and now. (Michelle)

> I'm guessing librarians don't live their work lives like that. I guess students need help at the last minute for papers, but there aren't really . . . aren't really library emergencies, I guess? (Miguel)

CONCLUSION

The focus groups with the participants yielded insights into how student affairs professionals likely view their roles in higher education. They are deeply committed to students and perceive themselves as chiefly responsible for preparing students to succeed in their postcollege lives by developing students' cognitive and interpersonal skills and helping them navigate experiences that translate into marketable job skills. They are committed to student success by identifying the barriers that make it difficult for individual students to attain their degrees, and they mediate between the student and the bureaucracy of the universities to reduce those barriers. The participants took different interpretations of how they tend to students' success by understanding clearly the predominant challenges students face at their particular institutions and framing their work around those challenges; this suggests student affairs is indeed a value-relational profession.

The participants saw themselves quite clearly as teachers and as advocates for students, but they noted limitations in the methodology of their teaching. Their method of challenge-and-support relied on the participants' ability to forge close relationships with students, but they conceded this reliance meant their impact was limited to only those students they knew reasonably well and that they missed a great many other students. Their ability to advocate, too, required a fine balance between representing the students' interests and working for an institution whose culture may not value the advocacy role.

The participants were less certain of their perceptions of librarians, as a number of them indicated they had no meaningful interactions with librarians. Their perceptions varied in whether or not they saw librarians as valued educators or as administrators too preoccupied with the daily business of running a library to be effective at teaching. In fact, these respondents doubted librarians' sincere commitment to students. The participants remarked, too, that librarians too often seemed invisible on their campuses, rendered to the marginality of their thoughts regarding potential collaborators.

While none of the participants reported significant collaborations with librarians, they were aware of past attempts at collaboration on their own campuses and at other institutions. They had heard that these collaborations did not meet with success and were abandoned. The participants felt librarians had not taken the time to evaluate what they could have done differently to make the collaborations more successful, and that librarians could demonstrate more flexibility in how they approach such collaborations. Some participants doubted librarians possessed very sophisticated interpersonal skills, making it difficult for librarians to relate to students and making them appear to be less convincing collaborators to the participants themselves. Lastly, the participants recognized that student affairs work is often disrupted by students' crises and abrupt changes to the logistics of program and activity planning endeavors. They acknowledged this need for immediacy in their work made it challenging to actively plan long-range collaborations with others, and that librarians in particular seemed desirous of advance planning.

Chapter Six

The Diverging and Sometimes Intersecting Worlds of Librarians and Student Affairs Professionals

In the two previous chapters, I shared the stories of the librarians and student affairs professionals as they responded to my interview protocols, and I organized their focused discussions into themes. In this chapter, I elaborate how the focused discussions shed light on librarians' and student affairs professionals' perceptions of their own and each other's roles, and what these perceptions mean for building prospective collaborations that improve student learning and student success. My findings highlight some of the reasons why collaborations between librarians and student affairs professionals might be difficult to achieve but are also suggestive of areas where collaboration might be more possible.

DIVERGING WORLDS

Differences in Predominant Roles

I noted the starkest distinction between the student affairs professionals and the librarians in their predominant roles, and that how they perceived these roles to be valued influenced their perceptions of each other. Across the focus groups, the student affairs professionals were very clear on the purpose of their work: to ensure students' persistence and to help them leave college with higher-order soft skills valuable to the working world and adult lives. The focus of this purpose varied, depending on the particular student issues troubling the higher education institutions most. Nonetheless, the student affairs professionals exuded confidence that their work was valuable and valued, regretting mostly that their usual teaching method of challenge-and-support, as explicitly noted by the student affairs professionals at University A, depended on a high degree of student contact, thereby limiting the reach and impact of any one student affairs professional.

Contrastingly, the librarians seemed somewhat uncertain as to how they fit into the larger educational mission of their institutions. Their primary role had shifted from one historically focused on collection building to support research to one of purveying to faculty and students a more curated collection of resources. They found this shifted role challenging, as demonstrated by the concern shared by the librarians at University A that they had a difficult time raising faculty and students' awareness. The librarians' emphasis on the information purveyor role was to ensure faculty, staff, and students knew about and used the collections the librarians acquired with increasingly scarcer resources. They were skeptical of the efficacy of their other predominant role—teaching students information-seeking skills and information literacy—as they found it hard to demonstrate evidence that their teaching made a difference. Their role in community development was still important, but reshaping the library into student hubs represented both opportunities and threats to the librarians.

Organizationally aligned with academic affairs at their higher education institutions, some of the librarians expressed discomfort, if not suspicion, about the increase of student affairs administrators while their own numbers declined along with the faculty. This discomfort suggested they perceived student affairs to be on the ascendancy while they perceived themselves to be on the decline in the context of the power structures of their institutions, as Howard at University D appeared to express. Lucy at University C alluded to this discomfort when she said student affairs professionals were "running a different university" in the struggle over primacy over the teaching of leadership skills. At the same time as the librarians were reimagining libraries as student spaces, they were also ambivalent about sharing those same spaces more permanently with student services, suggesting they found the conversion of library space into computer labs, coffeehouses, and spaces managed by student services to encroach upon their domain.

Because of the sharp distinction in confidence of purpose between librarians and student affairs professionals, I question the likelihood of these two groups reaching out to one another. The librarians may see the student affairs professionals more as vaguely defined threats rather than as partners, while if the librarians aren't clearly able to further student affairs professionals' goals, the student affairs professionals may not see a clear need to reach out to librarians at all. Yet the most profound barrier might be the lack of familiarity or, worse, the relatively poor impression the groups have of each other.

Lack of Familiarity, Structural Barriers, and Differing Perspectives on Expertise

It is difficult to find common ground if one does not know much about the other. Overall, the librarians were considerably confused as to who student affairs professionals were or what they did. They had a vague sense that student affairs professionals tended to student maintenance, such as housing or health services, but they had little notion of student affairs professionals' educational roles. When participants did demonstrate knowledge of student affairs professionals, they voiced considerable frustration. They perceived the student affairs professionals as contributing to the seemingly impenetrable "shuffle" that sent students—and librarians in their attempts to help students—between offices often without finding the help they needed. They also perceived student affairs professionals as demonstrating a lack of interest in working with the librarians, as evidenced by student affairs professionals' failure to respond to messages or to follow through with commitments.

The student affairs professionals suggested the nature of their work emphasized the "here and now," forcing them to juggle priorities constantly due to the needs of daily student crises. They acknowledged they had difficulty meeting librarians' apparent needs to plan out activities well in advance. At the same time, they criticized librarians' lack of persistence and perceived willingness to abandon plans when the outcomes of those plans did not immediately yield a return on the librarians' investment of time. The librarians indicated that "the Jenga pile" of many competing demands on their time, including absorbing other colleague's responsibilities when positions went unfilled, prevented them from focusing on work that did not have a relatively quick payoff. In fact, they were concerned that their reward systems did not reward trying new things, and several participants affirmed this for a newer librarian in the group. This lack of time, coupled with inflexible reward systems, poses a significant structural barrier that is very likely to inhibit prospective collaborations between librarians and student affairs professionals.

The student affairs professionals were more aware of librarians than vice versa, but they found the librarians to be "invisible people," confined to the library due to the many complexities of running such an organization. However, they were only marginally more favorably disposed to librarians than librarians were to them. Some participants indicated respect for the contributions librarians do make to student learning, but others were ambivalent about the value of the librarians' role, noting progress in technology reduced students' need to seek librarians' expertise. They perceived librarians to have a rather narrow skill set, suggesting librarians do not make the same impact on students' lives as student affairs professionals do, given the diverse skill sets and talent found in distinct areas of specialization in student affairs, such as cultural houses, student unions, counseling services, and residential life. To these participants, librarians seemed to have little to offer that the participants thought useful to the participants' work with students. This finding implies student affairs professionals and librarians may not have an appreciation for the expertise that each would bring to a collaboration, which Arcelus (2008), Kezar (2006), and Becher and Trowler (2001) claim is necessary in order for interdisciplinary work to be successful.

Becher and Trowler (2001) observed that collaboration between disciplines is most successful when the disciplines share a common language. The shared technical language of the disciplines help the groups engage in mutually satisfying dialog, another crucial aspect to interdisciplinary collaboration (Kezar & Lester, 2009; Becher & Trowler, 2001). However, the student affairs professionals noted differences in the ways librarians spoke about students or about their services. Nearly consistently, the librarians employed impersonal or clinical language to describe their relationships with students, such as "patron," "user," and "instruction." Some student affairs professionals found the language off-putting and ascribed a lack of commitment to students to librarians partly because of the impersonality of the language they used. While the librarians drew no particular observations about the language student affairs professionals use, I did note the student affairs professionals often spoke very personally about their work with students, perhaps reflecting the closer relationships they developed with the students whose growth they supported and challenged. The lack of a shared language portends that librarians and student affairs professionals may not have the utility to engage in mutually satisfying dialog, particularly if student affairs professionals find the impersonal language librarians use to be uncomfortable.

Differing Interactions with Students

Arcelus (2008), Kezar (2006), and Becher and Trowler (2001) claimed collaborative work based on improving the student experience necessitates a shared understanding of students and of student learning. Librarians and student affairs professionals appear to diverge considerably when it comes to their types of interactions with students. While both librarians and student affairs professionals communicated a commitment to students, they experienced their commitment in fundamentally different ways. Librarians' interactions with students were predominantly of a transactional nature, whether at the reference desk or circulation desk. They had a limited presence in students' cocurricular activities; although they sometimes attended programs in residence halls or advised student organizations, those participants expressed profound uncertainty about the roles they were expected to perform with those students. Even in librarians' teaching environments, they did not often have the opportunity to develop relationships with individual students unless students sought them out for more personal research consultations following instruction sessions.

The librarians were more focused on creating environments that supported student learning than perhaps impacting students directly. They wanted to inspire students, as the librarians did by putting up posters of student leaders at University C. They wanted to provide students with the technology and spaces they needed to do well in their courses, as the librarians did at University A by creating music practice rooms in the library and participating in Student Success Week to help students set up their various technology accounts. However, there was not much evidence that librarians changed students' lives, as the student affairs professionals set out to accomplish by challenging the way students conceived their identities, enabling students' leadership skills by putting them in charge of programs and organizations, and negotiating relationships by helping students understand others' perspectives. In the end, I believe student affairs professionals and librarians have very different perspectives on the ways they interact with students. Given these different perspectives, it would prove difficult for librarians and student affairs professionals to collaborate unless they focus the collaboration on student affairs professionals' more direct impact role in student learning or on librarians' more facilitative role in student learning.

SOMETIMES INTERSECTING WORLDS

Teaching Students Transferable Skills

Despite the widened gap that appears to exist between the worlds of librarians and student affairs professionals, their worlds do appear to sometimes intersect. These are perhaps the best areas in which collaborations between librarians and student affairs professionals are likely to be successful. The most significant intersecting area between the groups is teaching students skills that the curriculum may not be teaching and that students could easily transfer to their professional experiences in the working world. The librarians explained that they view the library as a "laboratory for learning," and they want to offer programs, services, and experiences that enable students' creativity and identity development. As employers of student assistants, they teach students skills relevant to the working world, such as customer service and time management. Similarly, the student affairs professionals were highly interested in helping teach students skills that allow them to enter the job market easily.

Both groups appear to have teaching students transferable skills in common, but librarians appear to have more limited means to teach students those skills, working primarily through the relatively few students they employ. The student affairs professionals may be able to create opportunities to teach a greater number of students, both those they employ and those they reach through the many programming options and student organizations they manage. This suggests that librarians and student affairs professionals might have a converging perspective on the direct teaching contributions each group thinks it is able to make to student learning and to student success.

Student Learning

Although their interactions with students differed significantly, the librarians and student affairs professionals appear to intersect in regard to their understanding of student learning. While the librarians saw their influence on students' critical thinking skills as the most significant way they could contribute to student learning, they did envision ways they could influence students' identity and psychosocial development. Very similar to the student affairs professionals, they focused on creating experiences that stimulated students in different ways. The student affairs professionals were more directly involved in these experiences, such as organizing service learning experiences or overseeing the work of student leaders managing programs or student organizations. The librarians employed more subtle means, such as making 3-D printing technologies available for students to explore their sense of creativity or practice their problem-solving skills. Librarians and student affairs professionals both appeared to teach from afar, deliberately creating experiences or environments that stimulated students' personal growth.

Themes that emerged from the previous chapters suggest the worlds of librarians and student affairs professionals diverge in profound ways. Librarians' roles have evolved from a predominant focus on collection building to a new focus on information purveyance, although a teaching role is also still significant. However, the librarians' focused discussions revealed uncertainty about their purpose and place within their higher education institutions and acknowledged a distrust of student affairs professionals, recognizing their growth in number and teaching of students while their own numbers decline along with those of the faculty. Structural barriers, including a profound lack of familiarity with each other's roles, lack of flexibility in librarians' reward systems that might penalize collaborative work with student affairs professionals, and differing approaches to time and planning accentuate their diverging worlds and diminish the likelihood of librarians and student affairs professionals working together. Additionally, a lack of a shared language and differing perspectives on their interactions with students are significant divergences.

However, librarians and student affairs professionals do bear similarities. Their worlds intersect in regard to the way they approach student learning. Student affairs professionals strive for holistic student development, focusing on students' identity and psychosocial development. While librarians are focused on shaping students' cognitive development, they appear to have a growing interest in advancing students' identity and psychosocial development as well. Both student affairs professionals and librarians are approaching holistic student development largely by teaching from afar, in which they create experiences and environments that stimulate students. In the subsequent major section of this chapter, I revisit the book's research questions and elaborate how the focused discussions shed light on librarians' and student affairs professionals' perceptions of their own and each other's roles, and what these perceptions mean for building prospective collaborations that improve student learning and student success.

DESCRIPTIONS OF STUDENT LEARNING AND SUCCESS

How did librarians and student affairs professionals describe student learning and student success? Many of the librarians were not familiar with "student success," and had little more to say when I shared Tinto's (1987) definition as persistence to graduation, as well as an affirming satisfaction with their learning and overall experience. Moreover, they never specifically described what student learning looked like or meant to them but instead discussed what they do on behalf of students to facilitate their learning. Nonetheless, their perspectives on student learning may be inferred from their focused discussions.

Their perspectives on student learning are different but complementary: Librarians are chiefly focused on furthering students' cognitive development by teaching information literacy skills and helping students achieve information fluency, whereas student affairs professionals think of student learning more broadly in mutually supportive cognitive, psychosocial, and identity dimensions. Librarians and student affairs professionals do share greater similarities in student success, as each group recognizes they bear responsibility for supporting students by reducing barriers to persistence.

The librarians revealed a strong educator identity in their focused discussions. While they did teach students formally in classroom settings, they rarely described their activities as teaching in the traditional sense. Instead, they conveyed their instructional roles through their word choices, such as "coaching," "facilitating," and "creating experiences" that suggested their teaching opportunities were less formal and often more individualized with students. Their educational settings included one-on-one interactions at the library, often at the reference desk, or via interactive technologies. In these endeavors, their focus was usually, if not always, on furthering students' cognitive development.

The student affairs professionals ascribed a broader definition to student learning. They were focused on holistic student development, of which fostering students' cognitive skills was only a part. They aspired to imbue students with the skills they perceived as necessary for success in their post-college lives, such as leadership skills and cultural competencies. Many of the student affairs professionals specialized in specific functional areas, such as student conduct or service learning. They described how they design their services and programs to support holistic student development. They recognized cognitive, psychosocial, and identity development as interconnected and complementary, so they valued faculty and librarians' focus on students' cognitive development. They did, however, differ from the librarians on how they thought about cognitive development. Several of the student affairs professionals said the faculty and librarians teach students content knowledge, yet the librarians spoke about teaching students how to think rather than introducing content, suggesting at least some of the student affairs professionals may misinterpret the way their colleagues in academic affairs approach teaching.

The librarians were not entirely focused on advancing students' cognitive development. They believed heartily in creating experiences that enabled students to explore their own sense of creativity, aesthetics, and identity. They accomplished this largely through passive programming activities that included exhibits, art installations, and bulletin boards. Lucy and Lauren at University C described creating posters of student leaders and innovators so students might be inspired as they studied together in the library. Alan and Margaret at University B and Jeanette at University A described their planning of makerspaces, in which students learned to solve problems by designing objects with 3-D printing technologies. Lauren at University C referred to the library as a "laboratory for learning," which certainly conveys the sense that the librarians understood—and valued—that they are capable of positively influencing students' interpersonal and identity development. The concept of the library as learning center where students explore new technologies, practice presentations together, create media, solve problems in groups, and seek innovation through creativity is a rather new and emerging role for libraries and librarians (Lankes, 2011). This concept bears some similarity to Lozano's (2010) conclusions regarding the types of activities students perform together at cultural centers—often a domain of student affairs professionals—in order to stimulate their identity development in a culturally responsive and supportive space.

Interestingly, both the librarians and the student affairs professionals taught from "afar" by creating environments and experiences that deliberately stimulated students' personal growth (Moore & Marsh, 2007, p. 7). Yet both groups seemed to have a much stronger educator identity than Moore and Marsh (2007) credited the student affairs professionals with and Schulte and Sherwill-Navarro (2009) credited the librarians with. Both groups considered their one-on-one interactions with students to be forms of teaching. The student affairs professionals taught primarily through their concept of "challenge and support." However, this teaching method was predicated on a reasonably personal relationship with students or the participants believing the method risked failure when students were not close to the participants and thus not receptive to the participants' probing questions and direct feedback. Additionally, the student affairs professionals questioned the utility of this concept as they were able to make an impact on only a relatively small number of students.

On the other hand, the librarians had an arguably greater repertoire for teaching students. Like the student affairs professionals, they perceived that they bore at least some responsibility for preparing students for their postcollege years by teaching students skills necessary for the working world. They taught students customer service skills, time management skills, and organizational skills. The librarians' opportunities for teaching these skills were primarily through their personal relationships with the student employees they managed. However, the librarians also taught students information-seeking and information literacy skills through their transactional relationships at the reference desk and in their formal instruction sessions as part of students' curricular experiences.

It does appear that librarians and student affairs professionals' descriptions of student learning and student success are converging. Student affairs professionals perceive students' cognitive development, psychosocial development, and identity development as intertwined and mutually supportive. While the student affairs professionals are concerned with shaping students' interpersonal skills and sense of identity, they recognize and value faculty and librarians' traditional emphasis on teaching students critical thinking skills. While librarians remain more focused on shaping students' cognitive development than are student affairs professionals, they are reimagining the library as a vehicle for shaping students' interpersonal skills and identities as well.

This new emphasis on the library as a student hub potentially offers the best space for librarians and student affairs professionals to discover opportunities to shape student learning together. The librarians perceive the library as a central location for enhancing student learning by designing spaces where students study together in groups, practice presentations, and work collaboratively to solve problems. The student affairs professionals have largely not yet connected with the library as a hub for student activities, but several of the participants noted the libraries are evolving to meet student needs that they did not typically associate with the library historically.

O'Connor (2012) found that a lack of a shared understanding of student learning and success is one of the predominant factors that inhibit student affairs professionals and faculty from working together collaboratively, but my finding suggests that student affairs professionals and librarians are more likely to have common ground for collaborating. The greatest challenge is possibly that librarians are not yet conversant with student learning and student success as the other group defines it. To bridge the gap, Swartz, Carlisle, and Uyeki (2007) recommended that student affairs professionals "read the literature [librarians] are reading" (p. 118). While this advice is still commendable, the reverse should also be recommended. If librarians read the literature student affairs professionals are reading, they will become familiar with the grounded research that student affairs professionals use to design their services and programs focused on educating the whole student.

PERCEPTIONS OF LIBRARIANS' AND STUDENT AFFAIRS PROFESSIONALS' ROLES

How do librarians and student affairs professionals perceive their own and each other's roles in student learning and success? The librarians felt that they juggled several key roles, including information purveyor, teacher, and community developer. While the librarians carried out their teacher and community developer roles through their teaching activities and reshaping the library as a student hub, their primary role appeared to be information purveyor, in which they attempted to increase faculty and students' awareness of the library's information resources. They perceived this role to be their greatest contribution to faculty and students' research endeavors. Many of the librarians were assigned to certain disciplines, and they focused their awareness-building activities on the faculty and students associated with those disciplines. However, several of the participants were beginning to step outside of this traditional framework of information purveyance and were evangelizing information resources to student communities that shared interests, such as student organizations and living–learning communities in undergraduate residence halls. These participants tailored their messages differently to support interdisciplinary work.

The student affairs professionals' roles varied based on the overriding concerns of their institutions. While their emphasis on educating the whole student remained at the forefront of their work, they were attuned to the predominant issues the students at their institutions faced. These predominant issues included preparing students for the job market, reducing financial barriers to graduation, and helping students navigate very large campus environments. The student affairs professionals developed services, programs, and other experiences in order to reduce students' barriers to graduation and increase success.

Librarians' and student affairs professionals' perception of each other's roles in the educational process is arguably the most significant barrier to collaboration. Although the student affairs professionals demonstrated greater familiarity with the role of librarians than vice versa, a lack of familiarity with each other's work was prevalent among all participants. Several organizational factors appear to contribute to the lack of familiarity, including librarians' lack of time and their perceived widening gap between academic affairs and student affairs divisions. Additionally, the focused discussions revealed that both groups held somewhat negative perceptions of each other based at least in part on dissatisfying past interactions.

Many of the librarians had little impression of student affairs professionals at all; some remarked that they were uncertain which functions even constituted the student affairs division at their respective institutions. Despite this underdeveloped familiarity, the librarians perceived the student affairs professionals as playing an essential role in the provision of student services and student maintenance. In the words of Jodie at University A, the student affairs professionals served "almost like a support system" for the students and provided "everything [students] need in order to succeed" with their academic work. The librarians associated functions such as housing, student unions, financial aid, health services, counseling, and recreation with student affairs, but most participants had limited contact with these areas. If the librarians perceived the student affairs professionals to have roles beyond the provision of student services, they did not speak much of it. The profound lack of familiarity mirrors Peltier's (2014) finding that faculty's understanding of student affairs professionals' roles is limited to managing student issues outside of the classroom. This indicates that student affairs professionals must communicate their educational focus on student development differently—if they are communicating the message at all—to their colleagues in other divisions of higher education.

When the librarians did have reasons to interact with student affairs professionals, they were not satisfied with the quality of the interactions. Some of the librarians encountered a lack of helpfulness participants termed "the shuffle," in which students—and the librarians who attempted to help the students—were passed between different student affairs professionals or between different student affairs offices without receiving the information or help the student had been seeking. Consequently, they perceived student affairs professionals as disorganized or as poor communicators. They also perceived students affairs divisions as opaque, lamenting their difficulty identifying the right persons to contact in student affairs; the paucity of information shared by student affairs professionals (except by occasional brochures or guest speakers); and student affairs professionals' nonresponsiveness to librarians' inquiries.

Some of the participants were skeptical of student affairs professionals' motivations and suspicious of their seemingly increasing ranks compared to the dwindling number of faculty and librarians. Lucy and Molly at University C did perceive student affairs professionals as educators but did not find student affairs professionals open to their overtures of collaborating on outreach to students. They speculated student affairs professionals resisted collaboration out of fear they would lose their autonomy and authority as educators. Howard, Deanna, and Sabrina at University D believed student affairs professionals were outpacing faculty and librarians in terms of new hires, structurally displacing academic affairs' roles in teaching. Their thoughts were evident in two exchanges:

> You call it collaboration. I call it cannibalizing the library. Whether we want [collaboration] or not. It's not shared. It's been taken from us. And the computer lab here—it's not the library's [now]. If you want to use it, you have to jump through hoops. (Howard)
>
> The computer lab is on the third floor. It's not good either. (Deanna)
>
> It's just they [student affairs professionals] . . . (Howard)
>
> [The computer lab] is still going to be there for a while. (Sabrina)
>
> Good. (Deanna)
>
> For a while. But, um, I mean eventually, I think it will . . . sort of . . . be something else. (Sabrina)
>
> Phaw! See? Just wait, come back in six weeks, and there's going to be a student services office in it. (Howard)

At a different point in the focused discussion, Howard grimly offered the following words, and none of his peers in the focus group replied, perhaps indicating their acceptance of his perspective:

> I'm on the academic senate, representing the library. I'm very concerned—we're very concerned—about the number of vice presidents and other administrators the university is hiring. All student affairs, mostly. Diversity, first-year experience, consultants for retention, now second-year experience since the consultants told us we need that. Some vice president or some other administrator says we need a new person in charge of something, and we get it. It's like they're self-propagating over there in student affairs. But do we get new faculty, new librarians? No,

almost never. And when we do, they're hired on limited-term contracts. I've never heard of a student affairs person on a limited-term contract.

In Arcelus's (2008) study, faculty perceived student affairs professionals as diminishing faculty's "academic primacy" (p. 167). Certainly, the suspiciousness evinced by Lucy and Molly at University C and by Howard and Deanna at University D suggests librarians might harbor similar concerns. The importance of these negative experiences as potential barriers to collaboration should not be underestimated. Rodem (2011) identified trust, comfort, and effective communication as essential factors in successful collaborations between faculty and student affairs professionals. If librarians perceive student affairs professionals as ineffective communicators and are mistrustful, they are unlikely to be open to collaboration without some positive experiences to change their perceptions.

Although relatively few of the participants had interacted with librarians since their own student days, many of the student affairs professionals seemed more familiar with the work of librarians. Many participants recognized librarians as playing a critical educational role by teaching students critical thinking skills through information literacy. They indicated students' cognitive, psychosocial, and identity development were mutually supportive. Because of this, these participants suggested cognitive development was essential for the holistic student development that student affairs professionals espouse as a fundamental purpose of their work. Consequently, these participants perceived librarians as partners in higher education, and they gladly referred students to librarians when they encountered students with academic difficulties.

Not all the student affairs professionals shared this perspective. Others believed librarians were predominantly administrators, chiefly concerned with the mechanics of operating libraries. They also emphasized the difficulty they believed students had navigating the library and felt that librarians were too out of touch with students' needs to effectively design services or learning environments. The student affairs professionals' concerns mirror those of the faculty in Nilsen's (2012) study that librarians are too concerned with running a library to be effective educators. Nilsen's conclusion was that faculty and librarians may be simply too different to craft lasting, effective collaborations. However, the student affairs professionals seem like they should bear greater similarity with librarians since student affairs is similarly charged with managing services and offices.

HOW DO LIBRARIANS AND STUDENT AFFAIRS PROFESSIONALS SEE THEIR WORK INTERSECTING?

It is questionable whether the participants truly saw the work of librarians and student affairs professionals as potentially intersecting. They seemed more aware of barriers and perceptions that prevented them from exploring working together in a serious way. However, many of the participants implied librarians and student affairs professionals have similar goals in enhancing student learning outside of the classroom. Although the emphases of their work might be different, the librarians and student affairs professionals are concerned with holistic student development. Additionally, both groups teach students valuable skills that prepare students for their professionals lives through their management of student employees. Finally, they also act as information resources for students but may have varying levels of information-seeking proficiency and access to reliable information.

While the librarians did not altogether recognize the student affairs professionals' role, they did express a desire to positively effect students' holistic development. Because of their emphasis on information literacy, the librarians were certainly concerned with students' cognitive development; many participants described working with faculty to bring students to the library for instruction sessions, in which they taught students information-seeking and analysis skills specific to the courses' intended learning outcomes. Yet many participants acknowledged they could not demonstrate whether they effected meaningful change in students' critical thinking skills and thus doubted whether their focus on students' cognitive development was time well spent. At University A, the librarians discussed this skepticism intensely, summarized best by John:

> In effect, that, that's been kind of one of the big bugbears of instruction . . . is determining to what degree we are able to support those, those efforts. And are we "pissing in the wind?" Uh, or to what degree are we, we really being, being successful. And we don't know.

Despite their skepticism of their efficacy teaching critical thinking skills, they implied they were increasingly concerned with educating the whole student. Lucy at University C described her efforts at helping students decompress while they were studying at the library and using theories of wellness to design library spaces that enable students to relax. Lauren wanted to inspire students studying in the libraries at University C and identified student leaders and innovators who might serve as role models to students, in order to place them on posters in a display. Two librarians at University D advised student organizations or were involved in student conduct. Robert, a student affairs professional at University C, described a librarian mingling regularly with students at a cultural house for minority students and showing interest in the cultural issues those students faced at the university. Most of the participants indicated they saw the library as increasingly a student hub that provided students with not only information sources but spaces, technologies, student services, and aesthetic experiences that increased students' interpersonal and other skills.

While student affairs professionals appear to have more significant interactions with a greater number of students than might the librarians, the student affairs professionals and the librarians are both preparing students for the professional world. Lorraine at University C referred to this as "adulting" students. Kimberly at University B said this was a focus of the student affairs professionals' work: "I think we spend a lot of time helping students take what they are learning in the classrooms and apply them in the real world." As a manager of student employees, Greta at University C was explicit in that she taught students crucial skills such as customer service, time management, and meeting the expectations of supervisors. Lorraine and Michelle at University C described teaching students perspective-taking and empathy by helping students put themselves in other people's shoes and see problems through the lens of other people's experiences.

Librarians, too, taught these skills to students. The participants acknowledged they have a limited presence in students' cocurricular activities, unlike the student affairs professionals, but they do manage student employees. In fact, nearly all the librarians referenced student employees, whether they supervised students themselves or participated in student employees' training or worked alongside them at the circulation or reference desks. They found managing student employees to be highly rewarding and the experience had influenced the career decisions of more than a few such students. Paul at University B said "I think I teach students maturity. I really hold them to a high standard of customer service—answer the phone by the third ring, make direct eye contact, greet people as they enter." Sabrina at University D reported that she managed the greatest number of students at her library, and teaching these students job skills was one of the most important aspects of her work. She said:

> I ask them to think about how they are treated in customer service situations—what do the employees do to make you feel welcome and like you got the best service you could? I ask them to think about why making direct eye contact is related to customer service.

Paul and Sabrina were in agreement that they considered themselves to be teaching skills to students that they could directly translate to the working world, and that these were skills they might not be taught in a classroom setting. Jessica at University D had a different perspective—that she was providing students with job experiences that helped them gain a competitive edge over their peers. In response to Sabrina, she said:

> Of course customer service is an important skill, but I'm also giving them experiences that they could put on a resume. I have [my student employees] advise faculty and graduate students on digital publishing strategies. More than a skill in customer service, work in digital publishing is something employers will notice on a resume.

The emphasis on helping students find jobs certainly rang true for the student affairs professionals at University B, who prided themselves on their very high job placement rate for students after graduation, and at University A, where the student affairs professionals feared students couldn't find jobs with their majors despite the high cost of tuition and living expenses. Even at University E, Matt and Don noted that putting students in charge of developing programs, inviting guest speakers, and planning dances helped imbue students with skills directly translatable to the job market. The librarians' and student affairs professionals' mutual interest in teaching students skills they do not necessarily learn in their coursework and preparing students for entering the professional world does not appear to be an intersection explored in the literature. This may represent an area where librarians and student affairs professionals could come together to share ideas and discuss how they might work together to adequately prepare students for their transition from college to their postcollege years.

Lastly, the roles of librarians and student affairs professionals appears to intersect as providers of information to students. Alison made a poignant remark that I wish I had probed more deeply with the focus group of librarians at University C. In her story about transitioning from a student affairs professional working in career services to a new role as a librarian, she remarked on her surprise at learning that many academic affairs departments also perform some kind of academic and career advising to students. She observed, "everyone is running a student affairs function."

She said that student affairs professionals forget they could have partners to enrich their work. She implied that student affairs professionals—like librarians—steer students to information and help students make decisions based on that information. She recounted how career counselors refer students to books on interviewing, job search strategies, and websites for investigating potential employers. She felt career counselors and librarians could work together to ensure students have access to the best information possible, that librarians could teach career counselors better information-seeking and fluency skills and ensure that libraries' collections on career guides match the trends career counselors know. Her suggestion echoes ideas Forrest (2005) and Hollister (2005) proposed a decade ago. In the literature review, the substance of Forrest's and Hollister's arguments seem somewhat condescending to student affairs professionals, but perhaps these are worth revisiting if the framework is not librarians teaching student affairs professionals but working with them to ensure the information librarians and student affairs professionals provide to students is seamlessly curated.

There also seems to be opportunity for student affairs professionals to work with librarians to ensure the content librarians acquire for their collections is appropriate for students. Lucy at University C said that she attempts to use theories of student development to understand whether the complexity of information resources matched students' abilities. The librarians at Universities A and C were similarly emphatic that they wanted to design student-centered learning environments and understood libraries played a role in helping students integrate their academic and social experiences. Yet the librarians acknowledged their contact with students was limited, perhaps justifying the student affairs professionals' concerns that librarians were too disconnected from students' lives to truly comprehend their needs. This is perhaps not a new thought: Gatten (2005) argued that student affairs professionals, as experts in student development, have much to teach librarians about students that could ultimately improve the practice of librarianship. Gatten's work appears to have made little impression on library literature but perhaps the participants' focused discussions illustrate there is space for these discussions between librarians and student affairs professionals to take place.

However, there are opportunities for collaboration yet to be explored. Alison at University C noted that many academic departments—including the library—do perform some student affairs functions, such as advising. Jack at University B briefly described his experience as an academic advisor in student affairs; he practiced a strategy called "intrusive advising" and thought it a useful strategy librarians should consider. Both librarians and academic advisors note concerns that students—particularly first-year, first-generation, minority, and low-socioeconomic-status students—do not reach out for advising or research assistance early enough for help to be effective (Emmons & Wilkinson, 2011; Gordon, Habley, & Grites, 2008). Advisors are assigned to certain students and then identify the points of the semester when the students are likely to struggle academically and socially, based on information from residential life staff and from the course syllabi supplied by the advisees' faculty (Gordon et al., 2008). The advisors advise "intrusively" by contacting students of their own initiative during those pressure points rather than waiting for advisees to ask for help.

Librarians often have assigned students, too. However, Valerie at University D noted that most reference librarians are assigned students only when students declare a certain major. Moreover, she suggested that most reference librarians do not initiate contact with their students except perhaps at the time of assignment to greet the student and to explain how the student might reach the librarian. This was an area of special concern for the student affairs professionals at University D, who believed the students were already unfamiliar with the work of librarians. Kate at University A noted this, too, as she observed many students graduated from school districts with increasingly fewer librarians to guide them.

If librarians and advisors could partner together for intrusive librarianship and advising, they could proactively ask at different points of the year what the students are working on in their classes or have going on in their lives. Based on the information they receive, they could advise the student accordingly or help the student develop thesis statements and locate relevant resources. This strategy would help both librarians and advisors develop a more holistic understanding of their students' academic and social progress, but more importantly help students recognize the advisors and librarians' purposes. If advisors and librarians can assist students earlier and more consistently in the academic year, students will likely be better equipped to be successful and have greater academic performance and persistence. Certainly this idea should appeal to student affairs professionals and to librarians' core values of service to students and to equity and social justice, since lower-socioeconomic-status, minority, and first-generation students will then navigate their college experiences more easily.

At University A and University C, the librarians indicated an interest in bringing the student affairs professionals into the library to provide career services and advising to students at a central location, while they had also attempted to offer their services—albeit unsuccessfully—in the undergraduate residence halls. Rather than simply holding outreach hours, the librarians could consider taking a step further and embed in student affairs divisions rather than working predominantly within the library. How might the career center's programs and services change if a librarian belonged on the permanent staff? Such a collaboration might prove fruitful in regard to teaching citizenship and instilling social responsibility among students. A career services librarian could belong to the career center staff and research employers with good records of environmental and corporate responsibility. Additionally, a career services librarian could instruct students on issues to consider when applying for positions, such as identifying whether specific employers have family-friendly policies or support social issues that align with students' values. Such a partnership could help students bridge the transition between college and employment and aid students with finding satisfying positions.

A final example in which librarians and student affairs professionals could collaborate is embedding librarians into bridge or TRIO programs. These programs orient students to higher education, provide a peer mentoring program throughout the college years, and create the cultural capital students need to persist to graduation. Given Solis and Dabbour's (2006) and

Whitmire's (2004) studies that students from underrepresented-minority, lower-socioeconomic-status, or first-generation backgrounds are less likely to use the library, bridge and TRIO programs seem to provide fertile opportunities for student affairs professionals and librarians to collaborate. Student affairs professionals could integrate librarians into activities and programs so students could become familiar with librarians, the library, and how to use library resources effectively very early in their college experience. If students are enrolled in remedial education, perhaps librarians and student affairs professionals could design assignments together in which students must use library resources. Such a collaboration should appeal to student affairs professionals and librarians who are committed to equity and social justice and wish to support students who lack the cultural capital to navigate the campus environment easily.

HOW MIGHT LIBRARIANS AND STUDENT AFFAIRS PROFESSIONALS APPROACH COLLABORATION?

Firstly, librarians and student affairs professionals must simply gain greater familiarity with each other's work and how each contributes to student learning. However, other forces may need to push either group toward each other before they make meaningful steps toward collaboration. Kezar (2006) identified eight core elements that are necessary to create the conditions that enable collaboration between groups: mission, integrating structures, campus networks, rewards, a sense of priority from senior administrators, external pressure, values, and learning. At least some of those elements must be present before librarians and student affairs professionals are able to collaborate in ways that lead to meaningful and lasting ventures that effect student learning and success. Of these eight elements, the most crucial and the most foundational are mission and a sense of priority from administrators. These elements are also the most likely to propel librarians and student affairs professionals toward each other in order to gain greater familiarity with each other's work. Campus networks, rewards, and values were also implied or explicitly addressed by the participants in this research.

Clear Mission and Collaboration as Priorities from Administrators

In the librarians' focused discussions, a theme of mission confusion emerged as a significant impediment to the likelihood of collaboration with student affairs professionals or, perhaps, with any actor outside of the libraries. The librarians at University A, B, and D complained of a lack of coordination of the library, resulting in librarians who performed their duties very autonomously and a lack of confirmation that their energies were well spent. The librarians seemed distinctly aware that the libraries suffered from unclear goals. Even at the libraries where the chief library administrators had clearly expressed support for collaboration with student affairs professionals, the librarians remained uncertain as to the desired outcome. For example, Beverly at University A said "Our dean is really big into working with student affairs. She talks about it a lot, but I'm not really sure what that looks like for me." Seemingly, interpretation or clarification was not sought or did not produce the clarity the librarians felt they needed. Instead, they took little or no action.

This seems contrary to Whitchurch's (2013) descriptions of librarians as third-space professionals. In her study, she interviewed librarians who recognized the ambiguity of their libraries' missions. Her participants found the ambiguity freeing, and they were able to experiment with new services and roles by working with faculty and other actors in higher education differently. However, the participants in my research seem to fit Lankes's (2011) claim that "There is great advantage to working across boundaries . . . but without a strong sense of purpose . . . librarians can have great difficulty working in [interdisciplinary] teams" (p. 196). This underscores the importance of strong leadership to articulate the need for such collaborations and the benefit of working with experts that are organizationally outside the library. Lankes cautioned further that without leadership providing clear purpose, "[Librarians have] a form of professional insecurity that often sees other skill sets . . . as competition. . . . It leads to a sort of schizophrenia whereby members of the profession are looking for innovation and, when they find it, see the innovators as . . . a threat" (p. 196). In Whitchurch's (2013) study, participants were primarily at institutions of higher education in the U.K., and it is possible librarians at United Kingdom institutions work under different realities than might librarians at U.S. institutions, particularly in terms of reward systems. I will address reward systems presently but those reported by the librarians in my research appear to inhibit the librarians' willingness to try new things.

Seemingly, the student affairs professionals seemed to suffer much less from mission confusion. They recognized major student concerns at their respective institutions—retention at Universities A and E; career placement at University B; and adjustment to a large campus at University C—and oriented their work accordingly. However, they did not indicate they collaborated much with colleagues outside of student affairs, except to serve as resources for faculty and librarians when those colleagues encountered troubled students. If their leaders and the mission of the institutions encouraged the student affairs professionals to collaborate with colleagues in academic affairs, they gave no sign of such encouragement. However, the student affairs professionals felt much more comfortable with the ambiguity of their missions, seemingly enabling the autonomy that Whitchurch (2013) noted as a facet of blended professionals working in the third space, but also what the librarians noted and seemed to envy:

> Um, the fact that we have a mission and a vision so we're aligning ourselves with that. So for us right now, uh, uh, transformative learning is a big buzzword, which is broad and vague. So a lot of us are challenged to see, to think what this transformative learning means in context. There's not a lot [of] talking that goes between us [student affairs functions] and um, we're all doing our own things, it feels like at times. (Miguel, University C)

> That's the beauty, really, to being student affairs. No one is paying a lot of attention to us, meaning the academic side. They're preoccupied on research and their own teaching, and so we're out here to do our own thing. (Louise, University C)

Librarians and student affairs professionals seem to be converging in their perspectives of student learning and are demonstrating interest in student success. Therefore, it should be incumbent upon the chief library and student affairs administrators to create missions that emphasize holistic student development. The leaders should articulate clearly to librarians and to student affairs professionals that they value collaboration and see it as the best mechanism for carrying out the mission and vision for student learning. The leaders should also be prepared to have multiple discussions to demonstrate the importance of student learning and affirm that librarians and student affairs professionals understand what the leaders hope to achieve. This should be especially true for the chief library administrators, as the librarians seemed less willing than the student affairs professionals to create their own interpretations of the expectations for their work.

Campus Networks

Kezar (2006) suggested campus networks that bring diverse actors together must be present for collaboration to unfold as a meaningful activity. Kezar noted campus committees that cross organizational boundaries, centers, conferences, and other bodies may serve as such campus networks. However, there seemed to be a lack of campus networks that could bring librarians and student affairs together. This lack of space for cross-boundary discussion between librarians and student affairs professionals was evident in the student affairs professionals' claims that librarians were invisible people or were trapped in the library. Many participants noted that they rarely see the librarians at their institutions, except on the occasional committee, unless they had a reason to visit the libraries themselves. For their part, the librarians indicated that they rarely crossed into the student affairs professionals' terrains, except when invited for specific purposes such as attending programs in the residence halls or dining with undergraduate students.

It might be incumbent upon the chief library administrators and chief student affairs administrators to initiate the spaces that will allow campus networks to flourish. Applying Whitchurch's (2013) spaces dimension to the focused discussions suggests the library as a student hub may be a safe psychological—and literal—space to begin a campus network. Committees or working groups could be proposed that bring student affairs professionals and librarians together to identify the student services that might serve students best in a centralized location. Another opportunity may be cross-training or a campus service institute similar to centers for teaching, learning, and technologies but specifically between librarians and student affairs professionals on the expertise that each possesses. An example might be working together to address students in crisis: Louise and Greta at University C desired the librarians to demonstrate a greater commitment to students' well-being by learning how to identify and respond to students in crisis, particularly in regard to mental health. The librarians at University D indicated they desired to help such students. Although they were uncertain how or where to refer such students, they felt not making an effort to understand students' distress was akin to abandoning their duty to serve students.

Reward Systems

Kezar (2006) suggested that reward systems must accommodate and recognize collaborative activities in order for collaborations to be successful. The student affairs professionals' focused discussions suggested they did not perceive reward systems to be a barrier. While it was unclear if their reward systems valued student affairs professionals developing collaborations with persons outside of their functional areas, their discourse implied a degree of agency to chart the direction of their work unimpeded by the potential constraints of reward systems. Gee's (2011) intonation tool highlights the saliency of a speaker's messages by focusing on how they emphasize or modify words. The student affairs professionals emphasized certain words in their discussions by changing their tones. For example, Dorothy at University A said, "I've learned to *work* with faculty and deans," and "*I* share ideas *with* them at meetings." Dorothy's intonation contributed to the importance she placed on collaboration in order to enhance student learning. Her consistent emphasis of the word "with" in connection with both her student affairs colleagues and also with faculty and librarians emphasized that she considered collaboration a core value of her work; this emphasis was common among the majority of the student affairs professionals at all the universities.

When the student affairs professionals did reach out to faculty, librarians, and other people outside of student affairs, they stressed their agency by emphasizing their identities. Greta at University C said, "*I* saw an opportunity to talk with the faculty on this committee about plagiarism, and that led *me* to talking with the graduate school about maybe starting a program on plagiarism for international students starting their degrees here." They also suggested they had agency by having some latitude to write their own evaluations. Alice at University B said "I think the way we evaluate here, it's very informal. It's like 'I know you've been doing good work so just write something that says what you've done so I can submit it.' That was the conversation I had." Her statement resulted in agreements from her colleagues and essentially represented the extent of the importance they placed on performance reviews. At University E, Stan said "You sort of do a self-evaluation to, to an extent. It's more a sort of bulleted list of the things that you've accomplished that year. Your supervisor takes that and puts it in a template. So if you have an idea to do something, all you have to do is really just justify it," to which Marta replied with "I never get any real feedback," and Barbara with "We're doing good. You really have to screw up around here to drop to a 'no merit' or even a 'standard merit.'"

From the participants' focused discussion, the librarians' reward systems do not reward librarians for "stepping outside the box" as Greta at University C said librarians need to do. In fact, the reward systems seemed to reinforce librarians' traditional roles and inhibited the likelihood of collaborating with student affairs professionals. While the librarians at University B didn't comment on reward systems, the librarians at University A, University C, University D, and University E explicitly discussed tenure or methods of annual performance as disfavoring activities that rely on collaboration with units outside the library, as this exchange between John, Amy, and Jodie at University A suggests:

> For non-tenure track librarians, we write our own contracts, kind of. Like, we submit documents that's like eight or ten things I want to do this year and work with our supervisor to figure out, you know. So you can absolutely write it as "outreach" like I have, but it depends what you have worked out with your supervisor. (John)

> Well . . . it's just basically up to the supervisor how much they value that. I would say it pretty much depends on the supervisor. Some, some supervisors don't value it as much. So. There's that. Why take the risk? Especially if you never hear your supervisor talk about [collaboration] in the first place. (Amy)

I think, looking at the operating paper, you, it isn't really rewarded. It's something that if someone has a lot of energy, they can, and will do, but doesn't necessarily get them what teaching, publishing, you know, those core activities are going to get them. (John)

So, the person now doing the most outreach in the library is not even a librarian. She's, um, a [support staff]. She just took it upon herself. (Jodie)

Yes, in a lot of ways, it's a, it's a pursuit of passion. Ah, but we don't have a good, in my opinion, a good and sustainable reward system for anything along those lines. Where frankly or a way to evaluate its success which is one of the real nightmares of, of outreach, that you can do everything right, and timing could, could be such that nothing's going to happen. Or there could be a change of personnel in charge of a program, and they could decide "Oh, I don't like you, and so we're not going to be a part of this." Then how does your supervisor evaluate? Like, is there an A for effort or is there only for success? (John)

Clearly, the librarians' reward systems must adapt to imbue collaborations with value and to encourage librarians to undertake such collaborations. The librarians' reward systems serve as a barrier to collaboration with other actors in higher education similar to those Borst (2011) identified, indicating that faculty who move outside the traditional domains of their disciplines may not have their work understood or rewarded by supervisors or by tenure and promotion committees.

CHANGED ROLES AND IDENTITIES FOR LIBRARIANS AND STUDENT AFFAIRS PROFESSIONALS

How might the work and identities of librarians and student affairs professionals change because of collaborations they might pursue together? This question requires additional research to answer fully. The librarians and student affairs professionals in this book had relatively little familiarity with each other, making it difficult to parse how their professional identities might evolve when working in a third space that combines elements of each other's expertise. Nonetheless, the focused discussions suggest the librarians recognize a need to serve students more holistically, potentially reframing their expertise as student specialists rather than as information specialists. Similarly, the student affairs professionals appeared to desire a greater range of instructional skill sets at their disposal, as they recognized the limitations of their challenge-and-support method of educating students. By working with librarians, student affairs professionals might evolve from an educator identity to encompass a teacher identity.

Librarians as Student Specialists

If librarians augment their teaching role and skills with theories of student development, their teaching role expands to a more comprehensive educational role. Rather than teaching students how to find information that just serves their curricular needs, librarians will be able to diagnose students' information needs in other dimensions of students' lives. Teaming with academic advisors, they could assist students with locating and understanding financial aid information or assist with selecting majors by recommending sources that help students explore and understand the skill sets and competencies each major develops. This would complement the librarians' primary role as information purveyors but also expand their teaching roles. Essentially, librarians would teach not only information literacy but would also apply other theories of student development to their interactions with students. They would foster students' ability to synthesize information with their academic and daily activities. This change suggests librarians' roles would expand from a teaching role to a specialist on holistic education role.

However, librarians must forge personal relationships with the students they serve in order to perceive the connections between students' social and academic lives and aspirations. This engagement with students likely means that librarians must leave the library and participate more fully in students' lives—they must go where the students are. The librarians noted they have a limited presence in students' cocurricular experiences. This might represent a significant departure for some librarians who are wedded to the library. Yet this engagement would potentially introduce librarians to contact with students that moves beyond the largely transactional interactions they reported as representing the bulk of their contact with students, excepting their management of student employees.

Librarians as Active Programmers

By collaborating with student affairs professionals on programming, librarians might also change the way they create experiences for students. The student affairs professionals at University C noted librarians' and student affairs professionals' concepts of programming are different. Whereas the student affairs professionals design experiences that make students interact with each other, the librarians tend to rely on passive programming such as exhibits and displays. While the participants perceived this difference as a barrier to collaboration, this could yet represent an opportunity for student affairs professionals to teach librarians to develop active programs that enable students to work or to socialize together with an educational purpose. The empowerment of librarians to design experiences for students that influence their interpersonal or identity development may cause librarians to reinterpret their teaching roles and to articulate learning outcomes that are not applied exclusively to students' information literacy skills.

Student Affairs Professionals as Teachers

Student affairs professionals' collaboration with librarians appears to be a natural progression of their link to faculty partnerships. Student affairs professionals could shift from enablers of student learning to teachers and adopt a more traditional teacher identity. By collaborating with librarians, student affairs professionals could benefit from librarians' expertise in curriculum design and pedagogical principles that are designed to spur students' cognitive development. Together, they could create formal learning experiences that are designed to apply cognitive lessons to students' social interactions. Through integrating student affairs professionals' deep knowledge of students' out-of-class experiences and student development theories with librarians' instructional expertise, a partnership could emerge that brings student affairs professionals closer to the academic realm. Moore and Marsh (2007) noted student affairs must reframe their educational role from enablers to teachers and extend themselves from merely creating environments that usher student development to intentional teaching of individual students. By collaborating with librarians, student affairs professionals could learn curriculum design strategies that will enable them to move from teaching "far" to teaching both near and far.

CONCLUSION

Librarians and student affairs professionals enjoy similar—and converging—perspectives on student learning and student success on which they could found future collaborative work. Student affairs professionals value students' holistic development and recognize that cognitive, interpersonal, and identity development are mutually intertwined. They are deeply engaged with the issues students face at their higher education institutions, and they orient their work to ensure students face fewer barriers to persistence and are better prepared for their postcollege years. Despite the librarians' emphasis on shaping students' cognitive development by teaching information literacy, they are also influencing students' interpersonal and identity development by reinterpreting the library as a hub of student activity. Librarians are also interested in preparing students for their postcollege years by teaching students skills related to career development and by creating passive programming that shapes students' personal development.

Despite converging perspectives on student learning and student success, librarians and student affairs professionals demonstrate little familiarity with each other. Most of the participants developed their understanding of each other based on their own days as students rather than as professionals. The widening gap between librarians and student affairs professionals maintains a siloing effect between the two groups. Some participants' stories suggested strong negative perceptions, indicating the librarians perceive student affairs professionals as disorganized whereas the student affairs professionals perceive the librarians as uncommitted or too removed from students and somewhat lacking in interpersonal skills. These negative perceptions could be reduced by two committed leaders communicating a mission and vision for seamless learning and bringing the two groups into greater contact. Campus networks could be founded in which librarians and student affairs professionals work together to teach students skills in, perhaps, a center for teaching, learning, and technologies oriented to postcollege preparation. Although student affairs professionals seem to enjoy agency in directing their work, librarians appear to be less empowered and less likely to initiate collaborations due to the demands placed on their time and reward systems that do not value collaborative work.

Chapter Seven

Recommendations for Practice

The work of librarians and student affairs professionals intersects in some ways, but their work diverges in profound ways that makes the groups much less likely to collaborate successfully on improving the student experience without significant incentives. At the same time, the findings from this book may help librarians, student affairs professionals, and other educators approach prospective collaborations between the two groups in ways that may overcome the barriers.

In this concluding chapter, I review the preceding chapters and provide reflections on the book. I discuss the book's major conclusions and consider how this research has changed my own thinking on collaboration between librarians and student affairs professionals and revise my assumptions that initially guided the genesis and design of my research. Next, I address the book's implications for practitioners. Librarians, student affairs professionals, and other educators will develop insight into whether and how successful collaborations to improve the student experience might be approached. Finally, I offer opportunities for future research.

My first chapter outlined an argument that librarians and student affairs professionals have common ground, at least philosophically, on which to base potential collaborations, particularly when those collaborations are intended to increase student learning or improve student success. Hinchliffe and Wong (2012) and Swartz, Carlisle, and Uyeki (2007) found little evidence that librarians and student affairs professionals had worked together, while Strothman and Antell (2010) found the relatively few collaborations that had taken place had not endured. Arcelus (2008), Kezar (2006), and Becher and Trowler (2001) studied successful collaborations between interdisciplinary groups and concluded participants must have a shared understanding of student learning, ability to engage in mutually satisfying dialog, and appreciation for the expertise that each group brings to the collaboration. Therefore, understanding prospective collaborators' perceptions was vitally important in order to approach collaborative work focused on the student experience.

Tenofsky (2007) and Walter (2007) suggested librarians and student affairs professionals are largely unfamiliar with each other's work and do not fully understand how the other group contributes to student learning and to student success. In fact, student affairs professionals' roles were largely unexplained in, and their perspectives completely absent from, the few case studies in the literature where librarians discussed collaborative work with student affairs professionals—work that many of the authors reported as not persisting despite some of the librarians' efforts. How librarians and student affairs professionals perceived each other's educational roles was a gap in the scholarly literature. Therefore, this book addressed the question of how librarians and student affairs professionals perceive each other's roles and what their perceptions might mean for potentially working together to improve student learning and student success.

Several overlapping core values guide the work of librarians and student affairs professionals, including service to students, community development, equity and social justice, and citizenship (Alire & Evans, 2010; Crume, 2004; Laosebikan-Buggs, 2006; Leckie & Buschman, 2007; Reason & Broido, 2016; Roberts, 2003; and Rubin, 2010). Next, I explored the phenomenon of collaboration in higher education and found collaborative work between different disciplines requires those disciplines' members to have a shared understanding of students, a shared vision of learning, and the ability to foster mutually satisfying dialog (Becher and Trowler, 2001). The higher education institutions themselves must also nurture collaborative work by demonstrating a clear mission and interweaving integrating structures, campus networks, rewards, a sense of priority from administrators, external pressure, values, and learning in order to create contexts that enable collaboration in organizations (Kezar, 2006; Kezar & Lester, 2009).

When I reviewed case studies of collaboration between student affairs and academic affairs, I found most addressed structural issues that either impeded or facilitated the collaborations between faculty members and student affairs professionals, particularly the power of the siloing effect between academic affairs and student affairs, which isolated groups from each other and provided little reason for different groups to interact (O'Connor, 2012). Arcelus (2008) found the "widening gap" between academic affairs and student affairs was driven at least partly by lack of trust between the groups (p. 124). Predominantly, librarians' collaborations were with faculty and sought to enhance students' information literacy and other critical thinking skills or to integrate library resources into course learning outcomes. However, faculty found librarians' expertise narrow and only marginally helpful (Bowles-Terry, 2014; Nilsen, 2012; Schulte & Sherwill-Navarro, 2009; Raspa & Ward, 2000). Lastly, I examined case studies of collaborations between librarians and student affairs professionals but found that many of the initiatives undertaken in the case studies did not persist, and student affairs professionals' voices and perspectives on the collaboration were distinctly unclear or lacking.

In my third chapter, I reviewed my research method and data analysis. I utilized focus groups as my research method and drew the sample of focus group participants from five higher education institutions in the Midwest. The institutions represented a range of institutional types, including size of student enrollment and private or public in character as denoted by Carnegie classification. The participants were employed full-time at those five higher education institutions and had been employed in their respective profession for at least three years. I conducted 10 focus groups, involving 30 librarians and 25 student affairs professionals. I held focus groups for the librarians and the student affairs professionals separately. All the focus groups lasted approximately 90 minutes.

Following my treatment of conducting the librarians' and the student affairs professionals' focus groups separately, I similarly organized their stories separately in the fourth and fifth chapters. The themes that emerged from their stories served as the sixth chapter, which pulled the themes together to compare and contrast the librarians and student affairs professionals' primarily diverging and sometimes intersecting worlds and addressed the book's research questions. In the next section of this chapter, I reflect on the genesis for my research and my assumptions that guided my thinking as I crafted this book. Then, I review my major findings and reflect on how these findings have reshaped my own thinking on collaboration between librarians and student affairs professionals.

REFLECTION ON THE GENESIS OF THE RESEARCH

I am a librarian who, for several years, intruded into the work of student affairs professionals. I practiced my craft in a setting unusual for my profession—wholly within the undergraduate residence halls on the campus of a large research university. I managed eight small libraries whose collections and services supported the programmatic goals of the living–learning communities and were tailored to reflect and to challenge the identities and interests of the first-year students residing there. As I observed the work of my student affairs colleagues in the residence halls, I was intrigued by the great responsibility I perceived that these professionals bore. My colleagues counseled and mentored individual students, helped students navigate their first year at college, and created intentional learning environments. My colleagues both supported and challenged students' critical thinking, sense of identity, and interpersonal skills. I thought my student affairs colleagues and I shared much in common at the heart of our work: We stood outside of the university's established curriculum, but still we shaped students' learning as finely as the faculty by our one-on-one teaching moments with students and through the environments and experiences we designed to facilitate students' success. We were in league.

At the same time, I was also a stranger in a strange land. Each time I collaborated with student affairs professionals on a program, I wondered why the collaboration had been so difficult to begin. I had found myself frequently explaining the nature of my work as a librarian, why I was working outside the library, and how students benefited from my participation in a student affairs initiative. To my librarian colleagues, I had also found myself explaining the nature and purpose of the work of the student affairs professionals. I speculated that despite our mutual interest in student learning outside of the classroom, librarians and student affairs professionals were dwelling in different worlds. We were alike but our differences made us strangers. I asked myself: In which ways were we so different, and how profound were these differences in working together toward a common goal? In which ways were we alike, and could these likenesses frame successful collaborations together for the betterment of our students? These questions were the genesis of my interest in this research.

At the beginning of my journey, I assumed librarians and student affairs professionals had reason—and a desire—to collaborate in order to improve the student experience. After all, I had been employed in a position that led me to work with student affairs professionals on designing programming, services, and spaces to support students. Moreover, I knew service to students is not only a deep commitment but the very ethos for academic librarians and for student affairs professionals alike. We belong to helping professions, and students are the reason for our calling. This assumption guided my exploration.

When I began my journey, I assumed—quite naively—that if one cared deeply for a value and was willing to try something in a new way, one had only find like-minded people and the collaborative work would unfold. At worst, the collaboration might not yield the outcomes one had hoped, and one would revise one's strategies accordingly. Naturally, I approached this research with high expectations. I undertook this work with the intent of making a difference in the way librarians innovate and create a more deeply integrated learning environment for students. In her call for collaboration between librarians and student affairs professionals, Forrest (2005) asked "Do they even exist?" (p. 12). At the beginning of my journey, I said to myself "I will find them. And if I do not find them, I will find the germs of ideas among the librarians and the student affairs professionals. I will help those germs grow and bloom into the ideas that others will then emulate and adapt for their own institutions." Perhaps one day, I thought, higher education might even see the rise of libraries blended wholly with student services. Students might visit a single building on campus where they could exercise, attend a program in a space dedicated to underrepresented students, and find staff capable of providing academic and career advising as well as expertise on information in all its multitudinous domains. Perhaps librarians and student affairs professionals might experience such great change to their work and professional identities, their expertise might even expand to encompass the skills of both professions. These were exciting, even revolutionary, prospects to me.

At the five higher education institutions where I conducted my focus groups, I did not find librarians and student affairs professionals working in collaboration. Because I did not find collaborative work taking place between any of the librarians and the student affairs professionals in my research, I was not truly able to identify any specific conditions that facilitated collaborations between the two groups but instead found conditions that may impede collaborations, such as lack of familiarity and shared languages, differences between each other's ways of working, and the gap that isolates the two groups from each other. Only a couple of the student affairs professionals knew of collaborations—and unfortunately failed ones—between librarians and student affairs professionals undertaken at other institutions. In fact, I found few germs of ideas for working together at all. To many of the participants, the concept was completely new and maybe even a bit strange. In explaining the purpose of my research as I began to facilitate the first of my focus groups, a librarian interrupted me with the rather alarming question: "What is that phrase you're using—student affairs?" This seemed like an inauspicious but telling beginning to my research. In the next section of this chapter, I will summarize my major findings and then return to my reflection in order to illustrate how these major findings caused me to rethink whether librarians and student affairs professionals should and could collaborate to improve student learning and student success.

MAJOR FINDINGS

My purpose was to explore librarians' and student affairs professionals' perceptions of each other's roles in student learning and success, to identify opportunities for prospective collaborations, and to identify the conditions which impede or facilitate prospective collaboration. Through the voices of librarians and student affairs professionals at four higher education institutions, I explored the following research questions: How do librarians and student affairs professionals describe student learning and student success?

How do librarians and student affairs professionals perceive their own and each other's roles in student learning and student success? Where do they see the work of librarians intersecting with the work of student affairs professionals? How might they approach collaborations in these intersecting areas? How might the work and identities of librarians and student affairs professionals change because of these collaborations?

The librarians and student affairs professionals never specifically addressed their perspectives on students or, more specifically, on student learning. Instead, they discussed what they did on behalf of students, and I inferred their perspectives. They do not yet have a shared understanding of students or of student learning, but I believe they are capable of reaching a shared understanding. Student affairs professionals are strongly focused on the holistic development of students, while librarians are principally focused on teaching students critical thinking skills. However, some librarians were demonstrating a greater interest in holistic student development by emphasizing ways they could design programs, services, and spaces at the library that allowed students to practice problem-solving skills and creativity. This suggests librarians and student affairs professionals have begun to see students not as empty vessels to be filled up with content knowledge, but as growing in multidimensional ways and influenced cognitively, psychosocially, and self-conceptually by the environments and experiences each group creates.

However, librarians' and student affairs professionals' perceptions of each other's predominant roles are quite dissimilar. Many of the librarians had virtually no impression of student affairs professionals whatsoever, except in regard to student maintenance. Many of the student affairs professionals were ambivalent toward librarians and they emphasized librarians' rather narrow focus at helping students locate information, a need many of the student affairs professionals questioned in the face of improving technologies. They questioned librarians' commitment to students, suggesting the language librarians used to describe students and libraries' services was off-putting.

They did not really view their work as intersecting. Again, their negative perceptions of each other might have prevented them from imagining the possibilities. While they did acknowledge that libraries were changing and that bringing student services into the library might be beneficial for students and therefore desirable, the lack of interaction between librarians and student affairs professionals seemed profound. Arcelus's (2008) widening gap seemed a strong force at play here. The student affairs professionals remarked upon the librarians' invisibility, which was likely true and created by the librarians' sense of the "Jenga pile"—in which librarians' experienced increasing demands on their time—and an inflexible system of evaluation and tenure prevented them from taking risks outside their core job duties. I believe differences in their ways of working contributed to the widening gap as well. The student affairs professionals lived in the "here and now," a constant shuffling of priorities driven by immediate student crises, while librarians required planning to build opportunities for trying new activities into their schedule and then abandoned those activities quickly when they failed to see a significant return on their invested time. These are significant structural barriers that prevent librarians and student affairs professionals from spending time in each other's worlds. Therefore, they have little opportunity to form perceptions or change their somewhat negative perceptions of each other and begin to talk about how their work might intersect.

My assumption that librarians and student affairs professionals could and should work together to enhance student learning and student success framed this book. Now, I doubt the validity of my assumption. While the work of librarians and student affairs professionals does intersect in some interesting ways and their perspectives on students and on student learning do seem to be converging, other factors keep them farther apart than I had thought. Structural issues inherent in their work—such as the librarians' sense of being overwhelmed with responsibilities or the "here and now" nature of student affairs work—inhibit their ability to connect with each other and exacerbate their lack of familiarity with each other's educational roles. They are skeptical of each other's capacity to work together successfully, with, perhaps, librarians mistaking student affairs professionals' lack of follow-through or planning as disinterest and student affairs professionals doubting librarians' interpersonal skills could make them suitable collaborators.

Becher and Trowler (2001) claimed disciplines with relational values are more likely to reach consensus and build successful interdisciplinary endeavors. The disciplines must share a common vision of learning, a common perspective on students, a common language, and the ability to foster mutually satisfying dialog. John-Steiner (1998) suggested individuals must possess a set of relational dynamics, such as trust, autonomy, and creativity, in order to express both the desire and the capacity to engage in collaborative work. Consequently, librarians and student affairs professionals must demonstrate evidence of convergence in their perspectives on learning and students, they must trust the members of the other group, and they must be open to new ideas and experience sufficient independence to work in new ways without the reward systems penalizing their willingness to step outside their traditional domains and ways of working. My findings suggest librarians and student affairs professionals diverge more significantly than they converge in these areas, thereby making long-lived collaborations between the two groups less likely.

MY NEW THOUGHTS

I now believe that librarians and student affairs professionals dwell in different worlds and are more dissimilar than I had previously thought. Where I was idealistic in my belief that librarians and student affairs professionals could and should collaborate together to improve student learning and success at the beginning of my book, I am now skeptical that they are appropriate prospective collaborators. They do not appear to share sufficient similarities that allow them to experiment with new ideas and enable long-lived, successful collaborations to flourish. While their lack of familiarity with each other is profound, they doubted the validity of the other group's educational contributions, did not trust each other's interpersonal skills or planning abilities, and appeared to differ markedly in their sense of autonomy or agency. I think back to John-Steiner's (1998) assertion that collaborators must possess a set of relational dynamics that include intellectual ownership, trust, autonomy, and creativity in order to express both the desire and the capacity to engage in collaborative works with people outside their discipline. I did not find much evidence in the focused discussions to suggest these relational dynamics were shared by the participants in my focus groups, suggesting the desire and the capacity to engage in collaborative work may not be present at all.

At the beginning, I did not yet appreciate the invisible forces at play in higher education. I knew, at least abstractly, of the isolation most groups working on higher education institutions feel from each other. What I did not recognize until I thought deeply about my findings was the breadth and the incredibly powerful role of the widening gap between student affairs and academic affairs, to which librarians usually belong.

I am also concerned the implication is that librarians will become increasingly isolated in higher education without partners who find librarians' expertise valuable in the educational enterprise. Oakleaf (2010) reported librarians and libraries' value in higher education are increasingly questioned, and librarians must demonstrate greater accountability for student learning by establishing how they change students' lives. She recommended that librarians collaborate with student affairs professionals in order to demonstrate that librarians may positively contribute to student persistence and to student learning outside of the classroom. Melling (2013) found the cultures of librarians and information technologists to be too different to allow them to work together successfully. Nilsen (2012) and Schulte and Sherwill-Navarro (2009) concluded that faculty do not perceive librarians as valued collaborators in student learning. If librarians and student affairs professionals are also too dissimilar to work collaboratively on improving student learning or student success, librarians are left rather alone to craft the future of their profession. As a librarian, the implication brings me much disquiet.

SIGNIFICANCE OF THE FINDINGS

Hinchliffe and Wong (2012) and Swartz, Carlisle, and Uyeki (2007) noted that little collaboration between librarians and student affairs professionals appeared to have taken place. Strothman and Antell (2010) claimed collaborations between librarians and student affairs professionals were not successful and did not persist. Becher and Trowler (2001) and Kezar (2006) noted that successful collaborative work focused on improving the student experience requires interdisciplinary groups to have a shared understanding of student learning and an appreciation for the expertise that each group brings to the collaboration. In Arcelus's (2008) and Kezar and Lester's (2009) studies of successful interdisciplinary collaborations, the groups' perceptions influenced the willingness and ability of different professional groups to work together, but student affairs professionals' perspectives were absent from the relatively few case studies that explored collaborations between the two professions (Aguilar & Keating, 2009).

My research gave voices to student affairs professionals and shared the perspectives of both groups. While librarians and student affairs professionals do intersect in some ways in regard to student learning, they do not appreciate the educational contributions that each could potentially bring to collaborative work focused on improving the student experience. Based on my findings, librarians, student affairs professionals, and other educators may recognize that prospective collaborations between the professions may be fraught with difficulties. At the very least, readers interested in laying the groundwork for collaboration between the groups will need to assess the level of familiarity and the accuracy of the perceptions that each group has of the other at their higher education institutions. Negative perceptions or misperceptions may need to be counteracted with greater contacts between the groups, and each group may need to alter their message about how they contribute to student learning. This may be especially true for the librarians, whom student affairs professionals perceive as narrowly focused on information skills. Readers may find value in the germs of the ideas for improving the student experience that emerged from my findings and develop insights into the conditions that are likely to impede prospective collaborative work.

IMPLICATIONS FOR PRACTICE IN HIGHER EDUCATION

Librarians and student affairs professionals who hoped to find new and interesting collaborations to implement at their own institutions are sure to be disappointed with what they found—or, perhaps more accurately, with what they did not find—in my research. I am too, at least in that regard. Indeed, the challenge of collaboration between librarians and student affairs professionals is not about specific ideas for collaborations at all but how to reorient librarians and student affairs professionals towards collaborative work despite the realities of their diverging worlds. Collaboration between the two groups will not be easy at the best of times because of the differences I identified. Instead, a cultural shift may be required in order for librarians and student affairs professionals to perceive each other as worthwhile collaborators. The institutional cultures that support the necessary characteristics for interdisciplinary collaboration to occur must be present first.

Based on my findings, I do believe collaboration between two interdisciplinary groups with such marked differences as librarians and student affairs professionals can happen though a major policy change initiated by campus leaders. I agree with Kezar's (2006) finding that higher education institutions must demonstrate certain necessary conditions before collaboration between interdisciplinary groups can emerge with lasting success. Kezar identified those conditions as a clear mission, integrating structures, campus networks, rewards, a sense of priority from administrators, external pressure, values, and shared perspectives on learning. Arcelus (2008) concluded that institutions moving toward the cultivation of those conditions require "a combination of leadership, dialog, and willingness to re-evaluate one's viewpoint while learning about people's perspectives" (p. 416). Based on what I came to learn from the literature and from the focused discussions, I believe the widening gap between student affairs and academic affairs is the most serious barrier to collaboration for institutions who desire to create seamless learning environments. How are librarians and student affairs professionals to learn more about each other's work and change their perceptions of each other if the invisible force of the widening gap prevents them from truly coming together?

However, the gap may be overcome if institutions redefine their missions and guiding philosophies. The institutional leaders must work toward a mutually agreed upon educational philosophy that in turn guides the tenor of academic and cocurricular programs, the allocation of resources that support the philosophy, and the adaptation of reward systems that actually reward, or at the very least do not penalize, the librarians and student affairs professionals who are willing to blend collaborative work into the exercise of their roles. The gap will be narrowed by a shared ethos, and that shared ethos will emerge when librarians and student affairs professionals exhibit confidence and trust in each other, support each other's work, and then create a coherent campus experience for students. So I believe the greatest indicator for long-lived, successful collaborations between librarians and student affairs professionals will be at higher education institutions where institutional leaders are interested in the enhancement of student learning through the establishment of seamless learning environments.

Finally, Kezar (2006) noted "micro-changes" might also be potentially important in reorienting institutional culture to value collaborative work. As an example, she offered a story of faculty inviting faculty from another department for an informal coffee to talk about their work. Kezar did not examined these micro-changes but speculated these moments might be as powerful as the institutional conditions she had outlined. Although interactions between librarians and student affairs professionals are stymied by the differences in how they plan and use their time, individuals who wish to explore collaborations between the groups must find a way to interact, if at least quite informally. However, these informal interactions must unfold in a group context rather than between individuals who have a mutual interest in reaching out to each other. Alison, a librarian at University C, expressed interest in working with the career advisors, but the other librarians in her focus group discouraged her from doing so until after she had earned tenure. In order to counteract the negative reinforcement that individuals might experience from colleagues, chief library officers and chief student affairs officers should organize joint meetings to discuss librarians' and student affairs professionals' work.

At University A, the librarians remembered that the dean of students, or someone else from student affairs, had indeed come to speak to the library staff. However, they did not recall very much about what he had to say or even his name, but mostly that student affairs professionals were to serve as resources for librarians when they encountered students in distress. That meeting was about what student affairs professionals could do for librarians on behalf of students—but making students themselves the focus of the discussion may influence a new direction to their interactions. I suspect the two groups could go a long way toward demystifying each other if they were simply brought together with students as the focus of their meeting. It seems simplistic to change the purpose of joint meetings from talking about how, when, and where to refer students in crisis to about how students are learning and how both groups change students' lives through the intentional interactions they design. Yet there may be real gains in approaching the conversation in such a way to capitalize on librarians' and student affairs professionals' shared ethos of service to students.

In short, chief library officers and chief student affairs officers must place a shared emphasis on collaboration between the two groups. This emphasis must be explicitly stated, and the anticipated outcomes of collaboration must be clearly articulated for the benefit of librarians and student affairs professionals who may not understand how their work is expected to change. The chief library officer and the chief student affairs officer should make students the center of discussion between the two groups. In order to better understand the context of each other's work, librarians and student affairs professionals should share how they contribute to student learning and student success and specifically discuss the actions they take to carry out their work. Through mutual dialog, librarians and student affairs professionals should develop keener insight into each other's work and may develop ideas for working together to improve the student experience.

I recommend librarians and student affairs professionals focus their discussions on identifying and addressing social justice issues students face at their institutions. As a core value common to both professions, librarians and students affairs professionals should be able to survey the campus climate of their institutions to identify how and where students encounter systemic institutional barriers toward their persistence. Together, librarians and student affairs professionals might be able to develop new approaches or services designed to provide better outreach or address inequities.

OPPORTUNITIES FOR FUTURE RESEARCH

This book focused on small groups of librarians and student affairs professionals at five higher education institutions in the Midwest. I did not specifically seek out higher education institutions that demonstrated seamless learning experiences as a core institutional value. If I had, I might have found librarians and student affairs professionals with different perspectives, because presumably Kezar's (2006) eight conditions for intergroup collaboration might already be present, and the siloing effect of the widening gap might not have been the powerful factor I suspect it was for the institutions I selected for my research. An opportunity for study would be to explore whether collaborations between librarians and student affairs professionals exist at such institutions, or whether the librarians and student affairs professionals are more familiar with or perceive each other differently than did the participants at the institutions I selected.

Additionally, my work drew participants who did not report having significant past interactions or collaborations with members of the other professional group. Therefore my research does not include the voices and perspectives of librarians and student affairs professionals who may have made satisfying connections with each other. They may be fewer in number, but they are almost certainly out there somewhere in the world of higher education since the several case studies included in Hinchliffe and Wong's (2012) edited work drew upon librarians' experiences working with student affairs professionals, at least in a limited way.

Although the five institutions I selected had a large number of undergraduate students in residence on their campus, I realize now the number of undergraduate students enrolled is not a good indicator that institutions are actually strongly focused on undergraduate education. Several of the institutions were characterized as research universities, and research universities tend to lack a sharp focus on undergraduate students; their librarians, at least, are often juggling the very different needs of multiple constituent groups than are librarians elsewhere (Alire & Evans, 2010). I speculate that a similar study that drew upon participants from faith-based institutions or small liberal arts colleges might possibly lead to different conclusions due to the more focused missions of those institutional types. For practitioners, it would be helpful to compare the perceptions of librarians and student affairs professionals at research universities with those at faith-based or liberal arts institutions. It may be that collaboration between librarians and student affairs at some institutions is simply not very feasible because institutional type is a more controlling mitigating factor than are the dissimilarities between the professions.

An additional opportunity for study would be to explore the perceptions of librarians and student affairs professionals who might have already worked together and describe what conditions brought those actors together and how their collaborative work was enabled or impeded by the forces at play at their institutions. There may be value in understanding the ways these collaborators engage with each other so that mutually supportive collaborations might be explored between librarians and student affairs professionals. This might prove especially helpful for librarians who are weighing the merit of reshaping their libraries into student hubs and thinking about how they can influence the learning and development of students who are likely to frequent there.

CONCLUSION

In this book, I explored librarians' and student affairs professionals' perceptions of their own and each other's roles in student learning and student success. I found librarians and student affairs professionals may not be suitable partners for working together to improve the student experience because they do not share strong similarities. They do not recognize, or appear to value, the expertise that the other profession may offer to collaborative ventures. Some librarians perceived student affairs professionals as disorganized, while student affairs professionals perceived librarians as uncommitted or removed from students and somewhat lacking in interpersonal skills. Although they diverged in powerful ways, such as skepticism of each other's expertise, ability to engage in mutually satisfying dialog, and shared language and perspectives on interactions with students, librarians and student affairs professionals appear to be converging in their perspectives on students and their possible contributions to student learning. I concluded that collaboration between librarians and student affairs professionals may, in fact, be difficult, but it is still possible when the bases of collaborative work spring from the intersections of their worlds, namely supporting and challenging students' cognitive, identity, and psychosocial development.

Additionally, I suggested a few potential avenues for, and possible approaches to, collaboration between librarians and student affairs professionals such as the practice of intrusive librarianship or the embedding of librarians into bridge or TRIO programs. In addition to the differences between the professions that may impede collaboration, I identified other conditions that may also inhibit the likelihood of successful collaborations, including inflexible reward systems for librarians, librarians feeling overwhelmed by their duties, and the powerful siloing effect of the widening gap between student affairs and academic affairs at higher education institutions. The findings of this book should prove useful to librarians, student affairs professionals, and other educators who are seeking insight into the possibilities and limitations of building collaborations between these professions in order to enhance student learning and student success.

References

Abbott, A. (1988). *The system of professions: An essay on the division of expert labour.* Chicago, IL: University of Chicago.

Accardi, M. T., Garvey-Nix, R., & Meyer, L. A. (2012). Plagiarism education, prevention, and student development: A collaborative approach to supporting academic integrity. In L. J. Hinchliffe & M. A. Wong (Eds.), *Environments for student growth and development* (pp. 73–87). Chicago, IL: Association of College and Research Libraries.

ACPA—College Student Educators International and NASPA—Student Affairs Administrators in Higher Education. (2015). Professional competency areas for student affairs educators. Washington DC: NASPA. Retrieved from naspa.org/images/uploads/main/ACPA_NASPA_Professional_Competencies_FINAL.pdf

Aguilar, P., & Keating, K. (2009). Satellite outreach services programs to under-represented students: Being in their space, not on MySpace. *The Reference Librarian, 50*(1), 14–28. doi: 10.1080/02763870802546365

Alire, C. A., & Evans, G. E. (2010). *Academic librarianship.* New York, NY: Neal Schuman.

American Association for Higher Education, Task Force on Student Learning. (1998). *Powerful partnerships: A shared responsibility for learning.* Retrieved from acpa.nche.org/sites/default/files/taskforce_powerful_partnerships_a_shared_responsibility_for_learning.pdf

American Association of University Professors. (2017). Trends in the academic labor force, 1975–2015. Retrieved from https://www.aaup.org/sites/default/files/Academic_Labor_Force_Trends_1975-2015.pdf

American Library Association. (2018). *Number employed in libraries.* Retrieved from ala.org/tools/libfactsheets/alalibraryfactsheet02

American Library Association, Office for Accreditation. (2008). *Standards for accreditation of master's programs in library and information studies.* Retrieved from http://www.ala.org/educationcareers/sites/ala.org.educationcareers/files/content/standards/standards_2008.pdf

Arcelus, V. J. (2008). *In search of a break in the clouds: An ethnographic study of academic and student affairs cultures.* (Doctoral dissertation). Retrieved from ProQuest. (UMI 3414294)

Arzola, R. (2016). Collaboration between the library and office of student disability services: Document accessibility in higher education. *Digital Library Perspectives, 32*(2). doi: 10.1108/DLP09-2015-0016

Atkins, S. E. (2003). *The academic library in the American university.* Madison, WI: University of Wisconsin.

Barr, T. F. (2013). Utilizing student affairs professionals to enhance student and faculty experiences and mitigate risk in short-term, faculty-led study abroad programs. *Journal of International Education in Business, 6*(2), 136–147. doi: 10.1108/JIEB-05-2013-0019

Battles, M. (2004). *Library: An unquiet history*. New York: W. W. Norton.
Becher, T. (1989). *Academic tribes and territories: Intellectual enquiry and the culture of disciplines*. Milton Keynes, UK: Open University Press.
Becher, T., & Trowler, P. (2001). *Academic tribes and territories* (2nd ed.). Oxford, UK: Society for Research into Higher Education and Open University Press.
Bennett, S. (2007). Campus cultures fostering information literacy. *Portal: Libraries and the Academy, 7*(2), 147–167. doi: 10.1353/pla.2007.0013
Blimling, G. S., & Whitt, E. J. (1999). *Good student affairs practice: Principles to foster student learning*. San Francisco, CA: Jossey-Bass.
Bok, D. C. (2015). *Higher education in America*. Princeton, NJ: Princeton University Press.
Bolin, M. K. (2008). A typology of librarian status at land grant universities. *Journal of Academic Librarianship, 34*(3), 220–230.
Borst, A. J. (2011). *Evaluating academic and student affairs partnerships: The impact of living-learning communities on the development of critical thinking skills in college freshman*. (Doctoral dissertation). Retrieved from ir.iowa.edu/etd/927. (ETD 927)
Boss, G. J., Linder, C., Martin, J. A., Dean, S. R., & Fitzer, J. R. (2018). Conscientious practice: Post-master's student affairs professionals' perspectives on engaging social justice. *Journal of Student Affairs Research and Practice, 55*(4), 373–385. doi: 10.1080/19496591.2018.1470004
Bowles-Terry, M. (2014). *UNLV Libraries: Partners in student learning*. Poster session presented at the meeting of the American Library Association, Las Vegas, NV. Retrieved from digitalscholarship.unlv.edu/lib_openhouse_ala/2
Bozeman, B., & Boardman, C. (2013). Academic faculty in university research centers: Neither capitalism's slaves nor teaching fugitives. *Journal of Higher Education 84*(1), 88–120. doi: 10.1080/00221546.2013.11777279
Calhoun, D. W., & Taub, D. J. (2014). Exploring the gender-identity roles of men in student affairs. *College Student Affairs Journal, 32*(1), 35–51.
Clothier, R. C. (1986). College personnel principles and functions. In G. Saddlemire & A. Rentz (Eds.), *Student affairs: a profession's heritage* (pp. 9–20). Alexandria, VA: American College Personnel Association. (Original work published 1931)
Cohen, A. M., & Kisker, C. B. (2010). *The shaping of American higher education: Emergence and growth of the contemporary system* (2nd ed.). San Francisco, CA: Jossey-Bass.
Cook, L., Marthers, P., & Fusch, D. (2017). Student affairs: Trends to watch in 2017–2019. Retrieved from academicimpressions.com/blog/student-affairs-trends-to-watch-in-2017-19/
Cossette, A. (2009). *Humanism and libraries: An essay on the philosophy of librarianship*. Sacramento, CA: Litwin Books.
Cownie, F. (2012). Law, research and the academy. In P. Trowler, M. Saunders, and V. Bamber (Eds.), *Tribes and territories in the 21st century: Rethinking the significance of disciplines in higher education* (pp. 57–68). New York, NY: Routledge.
Crowe, K. M. (2010). Student affairs connection: Promoting the library through co-curricular activities. *Collaborative Librarianship, 2*(3). Retrieved from digitalcommons.du.edu/collaborativelibrarianship/vol2/iss3/5
Crowley, W. H. (1986). The nature of student personnel work. In G. Saddlemire & A. Rentz (Eds.), *Student affairs: a profession's heritage* (pp. 47–73). Alexandria, VA: American College Personnel Association. (Original work published 1936)
Crume, A. W. (2004). *The historical development of the Student Government Association as a student sub-culture at Florida State University: 1946–1976*. (Doctoral dissertation, Florida State University). Retrieved from http://diginole.lib.fsu.edu/etd/
Cummings, L. U. (2007). Bursting out of the box: Outreach to the millennial generation through student services programs. *Reference Services Review, 35*(2), 285–295. doi: 10.1108/009073207107
Cutler, H. A. (2003). Identity development in student affairs professionals. *The College Student Affairs Journal, 22*(2), 167–179.
Dahl, C. (2007). Library liaison with non-academic units: A new application for a traditional model. *Partnership: the Canadian Journal of Library and Information Practice and Research, 2*(1), 1–11.

Davies, D. W. (1974). *Libraries as culture and social centers: The origin of the concept.* Metuchen, NJ: Scarecrow.

Davis, D. M., & Hall, T. D. (2012). *Diversity counts.* Chicago: American Library Association. Retrieved from http://www.ala.org/offices/sites/ala.org.offices/files/content/diversity/diversitycounts/diversitycountstables2012.pdf

Dervin, B. (2003). Given a context by any other name: Methodological tools for taming the unruly beast. In B. Dervin, L. Foreman-Wernet, & E. Lauterbach (Eds.), *Sense-making methodology reader: Selected writings of Brenda Dervin* (pp. 111–132). Cresskill, NJ: Hampton.

Donoghue, F. (2018). *The last professors: The corporate university and the fate of the humanities.* New York: Fordham University Press.

Dungy, G. J., & Gordon, S. A. (2011). The development of student affairs. In J. H. Schuh, S. R. Jones, & S. R. Harper (Eds.), *Student services: A handbook for the profession* (5th ed.) (pp. 61–80). San Francisco, CA: Jossey-Bass.

Eberhart, G. M. (2006). *The whole library handbook 4: Current data, professional advice, and curiosa about libraries and library services* (4th ed.). Chicago: American Library Association.

Elguindi, A. C., & Sandler, M. A. (2013). The ILS as outreach: Cataloging campus partner collections. *Cataloging and Classification Quarterly, 51*(1–3), 291–310. doi: 10.1080/0163937.2012.722589

Emmons, M., & Wilkinson, F. C. (2011). The academic library impact on student persistence. *College & Research Libraries, 72*(2), 128–142.

Ender, S. C., Newton, F. B., & Caple, R. B. (1996). *Contributing to learning—the role of student affairs: New directions for student services, No. 75.* San Francisco, CA: Jossey-Bass.

Ferguson, J. (2016). Additional degree required? Advanced subject knowledge and academic librarianship. *Portal: Libraries and the Academy, 16*(4), 721–736. doi: 10.1353/pla.2016.0049

Finkelstein, M. J., Conley, V. M., & Schuster, J. H. (2016). *The faculty factor: Reassessing the American academy in a turbulent era.* Baltimore, MD: Johns Hopkins University.

Flashmobs in libraries. (2010, February 15). *Journal of the European Association for Health Information and Libraries.* [Web log post]. Retrieved from http://jeahil/wordpress.com/2010/02/15/flashmobs-in-libraries/

Flexner, A. (1916). Is social work a profession? In National Conference of Charities and Corrections, *Proceedings of the National Conferences of Charities and Corrections at the Forty-second annual session held in Baltimore, Maryland, May 12–19, 1915.* Chicago: Hildmann.

Forrest, L. U. (2005). Academic librarians and student affairs professionals: An ethical collaboration for higher education. *Education Libraries, 28*(1), 11–15.

Furr, S. (2018). Wellness interventions for social justice fatigue among student affairs professionals. (Doctoral dissertation, Loyola University Chicago). Retrieved from ecommons.luc.edu/luc_diss/2803

Gatten, J. N. (2005). Student psychosocial and cognitive development: Theory to practice in academic libraries. *Reference Services Review, 32*(2), 157–163. doi: 10.1108/00907320410537676

Gee, J. P. (2011). *How to do discourse analysis: A toolkit.* New York, NY: Routledge.

Gibson, H., Morris, A., & Cleeve, M. (2008). Links between libraries and museums: Investigating museum-library collaborations in England and the USA. *Libri, 57*(2), 53–64. doi: 10.1515/LIBR.2007.53

Gilchrist, D. L. (2009). *Academic libraries at the center of instructional change: Faculty and librarian experience of library leadership in the transformation of teaching and learning.* (Unpublished doctoral dissertation). Oregon State University, Corvallis, Oregon.

Gordon, V. N., Habley, W. R., & Grites, T. J. (2008). *Academic advising: A comprehensive handbook* (2nd ed.). San Francisco, CA: Jossey-Bass.

Gorman, M. (2015). *Our enduring values revisited: Librarianship in an ever-changing world.* Chicago, IL: American Library Association.

Greary, D. S. (2008). *Tribes and territories in library and information science education* (Doctoral dissertation). Available from ProQuest Dissertations and Theses database. (UMI No. 1434728)

Griffiths, J. M., & King, D. W. (2009). *A national study of the future of librarians in the workforce.* Washington, DC: Institute of Museum and Library Services. Retrieved from libraryworkforce.org/tiki-index.php

Guba, E. G. (1981). Criteria for assessing the trustworthiness of naturalistic inquiries. *Educational Communication and Technology Journal, 29,* 75–91.

Guido, F. M., Chavez, A. F., & Lincoln, Y. S. (2010). Underlying paradigms in student affairs research and practice. *Journal of Student Affairs Research and Practice, 47*(1), 1–22. doi: 10.2202/1949-6605.6017

Hailu, M., Mackey, J., Pan, J., & Arend, B. D. (2017). *Turning good intentions into good teaching: Five common principles for culturally responsive pedagogy.* Hershey, PA: IGI Global.

Hamrick, F. A., Evans, N. J., & Schuh, J. H. (2002). *Foundations of student affairs practice: How philosophy, theory, and research strengthen educational outcomes.* San Francisco, CA: Jossey-Bass.

Helfgott, S. R. (2005). Core values and major issues in student affairs practice: What really matters? *New Directions for Community Colleges, v. 2005*(131), 5–18.

Hinchliffe, L. J., & Wong, M. A. (2012). The power of library and student affairs collaborations. In L. J. Hinchliffe & M. A. Wong (Eds.), *Environments for student growth and development* (pp. 231–245). Chicago, IL: Association of College and Research Libraries.

Hollister, C. (2005). Bringing information literacy to career services. *Reference Services Review, 33*(1), 104–111.

John-Steiner, V. (1998). The challenge of studying collaboration. *American Educational Research Journal, 35*(4), 773–783.

Johnson, B. L. (1939). *Vitalizing a college library.* Urbana, IL: University of Illinois.

Kahl, C., & Paterson, J. (2012). Posters, programs, and perspectives on democracy. In L. J. Hinchliffe & M. A. Wong (Eds.), *Environments for student growth and development* (pp. 101–113). Chicago, IL: Association of College and Research Libraries.

Kezar, A. (2006). Redesigning for collaboration in learning initiatives: An examination of four highly collaborative campuses. *Journal of Higher Education, 77*(5), 804–838.

Kezar, A. J., & Lester, J. (2009). *Organizing higher education for collaboration.* San Francisco, CA: Jossey-Bass.

Kleiman, P. (2012). Scene changes and key changes: Disciplines and identities in higher education dance, drama and music. In P. Trowler, M. Saunders, and V. Bamber (Eds.), *Tribes and territories in the 21st century: Rethinking the significance of disciplines in higher education* (pp. 130–141). New York: Routledge.

Kosygina, L. V. (2005). Doing gender in research: Reflection on experience in the field. *The Qualitative Report, 10*(1), 87–95.

Krkoska, B. B., Andrews, C., & Morris-Knower, J. (2011). A tale of three disciplines: Embedding librarians and outcomes-based information literacy competency in business, biology, and communication. In C. Knevild & K. Calkins (Eds.), *Embedded librarians: Moving beyond one-shot instruction* (pp. 121–138). Chicago: American Library Association.

Krueger, R. A. (1998). *Developing questions for focus groups: Focus group kit 3.* San Francisco, CA: Jossey-Bass.

Kuh, G. D. (1996). Guiding principles for creating seamless learning environments for undergraduates. *Journal of College Student Development, 37*(2), 135–148.

Kuhlthau, C. C. (2004). *Seeking meaning: A process approach to library and information services* (2nd ed.). Westport, CT: Libraries Unlimited.

Lampert, L. D., Dabbour, K. S., & Solis, J. (2007). When it's all Greek: The importance of collaborative information literacy outreach programming to Greek student organizations. *Research Strategies, 20,* 300–310. doi: 10.1016/j.resstr.2006.12.005

Lankes, R. D. (2011). *The atlas of new librarianship.* Cambridge, MA: MIT Press.

Laosebikan-Buggs, M. O. (2006). The role of student government: Perceptions and expectations. In M. T. Miller & D. P. Nadler, (Eds.), *Student governance and institutional policy: Formation and implementation* (pp. 1–8). Charlotte, NC: Information Age.

Laufgraben, J. L., & Shapiro, N. S. (2004). *Sustaining and improving learning communities*. San Francisco, CA: Jossey-Bass.

Leckie, G. J., & Buschman, J. E. (2007). Space, place, and libraries: An introduction. In G. J. Leckie and J. E. Buschman (Eds.), *The library as place: History, community, and culture* (pp. 3–25). Westport, CT: Libraries Unlimited.

Ledwith, K. E. (2014). Academic advising and career services: A collaborative approach. In K. K. Smith (Ed.), *Strategic directions for career services within the university setting: New directions for student services, No. 148*. San Francisco, CA: Jossey-Bass.

Lee, P. (2011). The curious life of in loco parentis in American universities. *Higher Education in Review*, *8*, 65–90.

LePeau, L. A. (2012). *Academic affairs and student affairs partnerships promoting diversity initiatives on campus: A grounded theory*. (Doctoral dissertation). Retrieved from ProQuest. (UMI 3543589)

Lincoln, Y. S., & Guba, E. G. (1985). *Naturalistic inquiry*. Newbury Park, CA: Sage.

Lightman, H., & Ryan, M. (2017). Better together: Cultivating campus collaborations. In B. Albitz, C. Avery, & D. Zabel (Eds.), *Leading in the new academic library*. Santa Barbara, CA: Libraries Unlimited.

Long, D. (2011). Embedded right where the students live: A librarian in the university residence halls. In C. Kvenild & K. Calkins (Eds.), *Embedded librarians: Moving beyond one-shot instruction* (pp. 199–210). Chicago, IL: Association of College and Research Libraries.

Love, E., & Edwards, M. B. (2009). Forging inroads between libraries and academic, multicultural, and student services. *Reference Services Review*, *37*(1), 20–29. doi: 10.1108/00907320910934968

Lozano, A. (2010). Providing a sense of belonging and promoting student success. In L. D. Patton (Ed.), *Culture centers in higher education: Perspectives on identity, theory, and practice* (pp. 3–25). Sterling, VA: Stylus.

Luter, D. G. (2007). *The meaning of community: Exploring the view of student affairs officers*. (Doctoral dissertation). Retrieved from trace.tennessee.edu/utk_gradthes/306

Manning, K., Kinzie, J., & Schuh, J. H. (2006). *One size does not fit all: Traditional and innovative models of student affairs practice*. New York, NY: Routledge.

Marines, A., & Venegas, Y. (2012). Strategic partnerships across divisions: Aligning student affairs and the university library to increase diversity in an academic institution. In L. J. Hinchliffe & M. A. Wong (Eds.), *Environments for student growth and development* (pp. 219–231). Chicago, IL: Association of College and Research Libraries.

Maxwell, N. K. (2006). *Sacred stacks: The higher purpose of libraries and librarianship*. Chicago, IL: American Library Association.

Melling, M. (2013). Collaborative service provision through super-convergence. In M. Melling & M. Weaver (Eds.), *Collaboration in libraries and learning environments* (pp. 149–156). London, UK: Facet.

Miller, L. (2012). The library and the campus visit: Communicating value to prospective students and parents. *College and Research Libraries News*, *73*(10), 586–589.

Montiel-Overall, P. (2010). *Toward a theory of collaboration for teachers and librarians*. Chicago, IL: American Association of School Librarians.

Moore, E. L., & Marsh, R. S. (2007). College teaching for student affairs professionals. *New Directions for Student Services, no. 117*. doi: 10.1002/ss.228

Morgan, D. L. (1998). *Planning focus groups: Focus group kit 2*. Thousand Oaks, CA: Sage.

Morgan, D. L. (2002). Focus group interviewing. In J. F. Gubrium & J. A. Holstein (Eds.), *Handbook of interview research: Context and method* (pp. 141–159). Thousand Oaks, CA: Sage.

Myers, G., & Macnaghten, P. (1999). Can focus groups be analysed as talk? In R. S. Barbour & J. Kitzinger (Eds.), *Developing focus group research: Politics, theory and practice* (pp. 173–185). London, UK: Sage.

National Center of Education Statistics. (2016). Undergraduate student enrollment by race and ethnicity. Retrieved from https://nces.ed.gov/programs/raceindicators/indicator_REB.asp

National Center of Education Statistics. (2018). Postsecondary education enrollment. Retrieved from https://nces.ed.gov/programs/coe/indicator_chb.asp

National Center of Educational Statistics. (2016). *Digest of education statistics, 2016*. Retrieved from nces.ed.gov/pubsearch/pubsinfo.asp?pubid=2017094

Newbury, D. (2001). Diaries and fieldnotes in the research process. *Research Issues in Art Design and Media, 1*. Retrieved from http://www.wordsinspace.net/course_material/mrm/mrmreadings/riadmIssue1.pdf

Nilsen, C. (2012). Faculty perceptions of librarian-led information literacy instruction in postsecondary education. Paper presented at the meeting of the World Library and Information Congress: 78th IFLA General Conference and Assembly, Helsinki, Finland. Retrieved from conference.ifla.org/past-wlic/2012/ifla78.htm

Oakleaf, M. (2010). *The value of academic libraries: A comprehensive research review and report*. Chicago, IL: Association of College and Research Libraries.

O'Connor, J. S. (2012). *Factors that support or inhibit academic affairs and student affairs from working collaboratively to better support holistic students' experiences: A phenomenological study*. (Doctoral dissertation). Retrieved from ProQuest. (UMI 3535416)

Onwuegbuzie, A. J., Leech, N. L., & Collins, K. M. T. (2008). Interviewing the interpretive researcher: A method for addressing the crises of representation, legitimation, and praxis. *International Journal of Qualitative Methods, 7*(4), 1–17.

Ortlipp, M. (2008). Keeping and using reflective journals in the qualitative research process. *The Qualitative Report, 13*(4), 695–705. Retrieved from http://www.nova.edu/ssss/QR/QR13-4/ortlipp.html

Otto, J. L., Meade, Q. H., Stafford, J. L., & Wahler, P. (2016). Library lights out: A creative collaboration between the library, students, and university housing. *Digital Library Perspectives 32*(3), 192–208. doi: 10.1108/DLP-09-2015-0018

Pascarella, E., & Terenzini, P. (2005). *How college affects students: A third decade of research* (2nd ed.). San Francisco, CA: Jossey-Bass.

Pateman, J., & Vincent, J. (2010). *Public libraries and social justice*. London: Routledge.

Peltier, M. S. (2014). *The impact of faculty perception of student affairs personnel on collaborative initiatives: A case study*. (Doctoral dissertation). Retrieved from digitalcommons.unl.edu/cehsedaddis/172. ETD 172

Phillips, E., McDaniel, A., & Croft, A. (2018). Food insecurity and academic disruption among college students. *Journal of Student Affairs and Research, 55*(4), 353–372. doi: 10.1080/19496591.2018.1470003

Porterfield, K. T., & Whitt, E. J. (2016). Past, present, and future: Contexts for current challenges and opportunities for student affairs leadership. *New Directions for Student Services, v. 2016*(153), 9–17.

Pritchard, A., & McChesney, J. (2018). Focus on student affairs 2018: Understanding key challenges using CUPA-HR data. College and University Professional Association for Human Resources. Retrieved from cupahr.org/wp-content/uploads/Student_Affairs_Report.pdf

Quaye, S. J. (2016). Teaching and facilitation. In J. H. Schuh, S. R. Jones, & V. Torres (Eds.), *Student services: A handbook for the profession* (6th ed.) (pp. 437–452). San Francisco, CA: Jossey-Bass.

Ranganathan, S. R. (1931). *The five laws of library science*. Madras, India: Madras Library Association.

Raspa, D., & Ward, D. (2000). Listening for collaboration: Faculty and librarians working together. In D. Raspa & D. Ward (Eds.), *The collaborative imperative: Librarians and faculty working together in the information universe* (pp. 1–19). Chicago, IL: Association of College and Research Libraries.

Reason, R. D., & Broido, E. M. (2016). Philosophies and values. In J. H. Schuh, S. R. Jones, & S. R. Harper (Eds.), *Student services: A handbook for the profession* (5th ed.) (pp. 80–95). San Francisco, CA: Jossey-Bass.

Rentz, A. L. (1994). The emergence of student development. In A. L. Rentz (Ed.), *Student affairs: A profession's heritage* (2nd ed.) (pp. 257–268). Lanham, MD: American College Personnel Association.

Riehle, C. F., & Witt, M. C. (2009). Librarians in the hall: Instructional outreach in campus residences. *College & Undergraduate Libraries, 16*(1/2), 107–121.

Roberts, D. C. (2011). Community building and development. In S. R. Komives & D. B. Woodward (Eds.), *Student services: A handbook for the profession* (4th ed.) (pp. 539–554). San Francisco, CA: Jossey-Bass.

Rodem, M. R. (2011). *Collaborative relationships between faculty and student affairs professionals: A case study.* (Doctoral dissertation). Retrieved from ProQuest. (UMI 3493142)

Rubin, R. (2015). *Foundations of library and information science* (4th ed). Chicago, IL: Neal-Schuman.

Sandeen, A. (2004). Educating the whole student: The growing academic importance of student affairs. *Change: The Magazine of Higher Learning, 36*(3), 28–33.

Sapp, L., & Vaughan, K. T. L. (2017). Connecting the libraries and athletics through instruction and outreach. *Medical Reference Services Quarterly, 36*(2), 187–195. doi: 10.1080/02763869.2017.1293999

Schrage, M. (1990). *Shared minds*. New York, NY: Random House.

Schulte, S. J., & Sherwill-Navarro, P. J. (2009). Nursing educators' perceptions of collaborations with librarians. *Journal of the Medical Library Association, 97*(1), 57–66. doi: 10.3163/1536_5050.97.1.013

Schuster, J. H., & Finkelstein, M. J. (2006). *The American faculty: The restructuring of academic work and careers.* Baltimore, MD: Johns Hopkins University Press.

Shenton, A. K. (2004). Strategies for ensuring trustworthiness in qualitative research projects. *Education for Information, 22*, 63–75. Retrieved from www.credo.co.uk/docs/Trustworthypaper.pdf

Shera, J. H. (1967). *The sociological foundations of librarianship*. New York: Asia Publishing House.

Shera, J. H. (1972). *The foundations of education for librarianship*. New York: Becker and Hayes.

Smith, L., & Blixt, A. (2015). *Leading innovation and change: A guide for chief student affairs officers on shaping the future.* Washington: National Association of Student Personnel Administrators.

Solis, J., & Dabbour, K. S. (2006). Latino students and libraries: A US federal grant project report. *New Library World, 107*(1/2), 49–62.

Stewart, D. W., & Shamdasani, P. N. (2015). *Focus groups: Theory and practice* (3rd ed.). Thousand Oaks, CA: Sage.

Stolz, K. A. (2010). *Collaborative partnerships that promote seamless learning for students with disabilities.* (Doctoral dissertation). Retrieved from ProQuest. (UMI 3435112)

Streit, M. R., Dalton, J. C., & Crosby, P. C. (2009). A campus audit of student affairs-faculty collaborations: From contacts to compacts. *Journal of College & Character, 10*(5), 1–4.

Strothman, M., & Antell, K. (2010). The live-in librarian: Developing library outreach to university residence halls. *Reference & User Services Quarterly, 50*(1), 48–58.

Suskie, L. (2009). *Assessing student learning: A common sense guide.* San Francisco, CA: Jossey-Bass.

Swartz, P. S., Carlisle, B. A., & Uyeki, E. C. (2007). Libraries and student affairs: Partners for student success. *Reference Services Review, 35*(1), 109–122. doi: 10.1108/00907320710729409

Taub, D. J., & McEwen, M. K. (2006). Decision to enter the profession of student affairs. *Journal of College Student Development, 47*(2), 206–216. doi: 10.1353/csd.2006.0027

Tenofsky, D. (2007). Teaching to the whole student: Building best practices for collaboration between libraries and student services. *Research Strategies, 20*, 284–299. doi: 10.1016/j.resstr.2006.12.023

Tetreault, R. (2007). Beneficial spaces: The rise of the military libraries in the British empire. In G. J. Leckie and J. E. Buschman (Eds.), *The library as place: History, community, and culture* (pp. 30–39). Westport, CT: Libraries Unlimited.

Tinto, V. (1987). *Leaving college: Rethinking the causes and cures of student attrition* (2nd ed.). Chicago, IL: University of Chicago.
Thelin, J. R. (2010). *A history of American higher education* (2nd ed.). Baltimore, MD: Johns Hopkins University.
Thomison, D. (1978). *A history of the American Library Association 1876–1972.* Chicago: American Library Association.
Thompson, L. (1942). The historical background of departmental and collegiate libraries. *The Library Quarterly, 12*(1), 49–74.
Trowler, P. (2012). Disciplines and academic practices. In P. Trowler, M. Saunders, and V. Bamber (Eds.), *Tribes and territories in the 21st century: Rethinking the significance of disciplines in higher education* (pp. 30–38). New York, NY: Routledge.
U.S. Department of Labor, Bureau of Labor Statistics. (2016). Librarians. *Occupational outlook handbook.* Retrieved from bls.gov/ooh/education-training-and-library/librarians.htm
U.S. Department of Labor, Bureau of Labor Statistics. (2018). Postsecondary education administrators. *Occupational outlook handbook.* Retrieved from bls.gov/ooh/management/post-secondary-education-administrators.htm
Wainwright, A., & Davidson, C. (2017). Academic libraries and non-academic departments: A survey and case studies on liaising outside the box. *Collaborative Librarianship, 9*(2). Retrieved from digitalcommons.du.edu/collaborativelibrarianship/vol9/issu2/9
Walter, S. (2007). Using cultural perspectives to foster information literacy instruction across the curriculum. In S. C. Curzon & L. Lampert (Eds.), *Proven strategies for building an information literacy program* (pp. 55–75). New York, NY: Neal-Schuman.
Walter, S. (2009). Building a "seamless environment" for assessment of information literacy: Libraries, student affairs, and learning outside the classroom. *Communications in Information Literacy, 3*(2), 91–98.
Walter, S., & Eodice, M. (2007). Meeting the student learning imperative: Supporting and sustaining collaboration between academic libraries and student services programs. *Research Strategies, 20,* 219–225. doi: 10.1016/j.resstr.2006.11.001
Weaver, M. (2013). Student journey work: A new review of academic library contributions to student transition and success. *New Review of Academic Librarianship, 19*(2), 101–124. doi: 10.1080/13614533.2013.800754
Weiner, S. G. (2005). The history of academic libraries in the United States: A review of the literature. *Library Philosophy and Practice, 7*(2). Retrieved from https://digitalcommons.unl.edu/libphilprac/58
Weiner, S. (2008). The contribution of the library to the reputation of a university. *Journal of Academic Librarianship, 35*(1), 3–13.
Whitchurch, C. (2008a). Shifting identities and blurring boundaries: The emergence of *third space* professionals in UK higher education. *Higher Education Quarterly, 62*(4), 377–396. doi: 10.1111/j.1468-2273.2008.00387.x
Whitchurch, C. (2008b). Beyond administration and management: Reconstructing the identities of professional staff in UK higher education. *Journal of Higher Education Policy and Management, 39*(4), 375–386. doi: 10.1080/13600800802383042
Whitchurch, C. (2009). The rise of the blended professional in higher education: A comparison between the United Kingdom, Australia, and the United States. *Higher Education, 58,* 407–418. doi: 10.10007/s10734-009-9202-4
Whitchurch, C. (2010). Convergence and divergence in professional identities. In G. Gordon & C. Whitchurch (Eds.), *Academic and professional identities in higher education: The challenges of a diversifying workforce* (pp. 167–184). London: Routledge.
Whitchurch, C. (2013). *Reconstructing identities in higher education: The rise of third space professionals.* London, UK: Routledge.
Whitmire, E. (2004). Campus racial climate and undergraduates' perceptions of the academic library. *Portal: Libraries and the Academy 4*(3), 363–378.
Whitt, E. J. (2011). Academic and student affairs partnerships. In J. H. Schuh, S. R. Jones, & S. R. Harper (Eds.), *Student services: A handbook for the profession* (5th ed.) (pp. 517–532). San Francisco, CA: Jossey-Bass.

Wittenberg, J., & Elings, M. (2017). Building a research data management service at the University of California, Berkeley. *IFLA Journal, 43*(1), 89–97. doi: 10.1177/0340035216686982

Wolff-Eisenberg, C. (2017). US library survey 2016. *Ithaka S+R*. doi: 10.18665/sr/303066

Ylijoki, O. H. (2000). Disciplinary cultures and the moral order of studying. *Higher Education 39*, 339–362.

Young, R. B. (2003). Identifying and implementing the essential values of the profession. *New Directions for Student Services*, no. 61. San Francisco, CA: Jossey-Bass.

Yousef, A. (2010). Faculty attitudes toward collaboration with librarians. *Library Philosophy and Practice* (e-journal). Retrieved from digitalcommons.unl.edu/libphilprac/512. Paper 512.

Zahir, A. (2010). Third space professionals as policy actors. *Zeitschrift für hochschulentwicklung 5*(4), 46–61.

Index

"academic practice". *See* third-space professionals
Academic tribes and territories (Becher and Trowler), 33–34
access to information, xiii; librarian roles, xviii; student affairs, xviii
American College Personnel Association (ACPA), 18, 22
American Commitments Project, 35
American Council on Education, 20
Arcelus, Victor, xii, xiv, xvii, 37, 135, 136, 145, 170
athletics, 51

Becher, Tony, xvii, 1, 5, 32–34, 55, 115, 135–136, 161, 162, 167, 169
bibliographic instruction. *See* information literacy
bibliographic paradigm, 16

campus cultural centers, 50
career services, ix, xi
citizenship skills, xi
cognitive development, x, xi, xiv, xviii, 16, 18, 27, 34–35, 39, 44, 46, 111, 119, 131, 146
collaboration, areas of opportunity: academic advising, 149–150; bridge programs, 150; career development, xi, 150; embedding librarians in student services offices, 150; experiential learning, 138, 140; non-curricular learning, 137–138, 140, 141; transferable work skills, 141
collaborations, ix, xvii–xviii, 29–31, 161; admissions and enrollment management, 47; athletics, 51; barriers to, 162; citizenship skills, 54; common language, 136; complementary partnerships, 35; coordinated partnerships, 35–36; core elements (Kezar), 31, 151, 172; defined, 54, 144; disability services, 52; diverging understanding of programming, 157; diversity initiatives, 35; EOP services, 46; first year experience, 47–48; formal processes, 31; interdisciplinary, 29–30, 32, 33; and library missions, 103; marketing, 48; need for campus network-building, 153–154; need for clear goals and outcomes, 103–105; personal relationship, 157; pervasive partnerships, 35–36; relational dynamics, 31, 37, 41; residential life, 48–49; resource management, 53; reward systems, 31, 95, 103, 106–107, 135, 138, 154–156; seamless learning for students with disabilities, 36; shared values, xii, 27–28, 29, 41, 48, 136, 138, 141, 143, 162, 165–166; social justice, 54; student affairs perspectives on, 55; student development theory, 157;

student success, 54; sustainability of, xii, 46, 49, 50, 51, 55, 161. *See also* workloads, librarian
collaborations, barriers to, xii, 55–56, 58, 115, 134, 135, 140, 145, 157, 167, 170; isolation, 168; lack of familiarity, 151; mission confusion, 151; non-responsiveness, 143; overcoming, 170–172; perceived threat to role in university, 144–145; perceptions, 143. *See also* workloads, librarian
collaborations, stages of (Kezar): building commitment, 31; commitment, 31; sustaining, 31
collaborations between: librarians and academic affairs, 39–41; librarians and student affairs, 44–53; library and non-academic departments, 40–41; student affairs and academic affairs, 34–39
collaborations in higher education, 30–34; barriers to, 32, 37–39; misunderstanding of librarian expertise, 42–43
collection development, 10
College Student Personnel Point of View (CSPPV), 20
community development, 1, 13, 15, 18, 23, 24, 27, 28, 86–93
community gardens, 40
confidence of purpose, 133–135
counseling, ix
critical thinking skills, xvi–xvii, 18, 27, 40, 43, 110, 116, 120, 138, 141, 145

Dabbour, Katherine, xii, 50, 51, 55, 150
disability services, 52
diversity services: diversity initiatives, 35; diversity skills, xi
Dixon v. Alabama, 21

extroversion, 58

faculty: changing nature of work, 1–2, 3, 19–20; perception of student affairs, 37, 38–39, 134; perceptions of librarians, 42–43
Faculty Institutes (UNLV), 40
familiarity, lack of, 134
Forrest, Laura Urbanski, 44, 54, 148

Gatten, Jeffrey, 149
Gee, James Paul, 64–67, 154
Greek life, 50

health services, ix
higher education, changes in, 1–3, 4
holistic student development, 30, 37, 111–112, 138, 140, 145, 146
Hollister, Christopher, 53, 148

identities, professional: cross-boundary, xvi–xvii; disciplinary, 33, 33–34, 155–156; faculty, xi, 4; professional staff, 3–4, 156
identity development, xi
identity shifts, xv
information literacy, xi, 9, 10, 12, 16, 27, 39–40, 42, 45, 146
"in loco parentis", 19, 21
integrated learning paradigm, 26, 27
intersection of roles, 146; holistic student development, 146; information resources for students, 146, 148; librarian perceptions of, xv; student affairs perception of, xv, 135; transferable work skills, 146, 147–148
introversion, 58, 75

John-Steiner, Vera, 29, 30, 31, 54, 167

Kezar, Adrianna, xii, xiv, xvii, 1, 30–32, 55–56, 135–136, 151, 153, 154, 161, 162, 169, 170, 171; stages of collaborations, 31; core elements of collaborations, 31, 151, 172

Lampert, Lynn, xii, 50, 51, 55
Lankes, R. David, 140, 152
leadership skills, 8–10
learning, outside the classroom, 22
librarian participant demographics, 76, 77, 78, 79, 80
librarian perceptions of student affairs, xii, xiv, 97–105; confusing, 99–100, 135; lack of familiarity, 98–99, 135, 166; self-separating from the academic mission, 100–102; threat to academic primacy, 99, 134

librarian perceptions of student affairs for collaboration, 103–107; indifference from student affairs, 104; not rewarded, 103, 106–107, 135; personality-dependent, 104–105; unconsidered, 103–104; undervalued by library, 103; unsuccessful, 103

librarian roles, ix; assessment, challenges of, 80, 81, 83–84; cognitive development, 10; collection development, 9, 11, 15, 16, 21–22; community development, 9, 86–93, 134; cultural stewards, 9; expertise, 79; information literacy, xi, 9, 10, 12, 16, 27, 39–40, 42, 45, 146; information purveyor, 77–81, 134, 138; intellectual freedom, 15; liaison roles, 9, 42, 52, 76, 81, 106; library design, xi, 15; managing student employees, 94; marketing, 77–78; mission confusion, 103, 134, 151–152; need-based interactions with students, 95–96; outreach, 77, 80–81, 95; presence (limited) in student's activities, 94–95; programming, 9; protection of intellectual freedom, 9; relationships, 79; student engagement, 15; student learning spaces, xi, 15; in student spaces, 80; teaching, 9, 81–86, 134, 139–140, 142, 156, 158; teaching via coaching, 84; teaching via displays and exhibits, 85–86, 137, 140; teaching via instruction sessions, 81–84

librarian values, xi; community development, 13, 15; intellectual freedom, 13; roles in student success, 14; service, 13, 14; social justice, 13, 14; stewardship, 13–14

librarians, 8–11; approaches to collaboration, xv; collaborations with faculty, xiv; curriculum design, xviii; demographics, 8–9; introversion, 58, 75; isolation, 75; pedagogy, xviii; personality traits, 58, 75; student intellectual interests, xi; student interactions, 85–86; student learning and development, xiii; and third-space professionals, 27

librarians and the internet, 12

librarianship, embedded, 17, 18–20
librarians in student spaces, 51
library: defined, 8; roles in student success, xi
library as place, 12
library design, 10, 146
library history, ix, 7, 11–12, 69–70; campus climate, xi
living-learning communities (LLCs), 34, 163

marketing, 48
methodology: data analysis, 64–69; focus groups, xii, xv, 57–59, 63–64, 71–72; identifying participants, 59–62; journaling, 72–73
minority student services, ix
misunderstandings of expertise, 39

National Association of Student Personnel Administrators (NASPA), 18
Nilsen, Christina, 43–44, 56, 119, 145, 162, 168

Oakleaf, Megan, xiii, 168

perceptions: importance of, xiv; poor, 134
perceptions, absence of data, 56
perceptions, importance of, 56
plagiarism prevention, 52
profession, defined, 5
professional staff, 3–4

Ranganathan, S. R., 14, 16
relational dynamics, 167
residential life, 48, 163
resource management, 53
Rodem, Michelle, 37, 145

service, 1, 13, 14, 20, 23, 27
shared values: community development, 1, 13, 15, 18, 23, 24, 27, 28, 86–93; service, 1, 13, 14, 20, 23, 27; social justice, 1, 13, 14, 25, 27–28, 54
social justice, 13, 14, 25, 27–28, 54
Solis, Jacqueline, xii, 50, 51, 55, 150
student activism, 21, 23
student affairs, ix; academic advisors, 18; access to information, xviii; admissions

staff, 18; advocates, xi; approaches to collaboration, xv; campus climate, xi; career center staff, 18; community development, 23; conflict mediation, xi; demographics, 19; financial aid staff, 18; formal partnerships across campus, xiii; history, 18–23; personality traits, 58, 109–110; residential life staff, 18; roles in student success, x; student development theory, xviii; teaching via environments and experiences, xviii; and third-space professionals, 27
student affairs goals, student identity development, 110
student affairs participants demographics, 110, 111, 112, 113, 114
student affairs perceptions, 145; of faculty, 37; of librarian roles, 119–120, 135; of librarian roles as educators, 120–121, 122; of librarian roles as information managers, 120, 121; of librarians, x, xii, xiv, 135, 145, 166; of librarians as "invisible people", 123, 124, 125–126, 135, 153; of librarians as never leaving the library, 122–124; of librarians as out of touch, 121–123, 135, 145; of librarians as student-focused, 120, 121, 122–123, 124, 126
student affairs perceptions of librarians for collaboration, 126–128, 132; "business hours people", 127; lack of appropriate student training, 129–130; lack of communication skills, 129; lack of intersection, 166; lack of persistence, 127, 127–128, 135; lack of shared approach to scheduling, 130–131, 135; lack of shared understanding of "programming", 128
student affairs roles, 21, 111–115; academic advising, 18; activity coordination, 18; admissions and enrollment management, 18; advising, 18; advocacy, 18, 25, 115, 119, 132; assisting students in forming meaningful connections, 114–115; campus ministries, 18; "challenge and support", 117–118; citizenship skills, xi; community development, 18; diversity issues, xi, 18; educate the whole student, 110–112, 131; educators, 21–22, 27, 110–112, 131, 143; experiential learning, 110, 118; Greek affairs, 18; health services, 18, 20; holistic student development, 166; immediacy, 130–131, 135; leadership development, xi, 18; managing student employees, 116; new student programs, 18; psychosocial development, xi; recreation and fitness, 18; residential life, 18; retention, 112–113, 133; service, 20; shaped by their institutions, 112, 133, 152; shared value, 133; student conduct, 18; student development, xi, 18, 22, 110; student identity formation, xi, 18; student success, 110, 111–115; student unions, 18; teaching, 115, 116–117, 139, 142, 158; transferable work skills, 110, 113, 116, 133; transformative learning, 116–117, 137

student affairs values: community development, 24; educating the whole student, 23; service, 23; social justice, 25

student cognitive development, and libraries, 16

Student Development in Tomorrow's Higher Education: A Return to the Academy (Rentz), 22

student development paradigm, 26

student development theory, 44, 52

student journey lifecycle, 45

student learning and development, x, xi, xiii, 3, 56; citizenship skills, xi; cognitive development, xi; critical thinking skills, xi; as defined by librarians, xiv; as defined by student affairs, xiv; diversity skills, xi; ethical development, xi; identity development, xi; information literacy, xi; integrative experiences, xiii; intellectual interests, xi; interactions with faculty, xiii; leadership skills, xi; librarian understanding of role, xv; librarian understanding of student affairs role, xv; psychosocial development, xi; stewardship, xi; student affairs understanding of librarians role, xv;

student affairs understanding of role, xv; student development theory, 26; transferability of knowledge and skills, xiii
student learning spaces, xi
student services paradigm, 26
student success, 30; as defined by librarians, xiv; as defined by student affairs, xiv; librarian's perception of role in, 139
student union, ix
study abroad programs, 35

technology and change, 17, 22
technology professionals, 41–42
third-space professionals, xv–xvii, 4, 5–6; blended, xvi; *bounded*, xv; and librarians, 27, 152; and professional identities, 4; and student affairs, 27, 152–153
Trowler, Paul, xvii, 1, 5, 32–34, 55, 115, 135–136, 161, 162, 167, 169

university galleries, 40
user-centered paradigm, 16

values, shared: community development, 1, 13, 15, 18, 23, 24, 27, 28, 86–93; service, 1, 13, 14, 20, 23, 27; social justice, 1, 13, 14, 25, 27–28, 54

Whitchurch, Celia, xv–xvii, 3–4, 27, 152, 154
workloads, librarian, 97, 135; barrier to collaboration, 105–106
writing centers, 40

About the Author

Dallas Long is associate dean and associate professor at Illinois State University, where he oversees the university library's access and technical services, digital initiatives, scholarly communication, special collections, and university archives. Prior to his administrative position, Long served as the residential life librarian at the University of Illinois at Urbana-Champaign, where he was embedded in the division of student affairs and collaborated with student affairs professionals to provide workshops and programming for first-year students. His other previous positions include the head of access services, copyright officer, and reference and instruction librarian at university and community college libraries.

Long's research explores collaborations between librarians and student affairs professionals to promote student success. His scholarship has appeared in *The College Student Affairs Journal*, the *Journal of Academic Librarianship*, *The Reference Librarian*, the *Journal of Access Services,* and the *Journal of Library and Information Services in Distance Learning*. His 2016 dissertation *Librarians and Student Affairs Professionals as Collaborators for Student Learning and Success* won the W. Paul Vogt Higher Education Dissertation of the Year award and was featured in *American Libraries* as a notable dissertation of the year.

Long received his doctorate in higher education from Illinois State University, his master's degrees in library science and education from the University of Illinois at Urbana-Champaign, and his bachelor's degree in psychology from Webster University. He has held Fulbright awards in Qatar and Hungary where he has taught for library and information science programs and provided professional development for librarians.

www.ingramcontent.com/pod-product-compliance
Lightning Source LLC
Chambersburg PA
CBHW021828300426
44114CB00009BA/366